THE QUICK STUDY PROGRAM

PENSION & PROFIT SHARING

MERRITT PROFESSIONAL PUBLISHING

Written by
Harry G. Turner, CLU
President
Financial Services Institute
17187 N. Laurel Park Dr. Ste. 220
Livonia, Michigan 48152
(313) 464-0005

THIS MANUAL BELONGS TO:

NAME

ADDRESS

EDITION 2

THE MERRITT COMPANY
Making business and people more productive

The Merritt Company publishes many insurance and safety educational materials. For more information call TOLL-FREE: (800) 638-7597.

Written by
   Harry G. Turner, CLU

Editor
   Cindy Davidson, CIC
   Tracy Lovik, J.D.

Production
   Simone Hirzel

The Merritt Company
1661 Ninth Street/P.O. Box 955
Santa Monica, California 90406

Copyright © 1996 by The Merritt Company. All rights reserved. No part of this book may be reproduced, stored in a retrieval system, or transcribed, in any form or by any means, electronic, mechanical, photocopying, recording, or otherwise, without the prior written permission of the copyright owner, The Merritt Company.

ISBN 1-56343-061-4
B-7438(227)96 4 1M 1

INTRODUCTION

Most individuals constantly seek means by which to enhance their economic security. One cause of economic insecurity and a risk most of us will have to face is the probable reduction of earning power at older ages, namely retirement. As we approach retirement, we face the very real risk of living too long and possibly outliving our retirement resources.

It is estimated that by the year 2040, there will be over one million Americans over age 100. Longer life expectancies, healthier lifestyles and medical advances will greatly lengthen our retirement years. The risk of living too long and outliving our retirement income is reduced or possibly eliminated by means of personal savings and individual retirement plans, private pensions and government-sponsored programs.

The earliest employer pension plan in the United States dates back to the establishment of the American Express Company plan in 1875. This was followed by the Baltimore and Ohio Railroad Company plan established in 1880. The growth of private pensions for the next 50 years was modest.

The latter half of the 20th century has witnessed the installation of an increased number of employee pension plans with larger and larger groups of individuals covered. This growth is due in part to the advent of Social Security through passage of the Social Security Act in 1935 and the labor movement spearheaded by the development of unions in this country. Added to these factors are pressures exerted by society for employers to provide their employees with adequate retirement incomes and a greater awareness by the public in general of the need to protect and enhance retirement resources.

This text is designed to be an information resource for individual and employer-sponsored pension plans. As an insurance agent, it is in your interest and especially the interest of your clients, for you to be competent and knowledgeable regarding retirement planning and the use of pension plans. It should be noted that as an agent, you do not "sell plans".

You provide the funding for these plans and accordingly, you sell annuities, mutual funds, and other funding mechanisms. To be able to provide the funding for these plans requires knowledge of and competency in the plans themselves.

Also, as an agent, you are not a CPA or an attorney. Tax and legal considerations are the function of these other professionals. Although this text will address tax and legal concepts, it should be remembered that in the real world, the agent works with the CPA and the attorney as a team member, for the benefit of their mutual client.

This manual includes:

- Twelve chapters with review exercises in each chapter
- A Final Course Review
- Answers to the review exercises
- Answers to the Final Course Review
- A Final Exam**
- Abbreviated Glossary of Insurance Terms

**To be used only if you plan to submit the exam for continuing education correspondence credit, and have prepaid your grading fee.

Pension & Profit Sharing

Table of Contents

CHAPTER 1

BACKGROUND AND DEVELOPMENT OF PENSION PLANS

- The Risks of Old Age 1-1
  - Standards of Living 1-1
  - Employment Opportunities 1-2
  - Lack of Planning 1-3
- The Advantages of Private Pensions 1-4
  - Advantages of a Formal Pension Plan 1-5
  - Labor Unions Influence 1-6
  - Group Savings 1-6
- The Employee Retirement Income
  Security Act of 1974 (ERISA) 1-7
  - Purpose and Function 1-9
- Summary 1-12
- Review Exercises 1-13

CHAPTER 2

BASIC CHARACTERISTICS OF PENSION PLANS

- Qualified and Non-Qualified Plans 2-1
  - Qualified Plan Eligibility 2-1
  - Tax Advantages 2-2
  - Types of Qualified Plans 2-3
  - Non-qualified Plans 2-4
- Eligibility and Participation Requirements 2-6
  - Percentage Test 2-8
  - Ratio Test 2-8
  - Average Benefit Test 2-8
  - 50/40 Rule 2-9
- Contribution Requirements 2-9
- Retirement Ages 2-11
- Vesting 2-11
  - 3/7 Vesting Schedule 2-12
  - 5 Year Schedule 2-13
- Incidental Plan Benefits 2-14
  - 25% Rule 2-15
- Top Heavy Provisions 2-15
- Taxation and Penalties 2-17
- Summary 2-23
- Review Exercises 2-25

CHAPTER 3
DEFERRED COMPENSATION

- Factors for Selection of Deferred Compensation 3-2
- The Deferred Compensation Agreement 3-3
  - Standard Provisions 3-3
- Types of Deferred Compensation 3-5
  - Funded Plan 3-5
  - Unfunded Plan 3-6
- Employer/Employee Advantages and Disadvantages 3-7
  - Non-Compete Clause 3-7
  - Inexpensive 3-7
  - Recruiting 3-7
- Taxation 3-8
  - Employee Income Tax 3-9
  - Corporate Taxation 3-10
  - Estate Taxation 3-11
  - Other Tax Considerations 3-13
- Funding Deferred Compensation Plans 3-13
- A Case Study 3-15
  - Solutions to the Problem 3-16
- Summary 3-19
- Review Exercises 3-21

CHAPTER 4
GENERAL TYPES OF QUALIFIED PLANS

- Profit Sharing Plans 4-1
  - No Profit — No Contribution 4-2
  - Plan Design 4-3
  - Stock Bonus Plan (ESOP) 4-5
  - Plan Design 4-6
  - CODA Plan 4-7
- Defined Contribution Plans 4-7
  - Money Purchase Pension Plan 4-8
  - Target Benefit Plan 4-8
- Defined Benefit Plans 4-9
  - Plan Design 4-10
  - Plan Funding 4-12
- Summary 4-14
- Review Exercises 4-16

CHAPTER 5
IRAs AND SEPs

- Individual Retirement Accounts (IRA) 5-1
- Eligibility 5-2
- Contributions 5-3

CONTENTS

    Rollovers 5-3
    Vesting 5-7
    Tax Penalties 5-7
  Simplified Employee Pension (SEP) 5-11
    Eligibility 5-12
    Contributions 5-13
    Taxation 5-14
    Funding 5-14
  Summary 5-16
  Review Exercises 5-19

CHAPTER 6
ELECTIVE DEFERRAL PLANS

  Tax Sheltered Annuities (TSA) 6-1
    Eligibility 6-2
    Contributions 6-3
    Taxation 6-9
  Cash or Deferred Arrangements (CODA) 6-10
    Eligibility 6-12
    Contributions 6-13
    Taxation 6-13
  Thrift/Salary Savings Plan 6-15
    Plan Design 6-16
    Funding 6-17
  Summary 6-18
  Review Exercises 6-21

CHAPTER 7
KEOGH PLANS

  The Self-Employed as an Employee — Eligibility 7-1
  Plan Qualification 7-3
  Plan Contributions 7-4
  Taxation and Plan Distributions 7-5
  Vesting of Benefits 7-8
    Funding 7-8
  Summary 7-10
  Review Exercises 7-12

CHAPTER 8
CORPORATE QUALIFIED PLANS

  The Qualified Plan Decision 8-1
  Qualified Plan Considerations 8-2
    Employee Considerations 8-2
    Tax Considerations 8-3

Ability to Pay 8-4
The Type of Plan 8-4
    Defined Contribution Plan 8-5
    Defined Benefit Plan 8-5
    Other Plan Types 8-6
    Funding 8-8
Summary 8-9
Review Exercises 8-10

CHAPTER 9
POLICY PLANS AND FUNDING ARRANGEMENTS

Types of Funding 9-1
    Allocated and Unallocated Funds 9-2
The Fully Insured Plan — Individual Contracts 9-2
The Fully Insured Plan — Group Contracts 9-4
    Group Annuity Contracts 9-4
    Deposit Administration Contract 9-5
Trust Fund Plans 9-7
The Use of Life Insurance in a Qualified Plan 9-8
    Life Insurance Situations 9-9
    Life Insurance as an Incidental Benefit 9-11
    Life Insurance Coverage 9-11
    Life Insurance and Defined Benefit Plans 9-12
    Life Insurance and Defined Contribution Plans 9-15
    Taxation for the Plan Participant 9-15
    Taxation for the Beneficiary 9-17
    Federal Estate Taxation 9-18
Summary 9-19
Review Exercises 9-20

CHAPTER 10
EMPLOYER CONSIDERATIONS

Cost Considerations 10-1
Cost Factors (Assumptions) 10-3
    Number of Participants 10-3
    Mortality 10-4
    Amount of Benefit 10-5
Funding Considerations 10-6
    Cost 10-7
    Benefit Safety 10-8
    Flexibility 10-8
    Service 10-9
Summary 10-10
Review Exercises 10-11

CHAPTER 11
PLAN DESIGN

- Employee Considerations 11-1
  - Profit Sharing Plan 11-2
  - Defined Benefit Plan 11-3
  - Defined Contribution Plan 11-4
  - Combination Plan 11-4
- Benefit Formulas 11-5
  - Unit Benefit 11-5
  - Flat Percentage of Compensation 11-6
- Plan Conditions 11-7
  - Eligibility 11-8
  - Vesting 11-9
  - Definition of Compensation 11-10
  - Premature Death or Disability 11-11
  - Retirement Age 11-13
  - Distributions of Plan Benefits 11-15
- Sample Profit Sharing Plan 11-17
- Summary 11-27
- Review Exercises 11-29

CHAPTER 12
PLAN ADMINISTRATION

- Plan Installation 12-1
- Fiduciary Responsibilities 12-3
- Plan Reporting Requirements 12-5
  - Annual Return/Report 12-5
  - Summary Annual Report 12-6
  - Summary Plan Description 12-6
- Plan Termination 12-8
  - Alternatives 12-10
- Summary 12-12
- Review Exercises 12-14

FINAL COURSE REVIEW E-1
FINAL COURSE REVIEW ANSWER SHEET E-15
ANSWERS TO REVIEW EXERCISES A-1
FINAL COURSE REVIEW ANSWER KEY A-9
FINAL EXAM FOR CONTINUING EDUCATION CE-1
ABBREVIATED GLOSSARY OF INSURANCE TERMS G-1

CHAPTER 1

BACKGROUND AND DEVELOPMENT OF PENSION PLANS

The insurance industry entered the pension business with the issuance of the first group annuity contract in 1921 by the Metropolitan Life Insurance Company. The Equitable Life Assurance Society began offering a group pension service in 1924. Although the establishment of employer sponsored pension plans dates back to the 19th century, the real growth in private pensions began after World War II. Prior to 1940, less than 20% of employees in commerce and industry were covered by employer plans. Following the war, private plans began to steadily grow and today, more than 60% of employees are covered by some form of employer pension plan.

THE RISKS OF OLD AGE

As stated in the Introduction, due to better lifestyles, medical advances, and increased longevity, senior citizens are faced with the real risk of outliving their retirement incomes. The extent to which an older individual will have the economic resources to meet self maintenance expenses depends on the standard of living desired during retirement, possible employment opportunities, and the realization of effective prior retirement planning.

Standards of Living

Post-retirement **standards of living** do not necessarily decrease. The assumption is often made that the financial needs of the retiree decrease after retirement. To a certain degree, this may be true. Normally, the retired individual no longer has dependent children, the house may be paid for and often the general indebtedness of the retiree is less than during the person's working years.

However, other social and financial needs regularly take the place of some of these working year needs in the form of increased recreational activities, travel, civic and social opportunities, and frequently, medical needs (i.e., frequent prescriptions). Added to these needs is the erosion of the retiree's purchasing power due to inflation. As a result, when the employee reaches retirement, the individual's standard of living and financial needs may not decrease at all or may decrease only slightly.

Thus, a couple with budgeted monthly expenses of $3,000 before retirement will probably find that $3,000 of income is required at retirement to help maintain a desired standard of living and accordingly provide for the pleasures and necessities of retirement.

Employment Opportunities

Employment opportunities for the retiree are few in today's society. Often, employees elect not to take normal retirement (age 65) and work a few years longer. There definitely is a trend in today's society for workers to stay on the job and make valuable contributions past age 65.

To help maintain their standard of living, some senior citizens may seek post-retirement employment. There are frequently few employment opportunities for these seniors or few retirees who are able to work after retirement. The reasons for this lack of post-retirement employment include:

- Retirees with adequate financial resources choose to live retirement leisurely and not work
- Many retirees are physically unable to work due to age or physical disabilities
- In an industrialized society, often the retiree is not capable of functioning in an industrialized work environment due to automation, mass production, and computerization of the work function which places a premium on physical dexterity and current state-of-the-art knowledge or experience
- Economic factors such as recessions make employment opportunities scarce for the entire work force
- The establishment of the Social Security system tends to mandate retirement at age 65 and "penalizes" the retiree who may return to work (up to age 70) by offsetting Social Security retirement benefits for post-retirement earned income

BACKGROUND AND DEVELOPMENT OF PENSION PLANS

Lack of Planning

A third risk of old age is **lack of prior retirement planning**. A formula for an adequate retirement lifestyle could be:

Systematic Savings + Time = Financially Secure Retirement

Systematic savings refers to individual and/or employer programs whereby specific sums of money are set aside on a regular basis for retirement purposes. The element of time is critical to accumulating an adequate sum of retirement income. The earlier a plan is instituted, the better will be the result at retirement.

> At age 55, Charlie begins to save $200 per month for his retirement at age 65. Ralph, age 35, begins to save $75 per month for his retirement at age 65. Which of these individuals will accumulate the most for retirement?

Disregarding interest earned on their savings, Ralph will have a more financially secure retirement because his plan will run for 30 years whereas Charlie's will only have 10 years before he has to use the money for retirement.

Effective retirement planning (individual or employer-sponsored) requires specific sums of money be set aside for retirement purposes well in advance of retirement age. As an insurance agent providing financial planning advice to clients, it is critical to stress the formula for a financially secure retirement — systematic savings plus the element of time.

> Let's return to Charlie and Ralph and assume that each of them has $10,000 to deposit into a retirement account. Ralph makes the deposit at age 35 and Charlie, at age 55. Table 1-1 depicts the results of this $10,000 deposit with an interest rate of 8.75% and retirement at age 65.

TABLE 1-1

Single Deposit of $10,000 Interest Rate: 8.75%		Retirement Age 65
	Ralph	Charlie
Age 35	$10,000	
Age 40	15,229	
Age 45	23,165	
Age 50	35,235	
Age 55	53,594	$10,000
Age 60	81,520	15,229
Age 65	123,997	23,165

The element of time working on Ralph's savings results in a retirement benefit which is more than $100,000 greater than Charlie's.

To meet the needs of retirement at older ages requires a realistic acknowledgement of the financial needs and requirements of the senior citizen and the implementation of a plan which minimizes the risks of old age in favor of a financially stable retirement.

THE ADVANTAGES OF PRIVATE PENSIONS

Private or employer-sponsored pension plans have steadily increased over the years and have provided a means of helping to solve the economic risks of old age. The major reason for the growth of these plans is not the existence of old age financial risks but rather the advantages inherent in these plans for the both the employer and the employees.

Generally, just about every employee eventually reaches a point where, due to advanced age, he or she becomes less productive and more of a liability than an asset to the employer. When this occurs, the employer has several alternatives.

1. The employee can be terminated without any further compensation or any retirement benefits. Needless to say, this is not a very practical (or ethical) alternative.
2. The employee can be retained by the employer even though the employee's productivity is marginal at best. This too is not a desirable solution as it is very detrimental to the employer.

3. The employee can be retained and possibly transferred to a less demanding job at a reduced salary. This solution may be better than the first two but probably not much better as it really doesn't solve the problem of what to do with the older employee. It merely postpones it temporarily.

4. There is a formal employer pension plan. The existence of a pension plan enables the employer to terminate the employee in an ethical manner by providing a prefunded retirement benefit. The existence of a formal plan also permits the employee to plan his or her retirement accordingly.

Advantages of a Formal Pension Plan

Other employee-employer advantages of a formal pension plan include a sense of security on the part of the employee. This security or employee morale is frequently translated into increased productivity and loyalty which is beneficial to the employer. A formal plan also permits the systematic retirement of older workers and opens the possibility of promotions for the younger employees. Accordingly, the existence of a company pension plan should enable the employer to attract and retain key employees.

One of the major advantages of a qualified pension plan is that employer contributions are tax deductible for federal income tax purposes. This advantage results in a portion of the plan's liabilities being funded with very little cost to the corporation. Not only are the contributions tax deductible but investment income earned on the plan's assets are tax deferred and thus there is no current taxation to the employees.

The advantages mentioned here are undoubtedly some of the principal reasons for the growth of employer-sponsored pension plans in this country during the latter half of the 20th century. Other factors which have contributed this growth include:

- The impact of labor unions
- Business necessity and employee expectations
- Efficiency

Labor Unions Influence

The labor unions have had a major impact on the growth of private pensions. In the 1920s, labor leaders generally favored a government-sponsored retirement plan which materialized by passage of the Social Security Act in 1935. During the post World War II period, employees and the unions focused on wages in lieu of benefits. By 1950, there was a growing union interest and demand for the establishment of employer retirement plans. The position taken by many unions was that Social Security did not provide adequate retirement benefits and employer-sponsored programs were needed to supplement Social Security benefits.

This growth and renewed interest in employer pension plans was stimulated by a decision of the National Labor Relations Board in 1948. The board declared that employers had a legal obligation to bargain over the terms and benefits of pension plans. This decision was based on the premise that pension benefits constituted wages and plan benefits affected the individual's employment. As a result of this decision, labor unions displayed renewed interest in bargaining for employer-sponsored pension plans as well as revisions to existing plans.

Due to the impact of the unions on the growth and development of pension plans, non-union employees began to expect pension benefits as a condition of their employment. Non-union companies were slowly forced to give in to these employee expectations or else face the possibility of losing key personnel to unionized companies. For example, non-unionized companies in such unionized cities such as Detroit and Pittsburgh were forced into considering pension plans for non-union workers or face the possibility of being at a distinct competitive disadvantage in attracting and retaining personnel. In short, employer-sponsored pension plans have almost become a business necessity.

Group Savings

Another factor contributing to the growth of private pension plans is that "group savings" for retirement is more efficient that other methods of accumulating money for retirement purposes. As previously stated, a formal pension plan is an effective way of dealing with the labor problem of what to do with the older, less-productive employee.

Employer-sponsored pension plans are probably the lowest cost method of providing economic security for the older employee. This is due in part to the fact that employer contributions are tax deductible. In addition, other costs or expenses related to the plan can be passed on to the consumer in the form of slightly higher costs for goods and services.

Finally, a company pension plan is a form of forced savings. An individual may have honest intentions to systematically save money for retirement but somehow never gets around to doing it due to other financial concerns. Whether the plan is contributory or noncontributory, the condition of employment triggers the systematic savings element inherent with the employer-sponsored plan.

THE EMPLOYEE RETIREMENT INCOME SECURITY ACT OF 1974 (ERISA)

As employer-sponsored pension plans began to grow in the latter half of the 20th century, so too did certain plan abuses and inequities. After many years of discussion concerning reform of the pension system, the federal government passed the Employee Retirement Income Security Act (ERISA) in 1974. The basic purpose of this act was to reform or "clean up" the pension business by establishing specific filing and disclosure requirements.

Prior to the enactment of ERISA, there were many plan inequities which resulted in limited or no pension benefits when an employee reached retirement. Union plans were frequently in violation of laws governing pension funds. It was common practice for pension funds to be loaned out or borrowed and as a result, when the union member reached retirement, there would be discrepancies in the plan's benefit structure. Not only were the union plans suspect but other private pension plans also contained inequities which benefited the employer at the expense of the employees.

ERISA has had a lasting impact on private pension plans which has resulted in the elimination of certain abuses. Following is a brief review of ERISA requirements.

Department of Labor: Generally, ERISA contains specific rules governing employee eligibility, vesting, funding, and distribution of plan benefits. These concepts will be discussed in more detail in later chapters. In addition, the act details specific standards that all plan fiduciaries must meet.

ERISA also established the Pension Benefit Guaranty Corporation (PBGC), a division within the Department of Labor. The PBGC guarantees retirement benefits for certain types of pension plans such as a defined benefit plan. Employers pay a premium to the PBGC. If a plan is terminated without assets which are adequate to pay benefits to the plan participants, the PBGC will pay the plan benefits.

ERISA requires the following be filed with the Department of Labor (DOL):

- **Plan Description** — The plan description must be filed by the plan administrator within 120 days of the establishment of the pension plan. A revised or updated plan description must be filed at least once every five years following the initial filing. Any changes in the information contained in the plan description must be filed with the DOL within 60 days of such changes.

- **Plan Revisions** — The plan administrator must file any changes or amendments to the plan with the DOL within 60 days of such revisions.

- **Summary Plan Description** — Plan participants must be furnished with a summary plan description which simply and briefly outlines the rights of plan participants and beneficiaries. A copy of this report must be furnished to the DOL within 120 days following implementation of the plan.

- **Annual Report** — This report is filed with the DOL summarizing the plan activities for the plan year. The report must be filed within 210 days of the close of the plan year.

ERISA also requires certain filings with the IRS, including the annual registration statement, plan changes or amendments, and tax information returns for plan benefits paid to participants. In addition, an annual information return must be filed with the IRS which reports information relating to the financial condition and operation of the pension plan.

Thirdly, ERISA requires certain **disclosures to plan participants** and plan beneficiaries. These disclosures include:

- All reports required by the DOL must also be furnished to the plan participants. These include the summary plan description plus any revisions and a summary annual report.

- **Annual Registration Statement** — The plan administrator must provide a statement of rights to any participant who terminated employment or was eligible for deferred benefits under the plan during the plan year.

- **Statement to Terminated Employees** — Plan participants who terminate employment must be provided with information regarding the tax status of various plan distributions.

- **Statement of Rights** — The plan administrator must provide plan participants with statements regarding their rights under the plan. This includes any participant requests for summary plan descriptions or similar reports and agreements related to the plan operation or benefits provided under the plan.

- **Joint-Survivor Options** — An explanation of this option must be provided to the plan participant by the plan administrator.

- **Claims Procedure Information** — If a claim is denied under the plan, an explanation or notice must be given to the plan participant which outlines the reasons for the denial.

In summary, ERISA provides that specific types of reports and information be sent to the DOL and the IRS. It also mandates full and fair disclosure of the plan and plan benefits to all participants. No other legislation in recent times has had the impact on private pensions that ERISA has. It could be stated that the primary purpose of ERISA is participant protection.

Purpose and Function

The primary purpose or function of a pension plan is to provide retirement income. Pensions and other qualified plans are designed to be retirement vehicles. There are a number of factors which have an impact on effective retirement planning. These factors include, but are not limited to, the following:

Life Expectancy: An individual's retirement life could be a few years or possible 20 or 30 years. By the dawn of the 21st century, life expectancy in the United States will exceed 80 years of age. With better and healthier lifestyles plus medical advances, the danger of outliving one's retirement income is a very real risk. Also due to longer life expectancies, the individual is exposed to the impact of inflation and erosion of the purchasing power of retirement dollars.

Accordingly, there then is a need to assure that adequate funds are available for the retiree's lifetime following retirement.

Realistic Projection of Retirement Expenses: Statistics indicate that most retirees experience a reduction of income at retirement but very little reduction in day-to-day living expenses. It is a fallacy for an individual to project a substantially smaller need for income after retirement. Living expenses continue, inflation continues, etc.

Very possibly, the retired person may no longer have a mortgage to pay for example, but he or she still has taxes to pay on the home. Often, pre-retirement expenses which may no longer exist are substituted by new expenses such as recreation, travel, social activities, etc.

Realistically, the retiree often requries 80% or more of his or her pre-retirement income as a post-retirement income need.

Inflation: Effective retirement planning requires an awareness of the impact of inflation on the purchasing power of retirement dollars. Future inflationary trends are bound to occur. The retiree needs to consider ways of accumulating adequate sums of money in the right types of retirement products to combat the erosion of post-retirement income.

Retirement Income Sources: Planning for retirement should be a coordinated effort. This effort includes a study and analysis of all retirement resources — Social Security, employer plans, individual plans, savings, investments, etc. Once all the resources have been reviewed, an estimation of the amount of income should be determined. If there are shortages, then steps should be taken to eliminate these income shortages prior to actual retirement.

Urgency: Sound retirement planning necessitates the formation of a plan which is implemented well in advance of the desired retirement date. Typically, a 35-year-old individual is not very interested in retirement but age 35 (or younger) is the time to set aside sums of money for future delivery at retirement.

The individual who begins to plan and save for retirement beginning at age 45 or 50 will not have a very financially secure retirement unless he or she is able to set aside large sums of money. As was previously mentioned in this chapter:

A financially secure retirement = Time + Money

SUMMARY

Individuals face many risks in life — premature death, disability, unemployment, and living too long. Due to improved lifestyles and medical advances, senior citizens are living longer and are faced with the risk of outliving their financial resources during retirement.

To combat the financial risks of old age, a person must decide what his or her standard of living will be. It is generally not entirely true to state that after retirement, living expenses decrease. Most often, living expenses will stay the same or decrease only slightly. Employment opportunities for retired citizens are generally not available due to physical inability of the retiree to work, recessions, and obsolescence due to automation and computerization of job functions.

The key to effectively planning for the financial risks of old age and retirement lies in setting aside a specific sum of money on a regular basis over a long period of time. This of course can be accomplished in a very effective manner by means of a employer-sponsored pension plan.

The principal advantages of a pension plan include:

- It's an effective and ethical way to take care of an older, less productive employee at the time of retirement
- It improves employee morale and in turn employee productivity
- It enables the employer to attract and retain key personnel
- Employer contributions are tax deductible and assets grow tax deferred

The growth of private pension plans in the U.S. has been due to the impact of the labor movement, expectations of employees, and the necessity of employers to compete for competent personnel. Existence of a pension plan often enables the employer to attract and keep key personnel. In addition, an employer-sponsored plan is an effective mechanism to provide retirement benefits as it is essentially a forced method of saving on a systematic basis for retirement and old age.

The Employee Retirement Income Security Act of 1974 (ERISA) was implemented primarily to protect plan participants by mandating certain filings with the Department of Labor and the Internal Revenue Service. In addition, plan participants must be provided with certain disclosure information.

REVIEW EXERCISES

1. You have been attempting to sell Archie, an employer, on the concept of establishing a formal pension plan for his employees. He states that retirement benefits are the responsibility of the retiree and not the corporation. How might you respond to Archie?

2. Comment on your client's opinion that she can live on Social Security retirement benefits because her expenses and cost of living will decrease when she retires. In addition, she also feels that she can get a job after retirement to supplement her benefits if necessary.

3. Describe some of the factors which have contributed to the growth of employer-sponsored pension plans in this country.

CHAPTER 2

BASIC CHARACTERISTICS OF PENSION PLANS

There are certain basic features or characteristics which are common to most pension plans. These features may be slightly modified depending on the specific type of plan. These common characteristics include the following concepts:

- Qualified vs. Non-qualified plans
- Eligibility and participation requirements
- Contribution limitations
- Retirement ages
- Vesting
- Incidental plan benefits
- Top heavy provisions
- Taxation

QUALIFIED AND NON-QUALIFIED PLANS

Retirement plans can be classified as qualified or non-qualified. Both types of plans provide retirement benefits but a qualified plan meets certain IRS criteria whereas a non-qualified plan does not have to comply with specific IRS requirements. The fact that a retirement plan is non-qualified does not imply that it is illegal or unethical.

Qualified Plan Eligibility

To receive certain tax advantages and be eligible for **qualified plan status**, a plan must comply with the following:

- The plan must be in **written form** and established by an employer (corporation, partnership or sole proprietor). The plan must be a formal, written document which reflects its permanent nature and the basic provisions governing the the plan.

- The plan must **be communicated** to the employees. Typically, this is accomplished by means of providing the employees with a written summary of the plan.
- The plan must **benefit the employees** and/or their dependents. The plan cannot be exclusively for the benefit of the employer or other key personnel.
- The plan must be **permanent**. This implies that the plan cannot have a specific termination date established by the employer.
- The plan **cannot discriminate**. All employees who are eligible to participate in the plan must be included (unless an employee signs a waiver indicating he or she does not wish to participate). It is discriminatory to purposely keep employees out of the plan who are eligible.
- The plan must be **filed and approved** by the IRS. Required forms and information must be supplied to the IRS and Department of Labor for plan approval.
- The employer is deemed to be a **plan fiduciary**. That is, the employer is placed in a position of financial trust with regard to the plan and its participants. Other individuals may also be considered fiduciaries such as the plan administrator.

Tax Advantages

If a plan satisfies these requirements, it will be considered a qualified plan and both the employer and the employees will be able to enjoy specific tax advantages. These advantages include:

- The employer is allowed a current tax deduction for plan contributions
- Amounts contributed by the employer on behalf of the participants are not currently taxable to the employees
- Investment earnings on the plan contributions are tax deferred. They will only be taxed upon receipt by the employee
- Lump sum benefit payments may be rolled into another qualified plan (such as an IRA) and current taxation is thus deferred
- Lump sum pension benefits received by the employee may be eligible for income averaging with regard to taxation

BASIC CHARACTERISTICS OF PENSION PLANS

Needless to say, the principal advantage of a qualified plan is its favorable tax advantages. The employer enjoys a tax deduction for all contributions and the employees have the advantage of no current taxation on the amounts contributed or on the investment growth of the contributions.

Types of Qualified Plans

There are various types of qualified plans. However, most corporate pensions will be classified as one of the following:

- Defined Contribution plan
- Defined Benefit plan
- Profit Sharing plan

We will describe these plans here. A detailed discussion of these plans will appear in later chapters.

A **defined contribution plan** is simply a qualified plan in which the contribution is identified but the retirement benefit is not defined.

For example, an employer announces to the employees that a 10% defined contribution plan is being established. This basically means that the employer will contribute an amount (from business income) equal to 10% of the employees' compensation to the plan. If an employee should question the employer regarding the amount of the retirement benefit to be received, the best answer to the question is that the benefit will be equal to the sum of money accumulated at retirement.

Thus, the employer knows with certainty the annual contribution liability but the benefit at retirement is an unknown. In accordance with current tax law, the maximum contribution for a defined contribution plan is limited to 25% of compensation not to exceed $30,000 per participant.

Conversely, a **defined benefit plan** is one in which the benefit is predetermined and the amount of the contribution to fund this benefit becomes the unknown factor. A defined benefit plan might state that all employees will retire with a benefit equal to 10% of their compensation; with compensation possibly being defined as the average compensation for their five highest years prior to retirement. It is the employer's responsibility to fund this benefit.

Example: John is covered by a pension plan which provides him with a benefit at normal retirement equal to 15% of his compensation. Because the benefit is already known, this would be a defined benefit plan.

Generally, there is no limitation on the amount of the contribution to a defined benefit plan. However, in accordance with tax law, there is a limitation on the amount of benefit which may be provided. The benefit limitation is $90,000 which is indexed for changes in the cost of living. The 1992 limitation was $112,221.

A **profit sharing plan** is similar to a defined contribution plan in that the employer establishes a definite contribution to the plan, such as 5% or 10% of compensation. However, the major difference is that the profit sharing plan does not represent a fixed liability. Generally, a contribution is made to the plan only if the company realizes a profit. No profit — no contribution and no liability for the employer. The contribution limitation is also 25%/$30,000.

Non-qualified Plans

Although the purpose of this text is to concentrate on qualified types of pension plans, we will briefly discuss the characteristics of **non-qualified plans**.

A non-qualified plan must be in proper **written form** and it must be **communicated** to the affected employee(s). Typically, proper written form means a contractual agreement between employer and employee(s).

The plan may only benefit one or a few employees. It is not for all employees. In other words, the plan **may discriminate**. The plan is **not filed, nor approved** by the IRS for special tax treatment. There are **no current tax deductions** for any employer contributions. **Investment growth** on any plan contributions are **currently taxable** to the employer. When plan benefits are paid, the employer may enjoy a tax deduction for the plan distributions.

Often, non-qualified plans are used for specific key personnel. The plan enables the employer to provide extra benefits for those selected individuals who are very important to the business operation. A specific type of non-qualified plan is **deferred compensation**.

Cindy is the Sales Manager for the ABC corporation. Annually, she is responsible for more than $20,000,000 in gross sales revenue. Her salary and bonuses total $300,000 per year. George, her employer, wants to increase her salary by $50,000. Cindy replies that another $50,000 of income will only compound her tax problems and that most of any increase will go to the government anyway.

Cindy's problem may be resolved by means of a deferred compensation agreement between herself and her employer. Most deferred compensation plans are established as non-qualified plans as they are designed to only benefit key personnel such as Cindy in the above example. The plan is discriminatory in that it is only for Cindy and not all of the employees. The plan will not be filed with or approved by the IRS. As a non-qualified plan, it does not offer any current tax incentives for the employer.

Cindy and her employer will enter into a written agreement. In accordance with this agreement, delivery of the $50,000 of compensation will be deferred until some later date such as retirement, death, or disability. Since Cindy is not in receipt of this $50,000, she also defers taxation on this sum until it is actually received by her.

The deferred compensation plan may be funded or unfunded. If unfunded, Cindy's deferred compensation will be paid from corporate assets. If the plan is funded, then the amount of $50,000 may be invested in an annuity, life insurance, mutual funds or some other funding vehicle. If the plan is funded, any investment income earned will be currently taxable to the employer.

Naturally, when Cindy retires, the amount promised or accumulated in accordance with the agreement will be paid to her. When the benefits are paid to her, the employer may take a tax deduction and Cindy of course, will be taxed on the distributions.

One problem with deferred compensation arrangements is that if the business becomes insolvent, the employee simply becomes a creditor of the corporation. There is no guarantee that the deferred amounts of compensation will actually be available when the employee is ready to retire. An unfunded promise to pay a future benefit is nothing more than a promise to pay. There are no guarantees because deferred compensation is a non-qualified plan.

Chapter 3 of this text will discuss the use of deferred compensation plans as retirement vehicles. Later chapters will discuss various kinds of qualified pension plans.

Later chapters of this text will discuss several types of qualified pension plans. In summary, Table 2-1 illustrates the principal characteristics of qualified and non-qualified plans.

TABLE 2-1

KEY FEATURES OF QUALIFIED AND NON-QUALIFIED PLANS

THE PLAN	QUALIFIED	NON-QUALIFIED
Must be in writing	Yes	Yes
Must be communicated	Yes	Yes
Benefits all employees	Yes	No
Must be permanent	Yes	No
Cannot discriminate	Yes	May discriminate
Filed with IRS	Yes	No
Approved by IRS	Yes	No
Employer is a fiduciary	Yes	No
Provides current tax advantages	Yes	No

ELIGIBILITY AND PARTICIPATION REQUIREMENTS

Generally, eligibility requirements are specific conditions that an employee must satisfy to become a plan participant. Naturally, when an employer is "sold" on a pension plan, the motivation to adopt a plan is frequently due to the tax deductibility of plan contributions and the retirement benefits to be derived by the employer, personally.

It is possible for a plan to achieve qualified status even if the employer is the only employee as long as the plan provides for the participation of future employees if any are hired. For the typical employer-employee situation, the plan remains qualified as long as all eligible employees are included in the plan. Due to employee turnover and cost considerations, an employer naturally may have a desire to exclude certain employees. At the same time, there are always going to be a few employees who are considered more valuable to the organization and accordingly, the employer may want to provide greater benefits for this group.

The federal government also recognizes this corporate fact of life. Thus, there are federal regulations governing **eligibility requirements**. Generally, the IRS states that employers may exclude the following classes of employees from plan participation:

- Employees with less than one year of full time service — full time service is considered to be a minimum of 1,000 hours annually
- Employees who are less than age 21
- Part-time employees
- Employees covered by collective bargaining agreements such as union plans

Example: Mary Beth is age 19 and has just begun employment with the Ajax Corporation which has a qualified pension plan. Based on the eligibility requirements permitted by the IRS, Mary Beth may join the pension plan after two years of service or upon reaching age 21.

The following are examples of the types of employees who may be excluded from an employer-sponsored pension plan.

- Barbara, who does filing on a part-time basis.
- John, who only worked during July and August of the current year.
- Mary, who is covered by a local union plan.
- Charlie, age 18, who works a few hours two days a week.

It should be noted that if a plan requires employees to complete more than one year of service, the employees must be fully vested immediately upon joining the plan (vesting will be discussed later in this chapter).

The above limitations should be considered minimum eligibility requirements in terms of age or years of service. An employer may elect more liberal eligibility requirements such as permitting employees to participate in the plan with only 30 days or six months of service or who may be minimum age 18.

BASIC CHARACTERISTICS OF PENSION PLANS

Related to the concept of eligibility requirements are the IRS's **coverage and participation requirements**. It is not necessary for an employer to provide pension benefits for all employees. However, the IRS does require a qualified plan to satisfy minimum coverage and participation requirements regarding the employer's work force if it is to maintain its qualified status and its tax advantages.

The corporation's employees include all eligible employees of any affiliated or subsidiary group or company in which the employer is a controlling member. A plan will satisfy the coverage requirements of the IRS and maintain its qualified status if it complies with **one of the following tests** in accordance with Code section 410.

Percentage Test

The percentage test is satisfied if the plan benefits at least 70% of the lower compensated employees. This test focuses on the percentage of lower paid employees who benefit from the plan, not the percentage of the total employees benefiting from the plan.

For example, if a plan consisted of 10 employees identified as lower paid, it would have to benefit at least seven of them.

Ratio Test

The ratio test is satisfied if the percentage of lower paid employees benefiting from the plan is at least 70% of the percentage of highly compensated employees who benefit from the plan.

For example if 40% of highly compensated employees benefit from the plan, then 28% of the lower paid employees (70% x 40%) must also benefit from the plan.

Frequently, the above two tests are combined into one test — the ratio percentage test, which requires that the percentage of lower paid individuals benefiting from the plan must be at least equal to 70% of the percentage of highly compensated employees participating under the plan.

Average Benefit Test

This test is divided into two components. The first section allows an employer to establish a classification of employees to be covered under the plan. This classification may not discriminate in favor of highly paid employees.

BASIC CHARACTERISTICS OF PENSION PLANS

The plan's classification is considered non-discriminatory if the percentage of lower paid employees who benefit from the plan is at least 50% of the percentage of highly paid employees who benefit from the plan.

The second component of the Average Benefit Test requires that the plan does not adversely affect the average benefit provided to the lower paid employees. The average benefit provided to the lower paid employees must be at least 70% of the average benefit provided the higher paid employees.

The benefit percentage for an employee is the total value of employer contributions and/or benefits received by the employee, expressed as a percentage of the employee's compensation. For example if Jan's compensation is $50,000 annually and her employer makes a contribution of $5,000 on her behalf, Jan's benefit percentage is 10%.

In accordance with IRS regulations [Section 490.4(d)(5)], by definition, generally, a highly compensated employee is one who is at least a 5% owner or one who is identified as being highly paid based on compensation received from the employer. In accordance with IRS regulations, compensation is indexed to account for changes in the cost of living each year. Thus a specific dollar amount changes annually. As a general rule, highly paid compensation could be identified as amounts in excess of $75,000.

50/40 Rule

In addition to the coverage rules mentioned above, each qualified plan must benefit the lesser of 50 employees or 40% of the work force (the 50/40 rule) throughout the plan year to maintain its qualified status. Employees who have not satisfied the plan's eligibility requirements or who are covered under a union plan may be excluded from the calculation of the "50/40 rule".

CONTRIBUTION REQUIREMENTS

Qualified pension plans may be **contributory or non-contributory**. The majority of plans are non-contributory which simply means that all contributions to the plan are made by the employer. If it is decided to permit employee contributions, then the plan is described as contributory.

A contributory plan may require employee contributions as a participation requirement. Occasionally, employer contributions are geared to match or be a percentage of employee contributions. Normally, contributory plans will allow employees to voluntarily contribute a specific amount or percentage of their compensation to the plan. Usually the maximum voluntary contribution is limited to 10% of the employees compensation. Advantages of a contributory plan include the following:

- Employee contributions could reduce the total amount contributed by the employer
- Employee contributions, in addition to employer contributions, will result in a larger retirement benefit
- Employee contributions are usually not tax deductible but investment growth on the contributions is tax deferred. There are some specific types of plans whereby employee contributions are deductible. These will be discussed later in this text.

Employer contributions to non-contributory plans are of course tax deductible and the plan's assets grow tax deferred. The amount of these contributions is normally based on some percentage of the employee's compensation up to certain limits established by the IRS. These contribution limits will depend in part on the type of qualified plan which is in force.

For example, a defined contribution plan has a current limitation of 25% of compensation up to a maximum of $30,000 per employee. Two points should be made clear.

1. The contribution amount is part of the "annual additions" as defined by the IRS. The annual additions consist of the employer's contribution, any forfeited additions due to terminated participants and any voluntary employee contributions. Accordingly, the total annual additions cannot exceed $30,000 or 25% of compensation. Thus the employer's contribution is less any forfeitures and employee contributions.

2. Employee compensation which can be used for purposes of calculating the contribution to a qualified plan is limited to a base amount of $150,000 as indexed to reflect changes in the cost of living. An employee with earned income of $300,000 would lose one-half ($150,000) for purposes of contribution calculations.

BASIC CHARACTERISTICS OF PENSION PLANS

RETIREMENT AGES

All qualified plans will identify at what ages a participant may retire. Most plans will specify that **normal retirement** is age 65 or a minimum of 10 years plan participation. Age 65 retirement has been traditional in this country due to the fact that full retirement benefits under Social Security are available at age 65.

It should be noted that generally the concept of normal retirement at age 65 corresponds to normal retirement age for full Social Security retirement benefits. However, Social Security is phasing in a new normal retirement age of 67 beginning in the year 2000 and completing the process in 2027. By 2027, normal retirement age will be age 67. Possibly this will have an impact on normal retirement age for regular pension plans in the 21st century.

Not every employee will continue to work until age 65. Most plans will also specify an **early retirement** age, such as age 55. Normally, early retirement will result in a reduced retirement benefit. The reduced benefit for early retirement is due to the fact that less money has been accumulated on behalf of the participant and early retirement results in a longer retirement period in which benefits will have to be paid to the retiree. Life expectancy of the retiree is a factor which will affect the amount of the retirement benefit. Early retirement at age 55 results in the participant's life expectancy being at least 10 years longer and accordingly, a reduced retirement benefit will be paid.

Some qualified plans may also specify a **late retirement**, such as age 70. Plans which permit late retirement often specify that late retirement is with the consent of the employer. Frequently, a delayed retirement can result in an increased retirement benefit as the individual's life expectancy following late retirement is reduced and the money accumulated now has to be paid over a shorter period of time. Thus, an increased retirement benefit would be possible.

VESTING

Vesting refers to **ownership**. As the employer makes contributions on behalf of the employees, over a period of time, they will own these employer contributions. If an employee does not remain actively employed with the employer until normal retirement, the individual may own, or be fully vested in the employer's contributions.

BASIC CHARACTERISTICS OF PENSION PLANS

The employer recognizes that not all employees will remain with the firm until retirement. Some may quit after a short period of time. Others may get fired. Because of employee turnover, most employers will elect a vesting schedule which limits the amount of employee vesting until a certain period of time has elapsed. Vesting schedules are regulated by the federal government so that the employees' rights and interests are protected.

> Lisa has worked for the XYZ Company for four years. She terminates her employment and is told that as of her termination date, the company had contributed $2,000 into the company pension plan on her behalf. Further she is told that effective with her termination, she is 20% vested. This means that she is entitled to 20% of $2,000 or $400 upon her termination.

In the above illustration, Lisa owned 20% of her pension contributions. The remaining 80% will stay in the plan for the benefit of the remaining participants.

Maximum vesting schedules are regulated by the IRS and over the years have become more stringent, thus favoring the employee. These schedules do change relative to changes in the tax laws. Currently, the following vesting requirements exist:

- Employees are always considered to be 100% vested at all times in their own contributions
- If a plan has an eligibility requirement which exceeds one year of service, the participant must be 100% vested immediately
- Employees are always 100% vested upon attainment of normal retirement age
- Employees are automatically 100% vested if the plan terminates or upon discontinuance of employer contributions

3/7 Vesting Schedule

Further, the IRS provides that a pension plan will maintain its qualified status if it establishes one of the following two vesting schedules:

3/7 Schedule: This schedule provides that employees must be at least 20% vested after three years of plan participation and thereafter vested at the rate of 20% per year, thus becoming fully vested (100%) at the end of the seventh year. Table 2-2 illustrates the 3/7 schedule.

TABLE 2-2

THE 3/7 VESTING SCHEDULE

Completed Years of Service	Vesting Percentage
Less than 3	0
3 years	20
4 years	40
5 years	60
6 years	80
7 years	100

It should be noted that changes in vesting occur at the end of a year of service under the plan. A year of service is defined as a 12-month period identified by the plan (i.e., plan year or calendar year) during which the employee has worked a minimum of 1,000 hours.

Amy has worked at the ABC Company for two years and 11½ months and quits. She is not vested in any portion of the employers plan contributions. Conversely, if Amy quits her job after six years of service as a plan participant, she is entitled to 80% vesting in the employer's contributions.

Bob is covered by a qualified pension plan which uses a 3/7 vesting schedule. Bob terminates employment after 3½ years in the plan when the value of his account is $5,000. His vested benefit would be $1,000, or 20% of the account value.

5 Year Schedule

5 Year Schedule: An employee must be 100% vested after five years in the plan. This schedule provides a rather wide range of flexibility for the employer. This element is especially attractive for an employer who may experience considerable employee turnover in the early years of an employee's employment.

For example, an employer could establish vesting under this schedule which specifies 0% vesting for the first four years and then 100% vesting at the end of the fifth year. This would be a 0/5 vesting schedule.

Other examples could be no vesting for the first year and 25% per year with full vesting at the end of the fifth year; no vesting for the three years followed by 50% vesting at the end of the fourth year and another 50% at the end of the fifth year.

The employer has considerable latitude in determining the vesting schedule provided that all employees are fully vested after five years. It is fairly common to simply provide vesting under this schedule at the rate of 20% per year with full vesting at the end of the fifth year.

INCIDENTAL PLAN BENEFITS

The primary purpose of the vesting requirements is to protect the plan participants from discrimination with regard to employer contributions. The employer may amend the vesting schedule in accordance with current laws. However, any such amendment cannot restrict or reduce participant's current vested amounts. Thus, if a slower vesting schedule is established, it will not apply to current plan participants.

The primary purpose of a qualified pension plan is to provide retirement benefits to plan participants. However, it may also provide for the payment of **incidental death benefits** (profit sharing plans may also provide certain health insurance benefits). This death benefit would be paid if the plan participant died before retirement.

The participant's beneficiary or estate is always entitled to any vested retirement benefits upon the pre-retirement death of the participant. Depending on when death might occur, these vested benefits may be relatively small. The purpose of providing a pre-retirement death benefit in the form of life insurance is to enable the beneficiary to receive a value which approximates the intended retirement benefit.

The life insurance must be incidental to the plan. The incidental limitation applies when insurance is purchased on the life of a participant and benefits are payable to the participant, the participant's beneficiary, or estate. The IRS test to determine whether life insurance benefits are incidental is to determine the relationship of the cost of life insurance benefits to the total cost of providing all plan benefits.

BASIC CHARACTERISTICS OF PENSION PLANS

25% Rule

This test or comparison is known as the **25% rule**. If the cost of the life insurance benefits (the premium paid) is **less than 25%** of the cost of providing all plan benefits, then the incidental limitation is satisfied. For example, if the employer's pension contribution for plan participants is $10,000, then something less than $2,500 could be used to pay the premiums for incidental life insurance benefits.

XYZ Company wishes to have a pre-retirement death benefit funded by life insurance as part of the company's qualified pension plan. If the plan contributions total $20,000 annually, the life insurance premium must be less than $5,000 annually to satisfy the incidental limitation.

TOP HEAVY PROVISIONS

One of the characteristics of a qualified plan is the non-discriminatory requirement in terms of eligibility and coverage. The non-discrimination rules also apply to plan benefits.

A plan will be viewed as top heavy by the IRS if the value of plan benefits for key employees **exceeds 60%** of the value for all plan participants. A **key employee** is identified as:

- A company officer
- A 5% owner
- A 1% owner with compensation in excess of $150,000
- A highly compensated employee

A highly compensated employee is determined by reviewing the individual's compensation for the current plan year or for the preceding 12-month period (the look back year). An employee will be considered highly compensated with regards to a plan year if:

- Compensation is in excess of $99,000 (as indexed) during the look back year
- Compensation is in excess of $66,000 (as indexed) during the look back year and the individual is in the top paid group

The top paid group of employees is the group of employees in the top 20% based on compensation paid in the current year. Thus, in a relatively small firm of 25 employees, the top paid group would be the five highest paid employees.

When the IRS identifies a plan as top heavy, adjustments must be made. These modifications pertain to vesting and contribution requirements.

A top heavy plan must use one of following two vesting schedules:

1. 100% vesting after three years of service
2. A six year vesting schedule as follows:

Years of Service	Vesting Percentage
after 2	20%
3	40%
4	60%
5	80%
6	100%

For any top heavy plan year, the plan must provide a minimum benefit or contribution for each non-key participant. If a defined benefit plan is top heavy (defined benefit plans will be discussed in a later chapter), the non-key participant must receive a minimum accrued benefit equal to 2% of average compensation multiplied by each year of service (when the plan was top heavy) up to a maximum of 10 years.

If a defined contribution plan is top heavy (defined contribution plans will also be discussed in a later chapter), non-key employees must be provided a contribution equal to the lesser of 3% of compensation allocated to a key employee or the largest percentage of compensation allocated to a key employee.

The ABC Corporation is anxious to install a corporate pension plan which will provide an employer contribution of 5% of compensation.

Employee	Date of Hire	Position	Salary
J. Smith	1-1-70	50% owner	$100,000
P. Brown	1-1-70	20% owner	75,000
W. Black	6-1-80	5% owner	75,000
R. Jones	9-1-82	Vice President	75,000
P. Carson	3-1-83	Foreman	60,000
J. Able	1-1-88	Asst. Foreman	50,000

BASIC CHARACTERISTICS OF PENSION PLANS

M. George	7-1-88	Office Manager	30,000
J. Kim	3-1-80	Machinist	40,000
P. White	5-1-81	Machinist	40,000
K. Kelly	6-1-90	Machinist	35,000
W. Williams	6-1-90	Machinist	35,000
A. Smythe	8-1-91	Machinist	30,000
W. Houston	9-1-91	Machinist	30,000
G. Knoll	1-1-92	Machinist	24,000
P. Johnson	1-1-92	Machinist	24,000
B. Turner	2-1-92	Machinist	22,000
W. Warren	2-1-92	Machinist	20,000
M. Ackerman	6-1-90	Secretary	20,000
S. Reed	7-1-91	Secretary	18,000
A. Keller	8-1-89	Bookkeeper	18,000

Total: $694,000

The top paid employees include: J. Smith, P. Brown, W. Black, R. Jones, and P. Carson. The key employees are the three owners and the vice president. The plan is probably not top heavy as the salary of the four officers totals $325,000. This represents less than 50% of the total payroll and correspondingly, plan contributions would also represent no more than 50% of the total contribution. Even if the plan were a defined benefit plan, there is probably enough "room" in terms of compensation for the owners compared to the rest of the employees, to prevent the plan from being top heavy.

TAXATION AND PENALTIES

Qualified plans offer distinct tax advantages as previously noted. A discussion of taxation requires knowledge of what is considered tax basis and cost basis. By definition, **cost basis** is money which has already been taxed by the federal government. **Tax basis** is that which is yet to be taxed.

Bill deposits $100 in his savings account. This $100 came from his paycheck and was already taxed. Bill's cost basis is $100. During the year, his $100 deposit earns $5 interest. This $5 has yet to be taxed and is identified as tax basis.

When an employer makes a contribution to a qualified pension plan, the contribution is tax deductible. It has not been taxed and this contribution will be tax basis. The pension contribution grows tax deferred. Thus, this investment return has not been taxed and is also considered tax basis.

When the plan participant receives the retirement benefit, the money received has never been taxed. It is all tax basis. Therefore, the entire amount received is **taxable at ordinary income tax rates** to the participant. This taxable event occurs when the participant receives plan benefits due to retirement, termination of employment, termination of the plan, death, or disability.

Example: Barbara is a participant in a non-contributory qualified pension plan. She is nearing retirement and the value of her account is $85,000. When she retires, her cost basis will be $0. This is because the employer's contributions were tax deductible and the contributions grew tax deferred. This money has never been taxed, so the full amount is tax basis.

If the participant has made after tax voluntary contributions to the pension plan, then those contributions would be considered cost basis as they have already been taxed. The voluntary contributions grow tax deferred. When the participant receives the voluntary contributions at retirement, part of the distribution is considered a return of cost basis (and not taxable) and part will be identified as tax basis and taxed under ordinary income tax rates.

> Jan has a $5,000 voluntary (after tax) contribution in her total pension benefit. The total value of her pension benefit including the employer's contribution and investment growth is $100,000. Jan's cost basis is 5% ($5,000/$100,000). Five percent of each benefit payment represents a return of her cost basis (up to $5,000). Ninety-five percent is taxable as tax basis.

Instead of a series of payments at retirement, the participant can elect a **lump sum distribution**. In this situation, any employee cost basis is recovered tax free. Any tax basis may be calculated using a five-year averaging formula. Five year averaging is available if the lump sum distribution is received after the participant attains age 59½ and the individual elects to treat all such amounts received during the tax year in the same manner.

The purpose of income averaging is to soften the tax blow for an individual who receives an unusually large amount of taxable income in a given year.

BASIC CHARACTERISTICS OF PENSION PLANS

Betty has averaged $30,000 of earned income for several years. She then realizes a taxable lump sum pension distribution of $100,000 which suddenly increases her taxable income to $130,000.

A graduated income tax structure as we have in the United States would result in a substantial amount of tax owed. Five year averaging of the $100,000 pension distribution should reduce Betty's tax liability.

Five year income averaging provides for the following calculation in Betty's situation:

A distribution allowance is deducted from the total taxable amount. The allowance is equal to the lesser of $10,000 or 50% of the taxable amount. However, this allowance is then reduced by an amount which is equal to 20% of the amount by which the taxable amount exceeds $20,000.

Betty's total taxable amount is $100,000 less the distribution allowance of $10,000. However, this allowance is wiped out by then reducing this amount by 20% of the taxable amount in excess of $20,000. $100,000 - $10,000 = $90,000

Difference between $90,000 and $20,000 = $70,000.

$70,000 x 20% = $14,000

Betty's tax is then computed by taking 1/5 of the taxable amount ($100,000) which equals $20,000; computing the tax on $20,000 and multiplying this amount by five. The tax is calculated at single tax payer rates without any deductions. Using 1992 tax tables, this calculation would be as follows:

Tax on $20,000 = $3,273 x 5 = $16,365.

Without five year averaging, the tax on $100,000 would equal $27,377.

From the above, it can be easily determined that five year averaging reduces Betty's tax bill by more than $10,000.

Another alternative available to plan participants who receive a lump sum pension distribution is to roll this distribution into another qualified plan such as an Individual Retirement Account (IRA). Rollover provisions allow for the rolling or transfer of qualified plan distributions into an IRA, provided such rollovers occur only once per year and the rollover funds are deposited in the IRA within 60 days of the distribution.

Using the rollover alternative for a lump sum pension distribution does not eliminate the tax liability, it merely postpones it until a later date. Sooner or later, the tax will be paid. There may be an advantage to paying the tax at a later date because the individual may be in a lower tax bracket.

Not only will the government eventually receive the taxes due but they can also impose **tax penalties** for violation of tax rules.

A **premature distribution** is any distribution from a qualified plan received prior to the participant's attainment of age 59½. Any such distribution is subject to ordinary income tax on the amount distributed plus a **10% penalty tax**.

> Sam, age 45, decides to spend his summer in Europe and to finance his trip, receives a qualified plan distribution of $10,000. If we assume that Sam is in a 20% tax bracket, he will pay approximately $2,000 in income taxes on this distribution plus another $1,000 due to the 10% penalty tax.

There are some exceptions to the 10% penalty rule. These include:

- Distributions due to death or disability of the participant
- Distributions received by a participant who is at least age 55 and who has satisfied the plan's early retirement rules
- Distributions to a former spouse or dependent child as the result of a divorce decree
- Distributions which are part of a series of periodic payments which are made for the life expectancy of the individual or joint lives of the individual and his or her survivor. This exception also accommodates early retirement situations.

- Distributions which are due to removal of excess contributions
- Allowable plan loans

It should be noted that these exceptions only remove the 10% penalty tax. Ordinary income tax still has to be paid as distributions received usually have a zero cost basis. A plan loan will not be taxed as a distribution if it is repaid within five years or if the purpose of the loan was due to the purchase of the principal residence of the individual.

Any excess distributions are also subject to a penalty tax of 15%. Tax law limits the total retirement benefits which may be paid to a qualified plan participant in any one year to $150,000, as indexed. However, this indexed number will only increase when inflation adjustments equal or exceed $10,000.

Exceptions to this penalty include:

- Amounts received which are attributable to after-tax participant contributions
- Excess amounts received due to the death of the participant
- Excess amounts which are paid due to a divorce decree

The government has also implemented regulations which penalize an individual for **delayed distributions** from a qualified plan. The purpose of a pension plan is to provide income during retirement. It is not to indefinitely shelter money from taxes. Therefore, plan participants must begin to receive plan distributions not later than April 1st of the year following the year in which the participant attains age 70½.

> For example, if Mary was 70½ years of age in the year 1991, she must begin a systematic withdrawal or distribution from her qualified plan by April 1, 1992. In addition, there is a minimum required amount which must be distributed relative to the individual's life expectancy and the type of qualified plan.

Failure to comply with this requirement subjects the participant to a penalty equal to 50% on the amount which should have been distributed.

Mark does not begin a systematic distribution in accordance with the law. Based on his life expectancy and the amount of money in the plan, it is determined that he should receive $5,000 annually. Mark will have to pay a 50% penalty on the $5,000 ($2,500) as a result.

Again, it should be remembered that the individual is subject to the 50% penalty plus ordinary income tax on these distributions.

Table 2-3 summarizes the taxation and penalties.

TABLE 2-3

TAXATION SUMMARY

Contributions by the	
Employer	Tax deductible
Employee	** Not tax deductible
Investment Income due to	
Employer Contributions	Tax deferred
Employee Contributions	Tax deferred
Distributions from	
Employer Contributions	Taxable — all tax basis
Employee Contributions	Taxable — less cost basis
Penalties	
Distributions prior to 59½	10% of the amount withdrawn
Excess distributions	15% of the excess
Delayed distributions	50% of the amount that should have been withdrawn by 70½

** It should be noted that there are a few qualified plans which provide tax-deductible employee contributions. These will be discussed in a later chapter.

SUMMARY

Retirement plans may be qualified or non-qualified. A plan must meet certain requirements to be qualified. These requirements include that the plan must be in writing, communicated to the employees, may not discriminate, must be permanent and for the benefit of the employees or their beneficiaries, and the plan must be filed and approved by the IRS.

Once a plan is approved as a qualified plan, the employer and the participants enjoy certain tax advantages. Contributions are tax deductible; investment income is tax deferred; and contributions are not taxable to the employees. A non-qualified plan, such as deferred compensation, is not filed with or approved by the IRS. It may only benefit one or a few key employees. As a non-qualified plan, it does not enjoy the tax advantages of a qualified plan.

Qualified plans must comply with certain eligibility and participation requirements. Typically, eligibility for participation in a plan means one year of service and minimum age 21. An employer is not required to cover all employees. However, if the plan is to maintain its qualified status, it must meet certain tests as to participation of employees.

Plans may be contributory or non-contributory. The majority of pension plans are non-contributory — the employer pays all. Contributory plans normally require that all participants contribute a certain amount to the plan. Some plans may allow voluntary contributions whereby a participant may elect to contribute a predetermined after tax amount. These voluntary contributions will grow tax deferred.

All qualified plans will establish a normal retirement age (usually age 65) and many of these plans will also permit early retirement. Usually, early retirement will require a minimum age be attained (age 55) and the participant must have been a member of the plan for a minimum number of years, such as 10.

Vesting refers to an employees non-forfeitable right to employer contributions. Vesting means ownership. To maintain its qualified status, a plan must comply with the 0/5 or 3/7 vesting schedules. A qualified plan may also offer 100% immediate vesting but it cannot restrict 100% vesting to more than seven years of plan participation.

Often, plans may provide incidental benefits such as a pre-retirement death benefit funded by means of life insurance policies. When this benefit is offered, the premium for the life insurance benefit must amount to less than 25% of the plan contributions made by the employer.

Due to the non-discrimination requirement of qualified plans, the IRS will review plans to determine if they are top heavy. A plan is considered top heavy if more than 60% of the plan's benefits or contributions benefit the key employees. A key employee is considered an owner or an employee who earns a pre-determined amount of income. This income measure is indexed in accordance with cost of living criteria. When a plan is considered top heavy, the IRS requires certain adjustments in contribution amounts and vesting schedules.

Qualified plans offer the tax advantages of deductible contributions and tax-deferred growth. As a result the cost basis of a qualified plan is usually zero. Normally, all retirement benefits are taxable, less the recovery of any possible cost basis by means of employee after-tax contributions. Lump sum distributions may receive favorable tax treatment by means of five year income averaging.

In addition to regular federal income taxation of plan benefits, the IRS also imposes certain tax penalties for premature distributions prior to age 59½, excess distributions and failure to begin a systematic distribution of plan benefits following the participant's attainment of age 70½.

REVIEW EXERCISES

1. John, an employer, cannot decide whether or not to install his company's pension plan with the option to have employee contributions. How might you respond to John regarding employee contributions?

2. Describe the vesting schedules which must be used when a qualified plan is top heavy.

CHAPTER 3

DEFERRED COMPENSATION

Chapter 2 briefly explored the situation of Cindy, the Sales Manager for ABC Inc. As both a key employee fringe benefit as well as a retirement plan, deferred compensation has been used for many years in the business world as well as the professional sports and entertainment worlds.

Even as a form of retirement benefit, one of the principal advantages of the deferred compensation plan is its deferral of current income and taxation for the individual. For example, many professional athletes use this device due to their extremely large salaries. Typically, some portion of their compensation is deferred for future delivery (typically at retirement). The deferral results in no current income taxes on the amount deferred.

Deferred compensation is a written agreement between an employer and an employee by which a specific amount of current compensation for present services is deferred until a later date or occurrence. This later date will normally be retirement, premature death, or disability of the employee.

Generally, deferred compensation can be established in one of two ways — a salary continuation approach or a salary reduction plan. The salary continuation approach means that the deferred compensation is actually an additional benefit over and above the individual's compensation. This is sometimes referred to as a **Selective Executive Retirement Plan (SERP)**. Since a SERP is selective (discriminatory), it is non-qualified. In accordance with the provisions of the SERP, the employer promises or elects to pay a deferred benefit upon retirement, death or disability of the key employee. The employee does not reduce his or her salary or defer any current compensation. The SERP is an additional benefit over and above current compensation.

Generally, deferred compensation means that the employee postpones current receipt of a salary increase in exchange for the employer's agreement or promise to pay this benefit at a later time. Thus, deferred compensation results in deferral or reduction of current compensation as part of the employee's salary.

FACTORS FOR SELECTION OF DEFERRED COMPENSATION

Just as every business is not necessarily ready for a qualified pension plan, not every business is a candidate for deferred compensation. Generally, prospects for deferred compensation can be found in profitable corporations, partnerships, sole proprietorships, and certain non-profit organizations.

The individual covered by deferred compensation may be an employee such as a manager, salesperson, key executive or even the businessowner. To these organizations and their key executives, deferred compensation can be promoted in various ways, depending on the company's needs and existing benefits. Some of the factors which might dictate the use of deferred compensation include the following:

- In lieu of a formal qualified pension plan, the employer needs to be discriminatory or selective as to which employees should be covered by the plan. As a non-qualified plan, there is no IRS approval necessary and the plan may be as selective as the employer desires.

- The employer has a formal qualified pension plan in existence but needs to provide supplemental retirement benefits to certain higher paid employees. In order to keep the costs of a qualified plan reasonable, the employer may have elected a relatively small benefit program which in a sense is discriminatory for the highly paid executive. A deferred compensation plan can alleviate this problem.

- The employer needs to provide retirement benefits for the older key executive who may have been hired at an older age. Due to the older age and the plan's eligibility requirements, this key individual may not even be eligible for the qualified plan or have extremely few benefits due to his or her late entry into the plan.

- Deferred compensation can be a valuable tool for purposes of attracting and hiring key executives. In addition, it also can serve as a means of retaining these key individuals. For the employer who has a problem in hiring and retaining these key individuals, deferred compensation could be the answer.

- The employer needs to make executive compensation more meaningful. Due to the graduated income structure, the key individuals receive raises or bonuses which often push the person into a higher tax bracket. By deferring receipt of these dollars, the value of these raises and bonuses may be more beneficial to the key person.
- Deferred compensation may be preferred in many close corporations in lieu of providing key persons with minority ownership. This enables the close corporation to remain in the hands of one or a few persons.

THE DEFERRED COMPENSATION AGREEMENT

Deferred compensation involves a written agreement between the employer and the employee whereby the employer promises to deliver future dollars to the employee upon death, disability, or retirement. There are various types of deferred compensation plans which will be discussed in the next section of this chapter. Regardless of the form of the deferred compensation, a written agreement must exist between the employer and employee. This agreement governs the mechanics of the deferred compensation plan.

Standard Provisions

Generally, the employer and the employee will decide on the terms of the agreement based on their respective needs and objectives. The agreement will normally contain the following provisions and conditions:

- **Agreement Identities:** The effective date of the agreement, parties to the agreement, name and address of the employer will be identified.
- **The Employment Provision:** The employer agrees to employ the employee in a specific capacity and to compensate him or her according to a predetermined salary. A copy of the employee's job description might be included.
- **Retirement Benefits:** The amount and commencement of retirement benefits should be specified including a provision for early retirement and reduced benefits.
- **Disability Benefits:** The amount of benefits, date on which benefits will begin, and duration of benefits

should be specified. In addition, a determination should be made with regard to what constitutes a disability.

- **Pre-Retirement Death Benefits:** The benefit amount, commencement date and duration of any pre-retirement death benefit to be paid to the employee's survivor should be identified.

- **Post Retirement Consulting:** This provision is optional and provides that as a condition for receipt of the deferred compensation, the employee agrees to provide consulting services for the employer after retirement.

- **Termination of Employment:** This provision will detail what will take place regarding the employee's termination prior to retirement with regard to the deferred compensation. Depending on the agreement, there may or may not be any payments made.

- **Termination for Cause:** If the corporation terminates the employee for adverse conduct or activity which is detrimental to the corporation, no deferred compensation benefits will be paid.

- **Forfeiture Provision:** This provision provides that any deferred compensation payments provided by the agreement may be suspended or eliminated due to breach of the agreement by the employee. It may also identify what will happen in the event that the employee does compete against the employer. The employer has very broad authority and discretion regarding this factor.

- **Communications Provision:** This provision specifies that all communication regarding the deferred compensation must be in written form. There will be no verbal agreements.

- **Claims Procedures:** Benefits due under the plan are detailed with regard to claims procedures as well as denial of any claims.

- **Plan Administrator:** A person should be identified as the plan administrator for the deferred compensation plan. This could be the employer or someone else appointed by the employer.

- **Non-Compete Provision:** The employee agrees to remain with the company until retirement and to refrain from becoming employed by a competitor at any time including after retirement.

These provisions are fairly common to all agreements. There may be other provisions included in the written agreement depending on the needs of the employer and employee. For

DEFERRED COMPENSATION

example, the agreement may contain a statement that the employer's agreement is no more than a promise to pay the deferred compensation in the future. In addition, there may be a provision which specifies that the employee has no secured or preferred claim to corporate assets, including any life insurance or annuity contracts purchased by the employer to fund the agreement.

TYPES OF DEFERRED COMPENSATION

Deferred compensation plans can be classified in several ways. Two such classifications are funded or unfunded.

Funded Plan

A **funded plan** is one in which the employer will actually set aside a sum of money or other property into an account or trust as security for the employer's promise to later pay this deferred benefit.

In accordance with current IRS regulations, a funded plan results in constructive receipt of the amount set aside by the employee. Accordingly, even though the employee has not actually received this money, he or she will be taxed on it. To avoid this taxation, the employee's right to these sums must be subject to forfeiture.

The element of forfeiture will be included in the written deferred compensation agreement between the employee and the employer. Thus, normally the agreement will specify that the employee loses or forfeits the right to this money due to:

- Terminating employment and going to work for a competitor
- Not remaining with the employer until retirement, death, or disability

In other words, the funded deferred compensation plan ties the employee to the company and the employer except for retirement, death, or disability. If the employee leaves for any other reason, the deferred amounts of money will be forfeited. Frequently, the agreement may even further specify that the employee must perform certain consulting services for the employer after retirement as a condition for receipt of the deferred compensation.

Thus, a funded deferred compensation plan normally results in a current tax liability for the employee unless the written agreement specifies conditions under which the employee will forfeit the benefit. It should be noted that funded deferred compensation plans are not that common. The more common type of deferred compensation is the unfunded plan.

Unfunded Plan

An **unfunded plan** is simply the employer's unsecured promise to deliver future benefits to the designated employee. The advantage to the employee is that since no money has been set aside, there can be no concern about constructive receipt and any possible tax liability. This applies to the normal deferred compensation arrangement as well as to a SERP.

The principal disadvantage with this arrangement is that the employee has no assurance that the promised future payments will be made. The employee or his or her estate must then be considered a creditor of the corporation should the employer not pay the promised benefits. This then means that the employee must stand in line with the other corporate creditors in order to hopefully receive payment. In his or her status as a creditor of the corporation, the employer could elect to pay other creditors ahead of the employee with the unfunded deferred compensation.

To help alleviate this situation to some degree, a **"Rabbi Trust"** can be utilized. The concept of the Rabbi Trust originates in an IRS ruling in which assets were placed in an irrevocable trust for payment to a Rabbi. The IRS ruled that these assets placed in the irrevocable trust did not constitute current income or economic benefit to the Rabbi, provided that the assets remained subject to the claims of creditors. Thus, if assets are placed in an irrevocable trust or escrow account to fund a deferred compensation plan, the assets are not considered as funding the deferred compensation plan. Thus, these assets can be placed in the trust for the benefit of the employee and provide some assurance as to the future delivery of these amounts.

Of course, these assets remain an asset of the corporation. As such, they too are subject to the claims of creditors. However, this apparent drawback is the reason that the employee is not considered to be in constructive receipt of the money and thus avoids current taxation. Funding for this trust can take just about any form — cash, mutual funds, life insurance, fixed or variable annuities, etc.

DEFERRED COMPENSATION

EMPLOYER/ EMPLOYEE ADVANTAGES AND DISADVANTAGES

From the **employer's perspective**, deferred compensation is a no lose situation. Assuming the agreement is formulated correctly, the employee is locked into his or her current situation. The possible forfeiture of the money in the event that the employee terminates employment with the employer may well be adequate motivation for the employee to "stick it out" and not terminate.

Non-Compete Clause

Naturally, the employer is freed from worry or concern about losing this key employee. The employer may be even more relieved that they probably will never lose the employee to a competitor because of the non-compete clause in the deferred compensation agreement.

Inexpensive

In addition, if the deferred compensation arrangement is unfunded, it costs the employer nothing to adopt this agreement since the unfunded plan is merely an unsecured promise to pay future benefits. The employer may or may not feel a moral responsibility to deliver those benefits at a later date. Naturally, we would assume that the employer accepts the ethical responsibility and will make every effort to provide the benefits promised.

As a non-qualified plan, deferred compensation represents a retirement plan which is inexpensive to install since it can be selective (discriminatory) as to participation. This is a plan for key personnel and not all employees. Typically, when a plan is qualified and covers all eligible employees, it becomes so expensive that the amount of benefits offered by the plan are minimal. These minimal benefits may affect all employees but they may more seriously affect the higher paid key personnel of the company. This group of executives which is highly compensated are "discriminated" against by being provided relatively smaller benefits compared to the other lower paid employees.

Recruiting

A deferred compensation plan can be an attractive recruiting tool for the employer who must compete with other companies for the services of highly qualified and skilled employees. Deferred compensation as a benefit can help the employer attract and retain key personnel.

Deferred compensation also offers several **employee advantages**, especially if it is a salary reduction type of agreement whereby normally current income is not received and not currently taxed to the employee. Secondarily, the deferred compensation represents a supplemental (or possibly a primary) retirement plan for the employee. In addition, it may also provide some protection against the risk of premature death or the economic death caused by total disability due to accident or sickness.

Possibly the principal **employer disadvantage** is the need to provide the deferred funds to the employee when required by the agreement. This is particularly true with regard to the unfunded plan. If the employer doesn't have the money upon the employee's retirement, this can create a financial drain for the corporation or possibly a lawsuit by the employee. In other words, this plan locks up the employee for his or her working life and will eventually cost the employer. Depending on how the plan is arranged and the employer's commitment to accumulating the necessary funds, it may or may not cause a financial problem for the employer.

Naturally, the employer's potential problem also becomes a major **disadvantage for the employee** — will the deferred money be there when the employee retires, dies, or becomes disabled? There is a certain degree of uncertainty regarding the delivery of the future dollars.

A secondary disadvantage for the employee could be current taxation if the plan uses a salary continuation approach such as a SERP. Sooner or later, taxes must be paid. With a SERP taxes are currently paid for the economic benefit of the plan to the employee as opposed to being paid at a later date when possibly, the individual's tax situation or tax bracket may be less.

TAXATION

Taxation of deferred compensation involves four categories of tax liability:

- Income tax to the employee
- Income tax to the corporation (the employer)
- Federal estate tax
- Other tax considerations

DEFERRED COMPENSATION

Employee Income Tax

Employee income tax is generally not a consideration during the period of time that the compensation is deferred. An actual salary reduction plan whereby the employee defers receipt of current income usually results in no current federal income tax liability to the employee during the deferral period.

The point has generally been made that at retirement the employee will be in a lower tax bracket and thus there is an additional tax advantage — lower taxes at older ages. In reality, this may or may not be an accurate picture of an individual's tax situation 10, 20, or 30 years from now. There appears to be a trend whereby tax rates are increasing thus resulting in possibly the same or even a higher tax bracket when a person retires and would be in receipt of the deferred compensation. In any event, when the benefit is received, the employee is liable for ordinary income tax on the amounts received.

If benefits are received as a result of the disability of the employee, these benefits are also subject to ordinary income tax as received.

If benefits are received due to the death of the employee prior to retirement, part of the benefits will not be taxable and part will be taxable. The first $5,000 of benefits paid to the beneficiary are not taxable. This exclusion from taxation is available provided that the deceased employee had a risk of forfeiture per the deferred compensation agreement. Amounts received in excess of $5,000 are taxable to the beneficiary as a receipt of the deceased's compensation.

Again, the key concept is the risk of forfeiture. This element must be present to prevent current taxation of the deferred amounts. The IRS occasionally changes its position on some of these tax implications. For example, a corporate owner and majority stockholder could run the risk of not having a substantial risk of forfeiture due to the fact that he or she is the owner and principal stockholder.

The reason that the IRS could take this position is that as owner and controlling stockholder, the individual is in a position to amend or end the agreement at anytime. The owner-stockholder actually controls the money and the income is available at anytime. There is less risk of the IRS taking this position if the employee is not a majority owner or controlling stockholder but instead, merely a very key person in the organization.

Corporate Taxation

The **corporate tax liability** is somewhat different than the individual situation. Generally, the corporation will receive a tax deduction for the deferred compensation amounts paid to the employee at retirement or disability; or to the beneficiary in the event of the employee's pre-retirement death.

To achieve this deductibility, the deferred compensation plan must be for a reasonable amount and must serve a legitimate or valid business purpose. A reasonable amount refers to an amount of deferred compensation which is reasonable relative to the individual's position in the company and the pay scale for key executives.

For example, if the key person is earning $100,000 annually and the amount of the deferred compensation is $1 million, then this amount would certainly appear as unreasonable in relation to the individual's position and current compensation.

The element of the plan providing for a valid business purpose relates to the fact that the plan cannot be primarily for the benefit of the owner or majority stockholders. A valid business purpose is considered to be the hiring and retention of key executives for the business. Thus, as a key executive benefit, the business benefits from the expertise and skill of the key person.

A special note should be made regarding the use of life insurance to fund a deferred compensation plan. If insurance owned by the corporation to fund deferred compensation is considered to be a reasonable business purpose or need, then there may be no adverse tax implications. However, the corporation must guard against the possibility of taxation on accumulated earnings.

When the corporation owns the life insurance to fund the deferred compensation, money must be generated or accumulated with which to pay the life insurance premiums. Again, this expense will be considered a legitimate business expense if it enhances business or corporate goals and needs as opposed to benefiting the individual goals or needs of majority stockholders.

Estate Taxation

Estate taxation refers to the fact that the value of the deferred compensation may be includible (and possibly taxable) in the employee's gross estate at death. Generally, life insurance proceeds are received federal income tax free. However, life insurance values are includible in the decedent's gross estate for federal estate tax purposes. Generally, this same concept applies to deferred compensation.

If the decedent was receiving or had an enforceable right to receive lifetime benefits in accordance with a deferred compensation plan, then the present value of benefits payable to a surviving beneficiary are includible in the decedent's gross estate. Generally, the deceased employee is considered to have an enforceable right to future benefits provided he or she has complied with the conditions of the deferred compensation agreement as of the date of death.

In the majority of situations, the key executive will have complied with the agreement and will be considered to have an enforceable right to the receipt of future lifetime benefits. Thus, the present value of any further benefits received by the decedent's estate or beneficiary following death will be includible in the gross estate for possible federal estate taxation.

A deferred compensation agreement which provides for survivor benefits only, and where the employee has no right to any post-employment benefits, may **not be includible** in the decedent's gross estate. Generally, this type of deferred compensation plan is referred to as a **death benefit only** plan (**DBO**).

A DBO is also referred to as a survivor's income plan or a widow's benefit plan. In accordance with a DBO plan, the employer agrees to pay a specified sum of money, normally in installments, to the key executive's beneficiary if the employee dies while still employed by the firm.

For these payments to be excluded from the decedent's estate, the employee cannot be entitled to any lifetime benefits such as retirement or disability benefits. Therefore, the DBO must provide only survivor benefits. If a separate agreement is implemented to include retirement and disability benefits, the IRS will consider these separate agreements as one. Accordingly, the present value of these benefits would then be included in the employee's gross estate.

One way to avoid this is to have the DBO operative until the employee retires at which point the employee and the employer will enter into a deferred compensation agreement which will provide retirement and/or disability benefits.

Since the primary purpose of the DBO is to provide survivor benefits, most often a life insurance policy will be used to informally fund the plan.

However, this estate taxation issue with regard to DBOs is always open to interpretation by the IRS and the tax courts. Currently, the IRS indicates that this type of plan is considered to be a completed gift of present interest as of the date of death. If the value of this gift of present interest exceeds the annual gift tax exclusion ($10,000), then a gift tax return must be filed. Gift tax may be due if the value of the gift exceeds the unified tax credit available ($192,800). The unified tax credit actually has an exemptive value of $600,000 for federal estate tax purposes.

The tax consequences of a DBO plan may be summarized as follows:

- During the employee's lifetime there is no amount includible in the employee's current compensation for tax purposes
- If the agreement is properly arranged, DBO benefits should not be includible in the key executive's gross estate
- The survivor may exclude the first $5,000 of the death benefit from taxable income
- The employer will receive a tax deduction for the payments made to the survivor provided they constitute reasonable compensation as a necessary business expense

Generally, a DBO does not provide any benefit for the key executive but rather for the individual's family. Accordingly, there are certain situations in which a DBO plan may be an attractive benefit for the key employee. These would include the following:

- The key person already has a substantial retirement benefit provided by a qualified retirement plan and is in need of increased pre-retirement death benefit
- The key executive has other benefit plans which can provide him with substantial retirement benefits (i.e., stock investments, split dollar life insurance plans, etc.)

DEFERRED COMPENSATION

- The key executive has a substantial estate and very little need for additional retirement benefits but does have a need to provide more estate liquidity through life insurance dollars

Other Tax Considerations

Other tax considerations regarding deferred compensation include Social Security taxation and federal unemployment taxes. If risk of forfeiture is part of the deferred compensation agreement, then Social Security and federal unemployment taxes are not applicable to the deferred amounts.

At the time of retirement, the deferred amounts may be subject to Social Security and federal unemployment taxes as they are received as compensation. Also at retirement, there is no longer any substantial risk of forfeiture. Any taxes due at this time will depend on the amount of income received in the first year of retirement. Generally, continued deferred compensation payments after the first year are not considered wages for Social Security or unemployment taxation.

In addition, deferred compensation benefits, treated as wages in the first year of retirement, could result in the retiree's Social Security benefits being reduced due to the amount of "wages" received. If the amount of deferred compensation benefits are substantial, then all of the Social Security benefits could be reduced to zero.

As a form of retirement or pension plan, deferred compensation is subject to some of the requirements of ERISA. Typically, deferred compensation plans are subject to limited reporting and disclosure requirements. The employer notifies the Department of Labor of the plan's existence and identifies the plan participants.

FUNDING DEFERRED COMPENSATION PLANS

As previously indicated, deferred compensation plans can be funded with any number of financial services products; i.e., fixed and variable annuities, stocks, bonds, mutual funds, etc. Deferred compensation can also be funded with life insurance. There are several advantages and reasons for using life insurance as the funding vehicle. These include:

- The employer's obligation to deliver the deferred benefits is triggered by death. Life insurance funding allows for an exact sum of money to be delivered exactly when it is required — at death.

- Life insurance also provides living benefits through the policy's cash values. The payment of the life insurance premiums results in a forced savings for the future delivery of the deferred benefits.

- The use of life insurance provides some assurance to the employee that there is a systematic plan in force to provide the promised benefits.

- If the employer is financially able to do so, the deferred benefits can be paid from corporate assets when the employee retires. The life insurance policy can remain in force and when the retired employee subsequently dies, the life insurance proceeds can enable the employer to recover the cost of the retirement benefits previously paid.

- Life insurance funding provides flexibility due to the living benefits, the death benefit, and the various settlement options contained in the life insurance contract.

- Generally, cash values grow tax free. Life insurance proceeds are also received tax free.

Naturally, other products can be used to fund the plan. Many of these alternatives do not offer the guarantees of the life insurance contract. Conversely, they may well provide greater opportunity for "investment growth". Life insurance is designed to protect against the risk of premature death; not as an investment product.

If the employer's objective is investment income or growth, then possibly some other products could be used in addition to or separately from any life insurance policies. However, as investment products, there will be a certain amount of investment risk involved which must be borne by the buyer (the employer).

If a certain sum of money is targeted for future delivery and the investment does not do well, the desired sum may not be fully available when the retiring employee expects to receive the plan benefits. Such products as variable annuities or mutual funds provide hardly any guarantees and thus their use as funding mechanisms for deferred compensation should be carefully considered.

DEFERRED COMPENSATION

A CASE STUDY

This case study is presented to provide a practical application of the concepts discussed in this chapter.

Cosmo Inc. is a closely held manufacturing company which currently employs 125 employees, most of whom are hourly workers. Five of the employees are key executives and stockholders with the firm.

Cosmo has averaged $6.5 million in gross income for the past 10 years. During this same period, they have also averaged 4% profit. The increasing cost of their group health insurance plan has steadily eaten away at their profits during this period. In spite of this, they are planning a substantial expansion of their operation within six months, by opening a second plant in a Southeastern city to serve as a distribution center for their products.

Currently, the company provides group life insurance in the amount of $15,000 for each employee and a group major medical plan for all employees and their dependents. Their group plan also includes some short term disability income which provides a benefit of 50% of pay to a maximum of $1,000 monthly, following a 30-day elimination period, payable for up to one year.

Cosmo Inc. would like to install a qualified retirement plan for all employees. In the past, they have looked at pension plan proposals on two occasions but were forced to reject them due to the cost. The five key executives are between the ages of 48 and 59. Because of these ages, Cosmo has reviewed defined benefit plans whereby retirement benefits would be equal to 30-40% of average pay and found them much too expensive.

The five key executives average $100,000 per year of income and management has discussed the feasibility of providing a qualified plan which would provide a retirement benefit of $25,000 per year for each of the key employees. Thus, they are again willing to look at a qualified defined benefit plan which would provide a retirement benefit of 25% of average compensation.

Management realizes that defined benefit plans are expensive, especially because of the ages of some of the employees and all of the key executives. They have considered increasing the deductible on the group medical plan from $250 to $1,000 and possibly eliminating the group disability benefits in order to create some additional dollars for a qualified plan.

Solutions to the Problem

The scenario of Cosmo Inc. is not atypical of many businesses. Cosmo is an established firm with minimal yet steady profits. They employ a substantial number of employees and offer a standard package of employee benefits except for a pension plan. They are a growing firm as evidenced by their expansion into the Southeast.

It is probably true that this profitable operation and its current growth are due to the efforts and skills of the five key executives. If one or more of these key personnel were to terminate their working relationship especially at a time when expansion is in the business picture, Cosmo could have serious difficulties. Therefore, it may be critical to provide some additional incentive for the benefit of these executives.

The primary goal of Cosmo is to provide a retirement benefit. Needless to say, the addition of a pension plan would be beneficial to all 125 employees. However, Cosmo has found this too expensive in the past. They have considered defined benefit plans on two occasions and rejected them due to the cost factor. They certainly aren't any younger today. Therefore, another defined benefit plan which would provide 25% of compensation as a retirement benefit will certainly be more expensive currently than it was in the past. This cost factor is due in part to the ages of the key executives but we will have to assume that there are a few other older employees in the work force as well. However, it is likely that these other older employees earn considerably less salary thus resulting in a smaller pension contribution. A large amount of the pension expense will be due to the ages and salaries of the key personnel.

Cosmo is considering cutting back in the group plan to free up some dollars for the pension plan. Increasing the deductible might result in a 3-5% savings in the group health premium. Eliminating the short term disability would probably result in a few thousand dollars more in savings. However, the disability income plan only provides a 50% of pay benefit (maximum $1,000 per month) payable for one year. The premium for this benefit may not be that substantial.

The question then arises, will these cutbacks produce an adequate sum of money with which to solve, at least in part, the pension expense problem? The answer is probably not, although it certainly would be helpful to some degree. Maybe a more important question is: What will be the impact on the employees of increasing the health plan deductible and eliminating the disability benefit in exchange for a pension benefit?

The answer to this question may be more important to the continued success of Cosmo than the amount of money created by the cutbacks! Typically, a manufacturing work force works for today. Health insurance and disability income benefits are "now" benefits. These are expenses that employees and their families incur today. A pension benefit is something for later, possibly many years later. Frequently, if an hourly worker is given the choice of a benefit which can be received now as opposed to a benefit 20 or 30 years from now, the worker will elect the "now" benefit. If the worker has no choice in the matter and current benefits are taken away, the worker is left with a choice. He or she can terminate employment and go elsewhere for the sake of these benefits.

Therefore, increasing deductibles and benefit elimination may not serve the overall purposes of Cosmo. They may do more harm than good. Thus, the following recommendations might be made to the management of Cosmo:

- Leave the current benefits alone. However, it may be feasible to increase the major medical deductible slightly to help control the cost of the health plan.

- Implement a simplified employee pension (SEP) plan or some other elective deferral program for use as a qualified retirement plan. The use of an elective deferral SEP or other similar type of plan provides for fewer or no employer contributions than a defined benefit plan. Elective deferral plans allow the employees to contribute to the plan on a tax deductible basis with or without some employer contributions. Thus, the employer's cost can be kept relatively low. If there is a change in the health plan deductible which may result in a savings of 3-5% of the premium, possibly this amount could be used as an employer contribution to the elective deferral plan. By implementing an elective deferral plan, the objective of a qualified retirement plan is achieved at minimal cost to the business.

- Implement a non-qualified deferred compensation plan for the benefit of the five key executives whereby each will receive a benefit equal to $25,000 at retirement. In addition, provisions can be made to include a pre-retirement death benefit as well as providing additional benefits in the event of a disability.

Another alternative for the Cosmo problem is simply to do nothing except to implement the deferred compensation plan for the key executives. Make no changes to the current benefit plan. The company's position that presently a qualified pension plan is too expensive can be maintained. One of the other advantages of deferred compensation is that the only employees who need to be aware of the plan are those affected by the plan — the five key persons.

The recommendation of using an elective deferral plan is made because it allows for the plan to be implemented with or without employer contributions. If the employer makes a minimal contribution, this will probably motivate more of rank and file employees to participate in the plan.

In addition, an elective deferral plan also is a form of a "now" benefit in that the employee is able to set aside a sum of money (for future use) and receive a current tax deduction. Thus, there is a present benefit to be realized by the employees. As the corporation's profit picture improves and the expense of expanding is taken care of, possibly then the corporation could increase its contribution to the plan or possibly give serious consideration to some other form of qualified plan in addition to the elective deferral plan.

Finally, management will have to make decisions regarding the implementation of the deferred compensation plan. These decisions would cover such elements of the plan as whether the plan is to be funded or unfunded, the provisions of the written agreement, normal retirement age, etc.

SUMMARY

Deferred compensation is a nonqualified retirement plan which provides for pre-retirement death benefits, disability benefits, and retirement benefits.

It is non-qualified because it may be discriminatory or selective in that all employees do not have to participate. Primarily, deferred compensation is a benefit for the key executive. As a non-qualified plan, it may discriminate, it is not filed or approved by the IRS and it does not offer the employer a current tax deduction.

Most deferred compensation plans involve a written agreement between the employer and the employee by which a specific amount of the employee's current compensation is deferred until a later date or occurrence.

Deferred compensation can be established as a salary continuation plan or a salary reduction plan. The continuation plan means that the deferred compensation is an additional benefit over and above the individual's salary. This type of plan is referred to as a Selective Executive Retirement Plan (SERP). Salary reduction plans are those in which the employee elects not to receive a portion of current compensation and that amount is deferred until a later date.

Not every business should be thought of as a prospect for deferred compensation. A business should have certain characteristics or needs to be considered a prospect for deferred compensation. These would include: the need to attract and retain key personnel; the need to benefit key executives only; a need for supplemental retirement income for key persons; or as an alternative to minority ownership in a close corporation.

Deferred compensation is implemented by way of a formal written agreement between the employer and the covered employees. This agreement will reflect the parties to the agreement, the employment provisions, the non-compete provision, the amount and duration of benefits, forfeiture provisions, etc.

Deferred compensation plans may be funded or unfunded. A formally funded plan is one in which the employer actually sets aside periodic amounts for future delivery in accordance with the deferred compensation agreement. An unfunded plan is simply an unsecured promise to pay future benefits.

Any assets held by the plan are considered assets of the corporation. As such, the employer's creditors can lay claim to these assets. Thus, even with a funded plan, the benefits may or may not be available when the employee retires.

To avoid any current taxation, the employee must at all times have an element of forfeiture of the benefits if he or she terminates prior to retirement or goes to work for a competitor. Generally, if the possible forfeiture of benefits is not present, then the employee may experience a current tax liability on any amounts deferred or amounts paid by the employer.

At retirement, the distributions from the deferred compensation plan are considered wages and thus taxed to the employee. At this time, the employer will receive a tax deduction for the amounts paid to the employee provided these amounts are reasonable relative to the employee's position and compensation and provided the benefits paid represent a necessary and reasonable business expense.

The employee should also be aware of the possible inclusion of the present value of these benefits in his or her gross estate for federal estate tax purposes, as well as the probability of Social Security taxation and federal unemployment taxation on the amounts received. A death benefit only (DBO) plan may or may not be includible in the deceased employee's gross estate.

Various financial services products can be used to formally fund a deferred compensation plan. These include life insurance, disability income insurance, fixed and variable annuities, mutual funds, etc. Life insurance is generally an ideal funding mechanism because of its many guarantees. It removes many of the uncertainties common to other funding products.

REVIEW EXERCISES

1. Briefly discuss the principal advantages and disadvantages of deferred compensation plans for both the employer and the employee.

2. Discuss the corporate tax implications of a deferred compensation plan as well as the federal income, federal estate, Social Security and federal unemployment tax considerations for the employee.

CHAPTER 4

GENERAL TYPES OF QUALIFIED PLANS

Chapter 2 presented general characteristics common to most qualified plans. Employer sponsored plans can be generally classified into three categories:

- Profit Sharing Plans
- Defined Contribution Plans
- Defined Benefit Plans

PROFIT SHARING PLANS

A profit sharing plan is a qualified plan for sharing profits with employees. Profit sharing plans may provide a definite formula for determining the employer's contributions to the plan such as 5% or 10% of compensation.

A profit sharing plan need not necessarily provide a definite formula for determining the amount of profits to be shared or contributions made to the plan. In the absence of any contribution formula, there must be evidence of some effort to provide substantial and recurring plan contributions by the employer.

Assets held in the plan must be valued at least annually. Plan assets are to be valued at current market rates and prices. Plan contributions may be invested in various investment vehicles such as mutual funds, certificates of deposit, stocks, bonds, etc.

Most newer businesses do not present a stable profit picture in the initial years of operation. Business income and profits usually fluctuate widely. Once the business becomes firmly established over a period of time, business income and profits become more stable and predictable. During these early years, a business may wish to provide certain types of employee benefits (including a retirement plan) in order to attract and retain key personnel.

Usually, the type of qualified plan selected in these early years of operation is a profit sharing plan. One form of a profit sharing plan is simply for the employer to share some of the company's profits, as earned, with the employees. However, a qualified profit sharing plan defers receipt of these profits until a later time, usually at retirement.

No Profit — No Contribution

Sam started the Ajax Corporation, nine years ago. Ajax manufactures small mirrors for the automobile industry. The auto industry is their primary customer. Generally, their profit picture has not been very stable due to the unpredictability of the auto industry for the past nine years.

For example, Ajax lost modest sums of money in the first two years of its operation. In the third and fourth years, it broke even. Years five and six witnessed a 10 and 12% profit respectively. Year seven resulted in a 4% loss and year eight, a 2% loss. Last year there was a modest 3% profit.

Sam is now 49 years old. He has 18 employees who range in age from 23 to 53. There has been some pressure, especially by the older employees, for a retirement plan.

It is evident that Sam should probably consider a profit sharing plan. Due to his age and the older employees, time to accumulate adequate sums of money for future delivery at retirement is a critical consideration. As the clock continues to tick, valuable time is lost which will effect the retirement status of the employees.

Due to the obvious unstable profit picture, Sam's liability becomes flexible with a profit sharing plan. If the money is earned, there will be a contribution. If Sam experiences a loss, there will be no liability for him to make a contribution.

Bill started his own business six years ago. He currently has nine employees (including himself) and wants to install a pension plan because last year he paid corporate taxes for the first time. His first two years of operation he lost money. In the next two years he made a modest profit but in the fifth year, made no profit. Last year was a particularly good year and he had to pay $6,000 in corporate taxes.

GENERAL TYPES OF QUALIFIED PLANS

It would appear that if Bill is to establish a qualified plan, it should be a profit sharing plan. The business has definitely exhibited an unstable picture with regard to income and profits. A profit sharing plan does not present a fixed liability.

The primary reason that an employer may elect a profit sharing plan in the early years of the business is due to the fact that the contribution does not represent a fixed liability. A profit sharing plan may be established whereby contributions are made only if the company realizes a profit. **No profit — no contribution**. Thus, this approach may more closely fit the unstable profit picture of a relatively new business.

In addition to the need for flexibility due to an unstable profit situation, an employer may wish to implement a profit sharing plan as a work related incentive. The more productive the employees are, the more profits will be realized and consequently, more frequent sharing of these profits, either in cash or in plan contributions.

Another type of situation which may indicate the feasibility of implementing a profit sharing plan is where there is a need to supplement another plan. For example, a firm already has a defined contribution plan. A "second plan", the profit sharing plan, is installed to supplement benefits to be derived from the defined contribution plan. There is the added advantage that the profit sharing plan can also serve as an employee production incentive.

The maximum deductible contribution which an employer may make on behalf of plan participants is an amount equal to 15% of the participant's compensation. This employer contribution may be fully discretionary in that it will only be made if the company declares a profit. As previously stated, this type of arrangement is most beneficial to the new business with unstable profits. On the other hand, the contribution could be based on a definite percentage which would constitute a fixed liability each year for the employer.

Plan Design

Employer contributions to a profit sharing plan may be discretionary or by means of a fixed formula. A discretionary contribution enables the employer to determine annually the amount of the contribution. The basic concept is that if there is a profit, the employer will "declare a contribution". However, even if there is no profit, the employer may, at his discretion, still make a plan contribution.

The employer can omit a contribution under a discretionary plan but the IRS requires evidence that over a period of time, attempts have been made to make recurring and substantial plan contributions. If there are no contributions for many years, the IRS will normally terminate the plan. At termination, plan participants are fully vested.

A plan with a fixed formula requires that a specific amount must be contributed to the plan each year that the employer realizes a profit. For example, the contribution formula may state that all participants are entitled to a contribution of 10% of compensation after the company has realized $20,000 of profits. Thus, the 10% formula kicks in at $20,000 of profits.

The plan must have a definite method of allocating contributions to participant's accounts. This method normally relates the individual's compensation to the total compensation. For example:

> Bob earns $50,000. Total compensation for all plan participants is $500,000. The employer makes a $50,000 contribution to the profit sharing plan. Bill's share of this contribution will be:
>
> $$\frac{\$50,000}{\$500,000} = 10\% \ (\$50,000 \text{ contribution}) = \$5,000$$

The plan must define compensation so that it is not in violation of non-discriminatory rules. For example, if "compensation" includes bonuses but excludes overtime pay, this could be discriminatory if we assume that only the higher paid employees receive bonuses.

Additional plan features are similar to most other qualified plans. Vesting schedules, 0/5 and 3/7, are used in a profit sharing plan. Typical tax penalties also apply such as the 10% penalty for a premature distribution prior to age 59½. Benefits are normally paid at normal retirement or upon an employee's termination which means the participant is entitled to his or her vested interest at the time of termination.

GENERAL TYPES OF QUALIFIED PLANS

Profit sharing plans frequently permit benefit payments prior to termination or normal retirement. Generally, this type of distribution is made for emergency or "hardship" reasons. Hardship would include medical emergencies, payment of tax bills, payment of college tuition, etc. The point is that what constitutes hardship will be specified in the plan's provisions.

These early hardship distributions may not exceed the participant's vested benefits. In addition, it should be noted that if a hardship distribution occurs, the distribution is fully taxable to the individual since all qualified plan money has never been taxed. The individual may also be subject to the 10% penalty for a premature distribution prior to age 59½.

To prevent the 10% premature distribution penalty, the plan may specify a loan provision whereby participants have access to their vested benefits for emergencies and hardships. In these situations, there would be no 10% penalty.

Stock Bonus Plan (ESOP)

A version of the profit sharing plan is a **stock bonus plan** (also referred to as an Employee Stock Ownership Plan). A stock bonus plan is similar to a profit sharing plan in that contributions are not a fixed liability each year. The plan contributions may or may not be made from profits. Plan contributions are made either in cash or in the form of the employer's stock.

An **Employee Stock Ownership Plan (ESOP)** is a stock bonus plan which is designed primarily as an investment vehicle for the common stock of the employer. An ESOP may borrow money from lending institutions to be used for the purchase of the employer's stock. The employer or the business uses the funds to finance various business-related projects. Annually, the employer then "repays the debt" by making contributions to the ESOP. These employer contributions are used to purchase stock and the stock is allocated to the accounts of the participants.

ESOPs provide certain advantages for the employees as well as the company.

> Employees own a piece of the company as stockholders. This can provide certain work related incentives, increased production, etc.

A market is established for the employer's stock which often helps increase the marketability of the stock.

ESOPs enjoy most of the same tax advantages common to all qualified plans.

Plan Design

As qualified plans, ESOPs and stock bonus plans must comply with all requirements which pertain to any qualified plan; ie., eligibility and participation, contribution limitations, vesting, tax penalties, non- discrimination, etc. There are certain features which are only common to ESOPs and stock bonus plans.

Usually, the participant's accounts reflect value in terms of shares of the employer's stock. Benefits are usually distributed in the form of stock.

When benefits are distributed in the form of stock, the employee has the right to require the employer to repurchase the stock in accordance with a valuation formula.

Employer's contributions may be in cash or stock.

Stock bonus plans and ESOPs must meet certain requirements:

- The participants must have the right to demand benefits in the form of the employer's securities (usually common stock)
- Benefits distributed under the plan may be paid in cash or in the form of securities
- Benefit distributions must occur within one year of the employee attaining normal retirement, dying, or becoming totally disabled or not later than the fifth year following the plan year in which the participant terminated employment
- Unless otherwise elected by the employee, plan distributions must consist of equal periodic payments for a period of not longer than five years. An exception to this five-year rule is in the case of a participant whose account balance exceeds $500,000. One additional year can be granted for each $100,000 (or fraction thereof) up to an additional five years.

GENERAL TYPES OF QUALIFIED PLANS 4—7

For example, Charlie has an account balance of $650,000. The plan must provide periodic payments for 6½ years unless Charlie elected some other payout.

The plan must provide for certain voting rights to plan participants or their beneficiaries as shareholders of the company's common stock.

It should be noted that tax laws do change frequently. As such, stock bonus and ESOP requirements can also change periodically. It is the agent's responsibility to keep abreast of these changes so as to properly discuss these types of plans.

CODA Plan

A variation of the profit sharing plan is a **cash or deferred arrangement** (CODA) plan. Most often, this type of plan is referred to as a 401(k) plan. A CODA is a profit sharing or stock bonus plan whereby participants may elect to have the employer make contributions on behalf of employees or as payments made directly to employees.

Typically, this arrangement is made possible by means of a salary reduction agreement whereby the employee agrees to have a portion of his or her salary reduced (before taxes) and this amount deposited in the plan. This amount is usually referred to as the **elective deferral amount**.

In addition to the 401(k) concept, elective deferral plans include tax sheltered annuities (TSAs) and simplified employee pensions (SEPs). The elective deferred amounts may not exceed the limit of $7,000 annually, as indexed for cost of living. Any amounts deferred in excess of the allowable amount must be included in the individual's gross income for tax purposes.

These types of plans will be discussed in detail in subsequent chapters of this text.

DEFINED CONTRIBUTION PLANS

Defined contribution plans specifically identify the amount of the employer's contribution to the plan but the retirement benefits are unknown. Defined contribution plans represent a fixed liability for the employer. An account is established for each plan participant wherein the individual's portion of the contribution and any plan forfeitures from terminated participants are maintained. The benefit to be received at retirement is based on the participant's account balance at the time of retirement.

Copyright © 1996 The Merritt Company

Contribution limits for most forms of defined contribution plans are 25% of the employees' compensation not to exceed $30,000 per year. For example, an employer may elect to establish a defined contribution plan which specifies that the contribution will be equal to 10% of compensation. This figure then becomes a fixed liability for the employer. Again, the retirement benefit remains unknown until the participant reaches retirement.

Defined contribution plans must comply with all qualified plan requirements in terms of eligibility, vesting, non-discrimination, taxation and tax penalties, etc. This type of plan is fairly common among many businesses. Generally, it is not as expensive as a defined benefit plan and it is more definite with regard to contributions than a profit sharing plan. If a newer company is likely to go into a profit sharing plan due to unstable profits, once profits and income become more stable, these firms may likely add a defined contribution plan.

Technically speaking, any pension plan which contains a specific contribution amount could be identified as a defined contribution plan. One such plan is a money purchase plan.

Money Purchase Pension Plan

A **money purchase pension plan** represents a fixed liability to the employer and accordingly, it is a type of defined contribution plan. A money purchase plan requires a specific contribution be made to the plan on behalf of each plan participant (i.e., 10%, 15%, etc. of compensation). At retirement, the individual's account balance is used to purchase an annuity (or similar retirement vehicle) which will provide a lifetime income to the participant.

Target Benefit Plan

Another version of the defined contribution concept is a **target benefit plan**. This type of money purchase or defined contribution plan targets a benefit on behalf of plan participants. For example, a plan may target a benefit of 10% of compensation. Separate participant accounts will then be established and maintained and the employer will contribute an amount each year necessary to fund this targeted benefit on behalf of each plan participant. Because the target benefit concept is considered a form of a defined contribution plan, the annual additions (contributions and forfeitures) to the employee's accounts cannot exceed the smaller of 25% of compensation or $30,000 annually.

GENERAL TYPES OF QUALIFIED PLANS

One of the main differences between a target benefit and a defined benefit plan is that the target benefit plan requires separate participant accounts whereas the defined benefit plan pools all contributions and there are no individual accounts to be maintained. Another principal difference is the contribution limitation imposed by the target benefit plan. There are no contribution limitations with a defined benefit plan.

DEFINED BENEFIT PLANS

In contrast to a defined contribution plan, a defined benefit plan specifically establishes the benefit to be received at retirement but the amount of the contribution to fund this benefit is not specified. For example, a defined benefit plan may specify that each plan participant will receive a specific dollar amount or a percentage of compensation (i.e. 5%, 10%, etc.) at retirement. It then becomes the employer's responsibility with the assistance of actuarial personnel to determine the amount of the annual contribution which will have to be made to assure that the defined benefit will be delivered to plan participants at retirement.

If a plan expresses the retirement benefit as a percentage of compensation, it will normally define this element of the plan as average compensation. Average compensation may mean the highest average obtained from the participant's highest five years of compensation. Thus, if an individual's highest five years of compensation were between ages 55 and 60, this figure would result in the average compensation upon which the defined benefit would be calculated.

> Mary has worked for ABC, Inc. for 27 years and has been covered by a 10% of pay defined benefit pension plan. The plan defines "pay" as the highest amount earned in a five consecutive year period prior to age 60. Mary's highest five year period reflects an average compensation of $30,000. Her defined retirement benefit will be $3,000 per year (10% x $30,000).

The annual contribution to the plan will vary depending on the ages of new plan participants, interest or investment income earned on the contributions, and the value of any plan forfeitures due to termination of participants. Unlike profit sharing or defined contribution-type plans, there are no limitations as to the amount of the contribution. Whatever amount is necessary to provide the benefit becomes the employer's responsibility. Consequently, the employer will incur a higher expense than with other types of plans but also will enjoy a higher tax deduction as long as the amount contributed to the plan is reasonable and necessary to satisfy the plan's benefit requirements.

If a plan consists mostly of older participants, then the contribution to fund the retirement benefit may be substantial. The older the participant the shorter the period of time to accumulate the necessary benefits and thus the higher the annual contribution. The cost of a defined benefit plan may increase dramatically during periods of low interest rates or losses regarding investment income. A defined benefit plan can be an expensive endeavor for the employer.

Due to the potential expense involved with defined benefit plans, their appeal is often to employers with extremely high incomes such as attorneys, doctors, dentists, etc. These occupational groups have the necessary income with which to make potentially large plan contributions.

Plan Design

Defined benefit plans provide benefits in accordance with a formula. There are several different methods or formulas used for determining benefits. These include the following:

Stated Amount: This method simply states the retirement benefit in terms of dollars and cents. For example, an employee will retire at age 65 and will receive $400 per month. This method does not allow for differences in individual compensation. Thus, a stock room clerk retires at $400 per month as does the company's president. Because of this, frequently this formula is used when there is little difference between the salaries of the participants.

Stated Percentage: This formula provides retirement benefits which are expressed as a percentage of compensation such as 5 or 10% or higher. Thus, a worker earning $50,000 per year would retire on an annual pension of 10% or $5,000 per year. This formula does account for individual differences in compensation so that the stock room clerk and the corporation president do not receive the same retirement benefit.

Often the plan will require a minimum service period for the participant to receive the full defined benefit. This service requirement might be expressed as 10 or 20 years of employment as a condition for receiving the full benefit. Let's assume to receive the full retirement benefit requires 20 years of service. The plan will normally specify what percentage of the benefit will be paid for those who don't have the necessary 20 years. Such a provision might specify that 10 years of employment will result in a 50% benefit; 15 years of service, 75%; and the full retirement benefit would be payable at 20 years of service.

Service Credit Formula: This formula ties the retirement benefit to years of service with the employer. For example the formula might specify 1% of earnings for each year of service up to 20 years. Thus, an employee would retire at 20% of average compensation. If average compensation was $100,000, the retirement benefit would be $20,000 annually.

An important element of this formula is the definition of compensation. Compensation could be based on a career average which means that all years of employment and compensation are averaged. This tends to produce a lower average compensation.

A final average method normally takes the final three, four or five years prior to normal retirement and only averages these years. The final average method usually results in a higher average compensation for purposes of determining the retirement benefit.

Regardless of which method is used to calculate average compensation, it should be noted that only the first $150,000 of salary can be used in accordance with current regulations.

Integration Formulas: As is true with many qualified plans, the contribution and/or benefit amounts may be integrated with Social Security. This approach recognizes the fact that the employer is already contributing to a retirement plan on behalf of the employees - Social Security.

For purposes of a defined benefit plan, often the benefit amount is integrated with Social Security. For example, the plans's benefit may be defined as a certain amount in excess of a specified Social Security benefit level. If a participant's benefit is identified as $1,000 per month and this person's projected Social Security retirement benefit is $750 monthly, the defined benefit for the plan becomes $250 per month.

Plan Funding

As is true with most qualified plans, defined benefit plans can utilize a variety of funding devices from life insurance to annuities to stocks and bonds. However, since the employer's responsibility is to provide adequate contributions to assure a specific future benefit, care needs to be taken as to the type of funding mechanisms used.

For this purpose, normally the services of an actuary will be required. The actuary will utilize various methods, formulas and assumptions in determining the amount of the annual contribution. The actuary has to make certain that the plan is properly funded at all times and not overfunded. Underfunded and overfunded plans result in possible tax penalties from the IRS.

Funding problems can occur when non-guaranteed products are used to fund the plan, such as stocks, bonds, mutual funds, variable annuities, etc. For example, if the stock market plunges so too will the value of the assets held in the plan. This can result in higher future contribution amounts to offset the plan losses. If the market increases greatly in value, then the plan may become overfunded.

Often, the use of life insurance and fixed annuity contracts can be used to minimize or reduce altogether these fluctuations in plan values. Accordingly, the actuary's job is made a bit easier, more predictable when guaranteed-type products are used for funding.

Unlike profit sharing and defined contribution plans, there are no separate account balances maintained for each plan participant. The entire amount contributed to the plan is held in trust for all plan participants. Thus, a defined benefit plan consists of a pool of money or assets from which each participant will be paid a definite retirement benefit.

Defined benefit plans do have restrictions or limitations on the amount of benefit to be received. The current benefit limitation is $90,000 per year as indexed. This indexed figure is currently about $120,000.

GENERAL TYPES OF QUALIFIED PLANS

The Pension Benefit Guaranty Corporation (PBGC), part of the Department of Labor, basically insures most defined benefit plans in the event that the plan does not meet the benefit requirement when participants retire. All employers with defined benefit plans pay a relatively small premium to the PBGC. In addition, the PBGC has the right to require reimbursement from the employer for any benefits it provides.

Table 4-1 summarizes the principal characteristics of these three classifications of pension plans.

TABLE 4-1

	Profit Sharing	Defined Contribution	Defined Benefit
Contributions	15% of salary up to $22,500 No fixed liability	25% of salary up to $30,000 A fixed liability	Amount required to fund benefit
Administration	Individual participant accounts	Individual participant accounts	Pooled assets
Retirement Benefits	Account values	Account values	Limited $90,000 indexed
Variations	Stock Bonus Plans ESOPs	Money Purchase Plans Target Benefit Plans	None

SUMMARY

All qualified plans contain certain characteristics as discussed in Chapter 2 such as contribution requirements, vesting, participation and eligibility, top heavy concepts, etc. Most qualified plans can be defined or classified in one of three general ways.

A profit sharing plan is a qualified plan which provides for a flexible contribution amount depending on the availability of company profits. No profits — no employer liability. Most often profit sharing plans are sold to those companies which display a pattern of unstable business income and profits.

A stock bonus plan or employee stock ownership plan is a type of profit sharing plan. Stock bonus plans do not involve a fixed liability with regard to contributions. ESOPs are primarily a method whereby employees can acquire company stock as the funding for retirement benefits. ESOPs must satisfy certain IRS requirements regarding acquisition of the employer's stock, benefit periods, and voting privileges.

A defined contribution plan is a qualified plan which specifically defines the amount of the mandatory employer contribution. The benefit at retirement will depend on the amount of money accumulated in each participant's account. The contribution is a definite liability for the employer. Currently, the maximum contribution is the lesser of 25% of the employees' compensation not to exceed $30,000 per year.

A money purchase plan is a type of defined contribution plan in which the participant's account value at retirement is used to purchase a lifetime retirement benefit.

A target benefit is part defined benefit and part defined contribution. A benefit is targeted for each plan participant and the employer is then required to establish individual participant accounts and make the necessary contributions to fund for the target benefit. However, target benefit plans impose the defined contribution limitations of 25% of compensation not to exceed $30,000 annually.

A defined benefit plan specifically identifies the retirement benefit for the plan participants but the amount of the employer's contribution is determined each year based on the age of the participants, plan forfeitures and investment performance. Usually a plan actuary will determine the annual contribution to the plan. Defined benefit plans can be expensive with regard to the annual contributions. Defined benefit plans do not limit contributions but there is a limit of $90,000, as indexed, on the annual benefit that a participant may receive.

REVIEW EXERCISES

1. Discuss the advantages and disadvantages of defined benefit pension plans.

2. Discuss the similarities between profit sharing and defined contribution plans.

CHAPTER 5

IRAs AND SEPs

The vast majority of qualified pension plans are classified as employer sponsored plans. These plans automatically infer an employer-employee relationship generally with employer contributions being made to the plan for the benefit of the employees. This chapter covers primarily an individual approach to pension plans by means of a discussion of Individual Retirement Accounts and Simplified Employee Pensions (SEP).

Individual Retirement Accounts (IRA)

ERISA gave birth to IRAs in 1974. ERISA created two retirement funds — individual retirement accounts and individual retirement annuities. Generally, these plans are simply referred to as IRAs. IRAs are used for individual retirement plans, rollover retirement plans and simplified employee pensions sponsored by employers. As a qualified plan, an IRA provides the same tax advantages as any other qualified plan; that is, tax deductible contributions and tax deferred growth.

An IRA is simply a plan by which an individual can set aside a specific sum of money for retirement and enjoy certain tax advantages normally only available to corporations and employers. IRAs may be established through a bank, with an insurance company, an investment company, a stock brokerage facility, etc.

IRA plans are generally exempt from many of the ERISA requirements specified for qualified plans. This is because an IRA is established by an individual and thus the plan is not considered an employer-sponsored plan. As such, participation, vesting, funding, and similar ERISA requirements do not pertain to IRAs.

ERISA does specify the funding vehicles which may be used for IRAs. IRAs may be funded with cash contributions, investments in stock, bonds, mutual funds, fixed or variable annuities, money market instruments such as Certificates of Deposit offered by banks or just about any other investment mechanism **except** life insurance contracts and collectibles, such as gold coins or works of art.

Eligibility

Eligibility requirements for an IRA specify that the individual must:

- Have earned income
- Be less than age 70½

> Sean, age 55, is a very wealthy individual. Last year he enjoyed unearned income in the amount of $300,000. This income was derived from interest payments, dividends, rental income, and some royalties from books which he authored. He had no other income. Does Sean qualify for an IRA?

Of course not, because his income, although substantial, was not earned. Only earned income can be considered as the basis for an IRA contribution. Earned income means wages, salary fees, and other compensation received for personal services rendered by the individual. Earned income also includes alimony payments. However, earned income does not include Social Security benefits or railroad retirement benefits.

> Debbie is a 19-year-old college freshman who works part time in the school cafeteria. She will earn approximately $1,500 this year. Does she qualify for an IRA?

Yes she does. The IRA regulations do not specify full- or part-time employment. They simply indicate that the individual must have earned income.

The limiting age of 70½ is in reference to the fact that as a qualified plan, some form of plan distribution must begin by April 1st following the year in which the person becomes 70½.

Contributions

IRA contributions are limited to $2,000 or 100% of the individual's earned income per tax year, whichever is the lesser of the two. Referring to our college freshman, Debbie, how much could she contribute to an IRA? Not $2,000, but she could contribute 100% of her earned income, $1,500.

In addition, a **spousal IRA** may be established for a non-working spouse. Contributions to a spousal IRA are limited to $250 per tax year. However, it should be noted that no more than $2,000 may be contributed to a single IRA (except for rollovers). Thus, two separate accounts would have to be established.

> George opens an IRA for himself and a spousal IRA for Martha, his non-working wife. The total contribution permitted is $2,000 + $250 for a total of $2,250. This total contribution could be divided in any number of ways provided no more than $2,000 was contributed to any one account. For example:

Total Contribution	George's Account	Martha's Account
$2,250	$2,000	$ 250
$2,250	$1,125	$1,125
$2,250	$1,500	$ 750

If Martha obtains a job, then both she and George may have IRAs and Martha could make a maximum contribution to her account.

Anita and John both work and earn in excess of $40,000 each. They file a joint tax return. Contributions are limited to $250 per tax year for non-working spouses, but only $2,000 may be contributed to a single IRA. Anita and John therefore may each contribute $2,000 to separate IRAs.

Rollovers

There is no limit for **rollover contributions**. A rollover is a transfer of qualified funds from a qualified plan to another qualified plan such as an IRA. Rollovers may occur due to:

- Distributions received from a terminated plan
- Lump sum distributions usually due to employee termination
- Distributions of any deductible employee contributions

An individual may not rollover a distribution to an IRA if the distribution is made to satisfy a minimum required distribution (i.e., the age 70½ rule) or if the distribution is one of a series of periodic payments made for the life of the individual or for at least a period of 10 years.

> Keith is terminating his employment with M&M Inc. Due to his termination, he will receive a $40,000 pension distribution. As a qualified plan distribution, this entire amount is subject to ordinary income tax plus, if Keith is less than 59½ years of age, an additional 10% penalty as a premature distribution.

To avoid paying these taxes currently, Keith can roll this distribution into an IRA since it is a distribution due to termination of his employment.

A rollover may be due to a total distribution from a plan or a partial distribution. If the rollover is due to a partial distribution, the distribution must equal at least 50% of the employee's plan value.

Other rollover requirements include the following:

- A rollover may occur only once in 12 months
- The funds being rolled over must be placed in the IRA within 60 days of the distribution
- If assets other than cash are being distributed, then those assets must be rolled over into the IRA. For example, if a plan distribution was in the form of stock, then the stock must be rolled into the IRA. The individual could not sell the stock and place the cash received from the sale in the rollover account

Rollover provisions only permit qualified plan distributions to be rolled over into another qualified plan, such as an IRA.

A distinction should be made between an IRA rollover and an **IRA transfer**. With an IRA transfer, the IRA owner is never in possession of the funds. There is no constructive receipt. Transfers are made directly from one IRA custodian or plan to another plan. For example, an individual has an IRA removed from the ABC Insurance Company's IRA plan and transferred to the custodian of the XYZ Insurance Company's IRA.

This concept of rolling over the distribution directly between the institutions involved has increased significance due to a recent change in tax law. The Unemployment Compensation Amendments Act of 1992 made changes to the rollover of qualified plan money into other qualified plans. These changes became effective January 1, 1993.

Under the new rules, an individual may elect a **direct rollover** which is defined as a rollover done directly from one institution to another institution. Direct rollovers or transfers are not subject to any withholding tax. However, if the individual elects a "regular rollover" whereby the funds are distributed to the participant and within 60 days rolled over into another qualified plan, 20% of the distribution must be withheld for potential tax purposes.

> Sue has elected a regular rollover of a $1,000 pension distribution into her IRA. As a regular rollover in which she will actually receive the $1,000, 20% or $200 must be withheld from the distribution thus resulting in a rollover of $800. Sue could choose to roll the $800 and add $200 from personal funds to achieve the full $1,000 amount.

It should be noted that the rollover rules apply to any qualified plan and are not only applicable to IRAs. Generally, most tax rules apply to any plan identified as a qualified plan.

As a qualified plan, an IRA offers the tax advantages previously discussed, provided the participant meets certain requirements. Generally, the individual's contribution of up to $2,000 ($2,250 with a spousal IRA) is tax deductible. The deduction is taken from gross income in the taxable year in which the contribution is made. Deductible contributions may also be made after the end of a tax year (December 31) if the contribution is made no later than the time that tax returns must be filed (April 15).

However, this **tax deduction may be reduced or eliminated**. The deductibility of the contributions depends upon whether the individual is an active participant in another plan and if so, upon the amount of the person's adjusted gross income. If an individual is participating in another qualified plan (pension, profit sharing, 401(k), TSA, SEP, etc.), any tax-deductible contribution may be limited or eliminated.

If an individual files a single return, the tax deduction begins to be reduced if the taxpayer's adjusted gross income is $25,000. If the individual's adjusted gross income is $35,000 or more, there is no tax deduction for the contribution. Thus, the deductible amount begins to reduce at $25,000 and totally disappears at $35,000.

The same concept applies to those individuals filing a joint income tax return, except the adjusted gross income range begins at $40,000 and extends to $50,000. Thus, a taxpayer filing a joint return will not be permitted an IRA deduction if adjusted gross income is $50,000 or more. Table 5-1 illustrates this point.

TABLE 5-1

IRA TAX DEDUCTION TABLE FOR ACTIVE PARTICIPANTS IN OTHER QUALIFIED PLANS

Single Return Taxpayer		Joint Return Taxpayer	
Adjusted Gross Income	Maximum Deduction	Adjusted Gross Income	Maximum Deduction
up to $25,000	$2,000	up to $40,000	$2,000
$ 26,000	1,800	41,000	1,800
27,000	1,600	42,000	1,600
28,000	1,400	43,000	1,400
29,000	1,200	44,000	1,200
30,000	1,000	45,000	1,000
31,000	800	46,000	800
32,000	600	47,000	600
33,000	400	48,000	400
34,000	200	49,000	200
above $35,000	0	above $50,000	0

According to Table 5-1, a single taxpayer with adjusted gross income of $30,000 may make the $2,000 IRA contribution but may only deduct $1,000. A married couple filing a joint return with combined adjusted gross income of $48,000 would only be able to deduct a total of $400.

Active participation in another qualified plan does not prohibit the individual from having an IRA or from making an

IRA contribution. The plan may exist and the full $2,000 contribution can be made. The contribution may not be deductible. Even though the contribution may only be partially deductible or not deductible at all, the investment income earned on the contribution will still grow tax deferred.

Jack earns $30,000 as a medical technician. Jack is covered by his company's qualified pension plan. He files his tax return as a single taxpayer and constantly complains about paying taxes. To this you have replied, "Jack, pay yourself first and then pay the government." You then suggest that he should establish an IRA.

Jack may contribute $2,000 to the IRA. However, because he is an active participant in another qualified plan, as a single taxpayer earning $30,000, he can only claim a tax deduction on $1,000. Even though he loses some of the tax deduction, he still retains 50% of the deduction plus his full $2,000 contribution will grow tax deferred.

Assuming that an individual's total IRA value has been tax deductible and investment growth tax deferred, the entire account value becomes the individual's tax basis and is thus taxed, upon receipt, at regular ordinary income tax rates. If the individual dies prior to distribution of the IRA amounts, the decedent's tax basis becomes the beneficiary's tax basis as well. The bottom line is that eventually someone must pay the tax due on the IRA.

Vesting

Vesting requirements are relatively simple with regard to IRAs. Vesting simply means ownership. Since this is the individual's money, the IRA participant is always 100% vested in his or her own contribution.

Tax Penalties

Due to its qualified plan status and the impact of ERISA, there are certain **tax penalties** associated with IRAs. The first of these is a **6% penalty for excess contributions**. Any contribution in excess of the allowable amount makes the individual liable for an excise tax of 6%. This penalty pertains to both deductible and/or non-deductible contributions. The penalty does not apply to rollovers unless the rollover contribution does not qualify as a rollover.

> Nancy contributes $3,000 to her IRA in the current tax year. She is liable for a penalty of 6% of the excess ($1,000) or $60.

Nancy is subject to the $60 penalty each tax year that the excess contribution remains in the account. To avoid the penalty in the current tax year, she could withdraw the excess amount. Such a withdrawal does not subject Nancy to any penalty or federal income tax liability. However, she must also withdraw any interest or investment income earned by the excess distribution. This investment income is taxable and subject to possible penalty (10%) as a premature distribution prior to age 59½.

If Nancy does not withdraw the excess until after the deadline for filing her tax return (April 15), she must pay the penalty. A final alternative is to contribute less in a subsequent year.

> Nancy contributes the $3,000 creating the excess and pays the 6% penalty for the current tax year. Next year she only contributes $1,000 to her IRA thus correcting the excess.

In the subsequent year, even though Nancy only contributed $1,000, she may take the $2,000 tax deduction for that year (assuming she is eligible for the deduction).

Premature distributions prior to age 59½ are subject to an **excise tax of 10%** on the amount withdrawn. This tax was discussed in the previous chapter. Premature distributions (prior to 59½) are taxed at the rate of 10% except for death, disability, divorce, early retirement by purchase of an immediate annuity for the life of the individual and/or the individual's survivor and correction of an excess contribution as discussed above.

It should also be remembered that in addition to any penalty, the individual must also pay ordinary income tax on such distributions.

There is also a **15% penalty for excess distributions** as discussed in the previous chapter. The IRS stipulates that the total retirement amounts payable to an individual cannot exceed the greater of $150,000 or $112,500 (indexed); the indexed amount for the year 1992 was $140,276. Thus, an individual with an IRA and who also retires as a participant in another qualified plan is subject to these distribution limitations.

Finally, IRAs are subject to the **50% penalty for a delayed distribution**. IRS regulations state that distributions from an IRA must begin not later than April 1st following the calendar year in which the participant becomes 70½. The initial plan distribution can begin by April 1st. However, subsequent distributions must occur by December 31st of each year. These distributions are generally based on the amount of money accumulated and the life expectancy of the person and/or his or her survivor (if the payout is based on a joint-survivor settlement).

> Julie turns age 70½ on September 1, 1991. Based on the value of her IRA and her life expectancy, she is required to have a distribution of $10,000 by April 1, 1992 (for the year, 1991). She will also have to receive another $10,000 by December 31, 1992, for calendar year, 1992.

Let's assume that the following takes place relative to Julie's situation.

| April 1, 1992, distribution: | $ 0 |
| December 31, 1992 distribution: | $5,000 |

Calculation of the delayed distribution penalty is as follows:

April 1 Distribution

>Required distribution: $10,000
>Actual distribution: 0
>Penalty Amount: $10,000 x 50% = $5,000

December 31 Distribution

>Required distribution: $10,000
>Actual distribution: 5,000
>Penalty Amount: $5,000 x 50% = $2,500

Unfortunately, Julie owes the IRS a total of $7,500 in penalties due to failure to begin a systematic distribution from her IRA.

In the event of death, the individual's interest in an IRA must be distributed in accordance with certain IRS rules, depending on whether death occurs before or after distributions have begun.

If **death occurs after** distributions have begun, any remaining balance in the account must be distributed at least as quickly as under the method of distribution in effect on the individual's date of death. In other words, any remaining account value will continue to be distributed in the same manner as before the individual's death.

If the IRA owner **dies before distributions begin**, the entire account value must be distributed not later than December 31 of the calendar year which marks the fifth anniversary of the individual's death.

> Gladys dies June 1, 1990, at age 44 with an IRA value of $50,000. No IRA distributions have been made. The entire IRA value must be distributed (and taxed) not later than December 31, 1995.

An exception to this rule exists if the individual has designated a named survivor (beneficiary). In such cases, the amount payable to the survivor may be distributed over the life of the named beneficiary as long as the distributions begin by December 31 of the year which follows the individual's death. In Gladys' case, had she named a beneficiary, then distributions would have to begin not later than December 31, 1991.

If the named survivor is the IRA owner's spouse, the distribution must begin by December 31 of the later of:

- The calendar year following the individual's year of death
- The calendar year in which the IRA owner would have attained age 70½

A final comment about IRAs. The purpose of an IRA as established by ERISA in 1974 was to motivate the average taxpayer to set aside money on a favorable tax basis for retirement purposes. The law has been modified from time to time.

One aspect of the IRA regulations which has not changed since 1974 is the $2,000 contribution limitation. The $2,000 contribution limit has never been changed and does not take into account the impact of inflation and erosion of the purchasing power of these IRA dollars. Other qualified plans do allow for periodic increases in contributions due to changes in the cost of living. Thus, one of the possible disadvantages of an IRA is the $2,000 contribution limitation.

Currently, another possible disadvantage of an IRA concerns itself with the "active participant in another qualified plan" rule. Again, the intent of the law was to persuade or motivate the average person to set aside money for retirement. Presently, the law discourages participation for those who are active participants in other plans and earn in excess of the allowable compensation. For this group of people, the tax advantage is lost. For example, an individual who is an active participant in another plan, earning $40,000 per year can contribute to an IRA but the contribution is not tax deductible. Conversely, a single taxpayer who is an active participant in another plan, earning $20,000 annually could make a tax deductible contribution but probably cannot afford to contribute any amount to an IRA.

There have been serious political discussions regarding this aspect of an IRA and it is possible that this disadvantage may be resolved by amending the law so that any person, regardless of participation in other qualified plans, may make tax deductible contributions.

SIMPLIFIED EMPLOYEE PENSION (SEP)

A close relative of IRA is SEP. A **simplified employee pension** is basically an IRA, owned by an employee, which will accept employer contributions on behalf of the employee.

> Paul, an employer has been considering establishing a company pension plan for a few years but is easily turned off by the fact that he would need to consult with his attorney and CPA. In addition, a qualified plan requires filings with the IRS and the Department of Labor. All of this administrative hassle and expense has resulted in Paul's continued procrastination.

A SEP may possibly solve Paul's problem. As a qualified plan for employees, the SEP must comply with the eligibility, vesting, discrimination rules and contribution requirements of any qualified plan. However, in a sense, a SEP is a "pre-approved" plan since it piggy-backs on an IRA which is already a qualified plan. Thus, there is little or no need for an employer to spend time and money in consultations with lawyers or accountants. However, as an employer-sponsored plan, a SEP must comply with the reporting and disclosure requirements of ERISA. Generally, a SEP offers the administrative simplicity of an IRA but with higher contribution limits.

Eligibility

Eligibility for a SEP in which the employer makes employee contributions requires that each participant:

- Must have an IRA
- Be at least age 21
- Must have performed services and earned at least $300, indexed for inflation, during the year in which a contribution is made
- Must have worked for the employer in at least three of the last five years

The "three-out-of-five rule" applies to current and past employees.

> Jane was a participant in her company's SEP program for three full years; 1989-1991. She terminated her employment June 1, 1992. The employer is due to make a SEP contribution, December 31, 1992. Will a contribution be made on behalf of Jane?

Since she was a participant and worked for the employer in at least three of the preceding five years and performed services during the year in which the contribution is to be made, Jane is entitled to the employer's contribution. The same rationale would apply even if Jane had died during the plan year of 1992.

Naturally, a plan could be installed with more liberal eligibility requirements but all employees must have an IRA. The IRA becomes the vehicle which receives the employer's contribution. Union employees subject to a collective bargaining agreement may be excluded from participation as well as foreign aliens who have not received income from U.S. sources.

IRAs AND SEPs

Contributions

Employer contributions to a SEP are limited to the lesser of 15% of an employee's compensation or $22,500.

Since the employees own the IRAs, they may treat the SEP as an IRA and make deductible or non-deductible contributions in the same manner that they would for any IRA. The employee's contribution would be limited to $2,000 (or 100% of earned income whichever is the lesser of the two). Since they are participants in a qualified plan (the SEP), these employee contributions may or may not be deductible, depending on the individual's compensation.

A SEP may also be treated as a **salary reduction SEP**. A salary reduction SEP permits an employee an election between taking the employer's SEP contribution in cash or having the contribution deposited in the SEP. The employee realizes no tax advantages if the election is made to take the contribution in cash as it will be treated as compensation and taxed accordingly.

When the employee deferral is elected, it is treated as a **salary reduction** and thus is not taxed to the employee and it will grow tax deferred. Salary reductions occur before taxes and thus are considered tax basis for purposes of taxation. Salary deductions occur after taxes. Accordingly, a salary reduction SEP provides the employee with tax advantages.

A salary reduction SEP must meet the following IRS requirements:

- The employer must have no more than 25 employees during the preceding year who were eligible to participate in the plan
- At least 50% of the eligible employees must "sign up" for for the salary reductions
- The salary reduction SEP cannot favor the highly paid employees

Employee salary reduction are limited to amounts of $7,000, as indexed. Thus, the salary reduction concept permits an employee to set aside considerably more money that provided by an IRA.

Taxation

As qualified plans, SEPs receive the **tax advantages** of deductible employer contributions and tax-deferred investment growth. SEPs are treated as defined contribution plans. If an employer has other defined contribution plans, then all such contributions must be totaled and deductible contributions are limited to the lesser of 25% of compensation or $30,000 for all plans.

Contributions to a salary reduction SEP are not subject to federal income tax. However, these contributions are subject to Social Security and federal unemployment taxes.

A plan participant is always 100% vested in SEP contributions. Since the plan is the participant's IRA, the individual employee is always 100% vested. Benefits of a SEP are totally controlled by the employee and are portable between jobs and employers.

Penalties for this employer-employee plan are the same as were discussed in Chapter 2. Excess contributions are subject to a penalty of 6% on the excess amount; premature distributions prior to 59½ incur a 10% penalty; excess distributions are subject to a 15% penalty. In addition, SEPs must also comply with the IRS's top heavy rules. Any employer sponsored plan must always comply with the government's discrimination rules in favor of highly paid employees.

Funding

It should be noted that with any of these qualified plans including IRAs and SEPs, they are just that — plans. They are vehicles. Insurance agents and other financial services personnel do not "sell" plans but rather the funding for plans. An insurance agent does not earn any compensation for motivating an individual to implement a plan, called an IRA. The agent is compensated by recommending suitable funding for the plan.

Funding an IRA or a SEP can be accomplished with almost any type of product — except life insurance and collectibles (works of art, jewelry, etc.). These plans may be funded with mutual funds, stocks, bonds, fixed and/or variable annuities, certificates of deposit and other bank instruments including simple savings accounts.

The funding mechanism used will be determined by the objectives and risk tolerance of the participant. For example, if an individual cannot tolerate the thought of losing any money via investments, then he or she is probably not a prospect for such investments as stocks, bonds, or mutual funds as these products definitely present various investment risks to the individual. Thus, this type of person with low risk tolerance is more likely to be interested in guaranteed types of products for purposes of funding his or her IRA.

SUMMARY

IRAs were created by ERISA in 1974. The primary purpose of the IRA is to motivate the average person to plan for retirement by systematically depositing money in the IRA. As a qualified plan, there are specific tax advantages for participation in an IRA. As a qualified plan, there must also be compliance with specific IRS requirements.

SEPs are related to IRAs in that one of the eligibility requirements is that the participant must have an IRA to receive employer contributions. As an employer sponsored plan, an SEP must comply with all eligibility, contribution, coverage, participation, and discrimination requirements of any qualified plan. Table 5-2 and 5-3 identify the major characteristics and requirements of these plans.

TABLE 5-2

PLAN FEATURES

IRA

Eligibility	Must have earned income and be less than 70½
Contributions	The lesser of $2,000 or 100% of earned income
	$250 contribution for non-working spouse Rollovers allowed
Taxation	Tax-deductible contributions and tax deferred growth
	Exception: If an active participant in another qualified plan filing a single return, deduction begins to be reduced at $25,000 of adjusted gross income and is eliminated at $35,000; if filing a joint return, the deduction is reduced at $40,000 and eliminated at $50,000
Vesting	100% immediate vesting
Penalties	Excess contribution — 6% excise tax on excess
	Excess distribution — 15% penalty on excess ($150,000 or $112,500 as indexed)
	Premature distribution — 10% excise tax if prior to 59½ with certain exceptions
	Delayed distribution — 50% tax on the amount which should have been distributed
Other Comments	IRAs are exempt from many ERISA requirements as an individual plan
	No more than $2,000 can be contributed annually to any one IRA except for rollovers
	Rollovers can occur once per year and must be completed within 60 days of the distribution

TABLE 5-3

PLAN FEATURES

SEP

Eligibility	Age 21 and must have an IRA
	Must have worked for the employer in the current year and for at least three of the preceding five years and earned at least $300 in the year that a contribution is to be made
Contributions	Employer contributions are the lesser of 15% of compensation or $30,000
	Employee contributions may be $2,000 in accordance with IRA regulations
	A salary reduction SEP is limited to $7,000 as indexed
Taxation	Tax deductible employer contributions — tax deferred growth
	Any employee IRA contributions may be deductible depending on the employee's compensation — tax deferred growth Salary reduction contributions are deductible — tax deferred growth
Vesting	100% immediate vesting for both employee and employer contrbiutions
Penalties	Excess contributions — 6% excise tax on excess
	Excess distribution — 15% penalty on excess over $150,000 or $112,500 as indexed
	Premature distribution — 10% excise tax if prior to 59½ with certain exceptions Delayed distribution — 50% tax on the amount which should have been distributed
Other Comments	Plans must comply with participation, coverage and discrimination rules
	Top heavy rules apply

REVIEW EXERCISES

1. Ralph, your client and a businessowner, tells you that an IRA is a rip off because he can only contribute $2,000 per year and then it may not even be tax deductible. How could you overcome his objection to an IRA through the use of an SEP?

2. Identify and discuss in detail, the various tax penalties associated with IRAs or SEPs.

CHAPTER 6

ELECTIVE DEFERRAL PLANS

Chapter 5 basically discussed an individual approach to pension plans through the use of an IRA. A participant elects to contribute a sum of money to the IRA and hopefully enjoys some specific tax advantages.

An employer may establish an SEP which requires that each participant have an IRA. The IRA will serve as the device to receive employer contributions. In addition, the participant may make an IRA contribution. However, since the individual is now an active participant in the SEP, this IRA contribution may not be deductible.

The SEP may also be established as a salary reduction plan whereby the employees can elect to defer receipt of current income by means of a salary reduction agreement with the employer. This arrangement will be tax deductible to the employee. Needless to say, this type of plan is attractive for the employees because of the tax advantages. An SEP is an elective deferral plan.

This chapter will discuss two other elective deferral plans — tax sheltered annuities (TSA) and what is commonly called a 401(k) plan; both of which offer specific tax advantages to the participant due to the elective deferral (salary reduction) concept.

TAX SHELTERED ANNUITIES (TSA)

Stephanie wishes to systematically save some money for a long period of time. If she saves the money in a bank account, any interest earned on the account is taxed to her in the year earned. If she decides to invest in mutual funds, any investment growth will also generate a tax liability. Investment in the stock market involves a considerable degree of investment risk and potential tax liabilities.

Stephanie's plan to systematically save money is hindered somewhat because of tax problems. She basically has to share her savings currently with the government. However, her tax problem could be solved if she happens to work for a non-profit organization and utilizes a tax sheltered annuity as her savings vehicle.

TSAs are also referred to as Tax Deferred Annuities (TDA). The term "TDA" is preferred by the Securities and Exchange Commission (SEC) when the individual is using the TDA for investment in a variable annuity or similar product regulated by the SEC.

Eligibility

TSA eligibility concerns itself only with employees of certain non-profit charitable, religious, scientific and educational organizations in accordance with section 501(c)(3) of the Internal Revenue Code. Examples of these non-profit organizations include:

- Non-government operated hospitals
- Medical and dental schools
- Churches and religious institutions
- Public, private, and parochial schools and colleges
- Social agencies such as the community chest
- Museums and symphony orchestras

State, county and city governments do not qualify for TSAs under 501(c)(3). However, certain institutions which are subdivisions of local or state governments may be eligible for TSAs. These governmental subdivisions typically must be charitable, educational or religious in nature. In addition, there are some organizations which are non-profit under 501(c)(3) and tax exempt under section 501(a) of the code which are not eligible for TSAs. Examples of these are:

- Civic leagues
- Labor and agricultural organizations
- Chambers of Commerce and boards of trade
- Fraternal societies
- Credit unions
- Benevolent life insurance associations

Only employees of eligible organizations can participate in a TSA. Independent contractors, for example, are not eligible to participate in a TSA even though they may perform work for a school system or similar non-profit organization. Typically, employee status is determined by such tests as the payment of Social Security taxes and workers compensation coverage as a condition of employment. In addition, it could be said that an individual is considered an employee if he or she has an office or desk and/or can be supervised and controlled by the employer in terms of work location, hours, etc.

This employee status qualification is an important concept for some TSA-eligible organizations such as a hospital. For example, it is not always clear whether certain "hospital employees" such as radiologists or pathologists are indeed employees. These medical specialists may in fact be independent contractors who share fees for their services with the hospital. In these situations, employee qualification usually is determined by whether the hospital covers the individual for workers compensation and pays Social Security taxes on behalf of the person.

There is no requirement whereby employees must comply with age or service eligibility to participate in a TSA. If an employer does not specify a period of service or a minimum age for eligibility, then the later of one year of service or age 21 becomes an eligibility factor. The age and service eligibility may be extended if the employee is 100% vested. For example, an employer may use two years of service instead of one, provided the employee is 100% immediately vested. Since most TSAs are based solely on employee elective deferrals, the individual is always 100% vested in his or her own contributions. In the case of employees of school systems, the age factor may be age 26 if after one year of service the employee is 100% vested.

Contributions

TSA contributions must be made by the employer. Most TSA contributions are employee pay all situations whereby contributions are made through a salary reduction agreement. In these situations, it is still considered that the plan contributions are being made by the employer. TSAs may be classified as employee elective deferral plans or employer contribution plans.

Typically, an **employer contribution plan** simply means that the employer establishes the plan for all eligible employees and complies with all necessary requirements similar to any qualified plan. The employer generally would make a contribution to an annuity, mutual fund, or some other approved investment for purposes of funding the TSA. This type of plan resembles any other corporate employer sponsored program. However, few TSAs are employer contribution plans.

Most often, a TSA program is established as an **employee elective deferral plan**. Under this arrangement, usually the contribution is only made by the employee in the form of a **salary reduction**. The employee enters a written salary reduction agreement with the employer which must be renewed annually. In accordance with the agreement, the employer will withhold a predetermined sum of money from the employee's paycheck and make the appropriate TSA contribution. As a salary reduction, this money is deducted before the calculation of any taxes thus providing the employee with a favorable tax situation. As a qualified plan, the TSA deferral is not taxed and the investment income is tax deferred.

> Martha is a high school teacher working in the Farmington Consolidated School System. Her employer, the school system, has established a TSA program for those employees who wish to participate by means of reducing their salaries and having this deferred income contributed to a fixed annuity. Martha agrees to a 5% reduction. This amount will be invested in a fixed annuity before taxes and will grow tax deferred.
>
> Martha meets the eligibility requirements and agrees to the salary reduction. Note, however, even though the TSA program is a qualified plan, participation in the employee elective deferral version of the TSA is voluntary. Not all employees need to participate but the plan must still contain eligibility requirements as a qualified plan.

When the TSA is an employer contribution plan, then it must meet the participation and coverage requirements outlined in Chapter 2, such as the 50/40 participation rule. In addition, the plan must comply with one of the coverage tests — the percentage test, the ratio test or the average benefit test.

Contribution limits for TSAs are dependent on whether the plan is an employer contribution plan or an employee elective deferral plan. There are three separate tax deductible contribution limits. These limitations include:

1. The maximum limit on benefits and contributions for qualified plans
2. The exclusion allowance for the individual's current tax year
3. The limits on elective deferrals through the salary reduction agreement

The first two limitations apply to employer contributions. The third limitation applies to employee contributions by means of a formal salary reduction agreement. Due to the fact that the majority of TSA programs are solely employee deferrals, the maximum deductible contribution will be the lowest of these three limitations.

1. Employer contributions to a TSA are limited to the lesser of 25% of the participant's compensation or $30,000. This 25%/$30,000 limitation is applicable to any qualified plan which is considered a defined contribution plan. Thus, if an employer maintained a TSA plan and a defined contribution pension plan, the aggregate contributions cannot exceed the 25%/$30,000 limitation.
2. The exclusion allowance is based on a formula which provides some benefits for past years of service. The formula is:

    20% of current salary times ($\times$) years of service less ($-$) prior year's employer contributions

    For example, Larry has been an employee of the Riverside School System for five years. During this period, the employer has contributed $10,000 to his TSA. Larry's current salary is $20,000. Applying the formula:

    20% x $20,000 x 5 = $20,000 less $10,000 = $10,000

    Thus, Larry could exclude up to $10,000 of the employer's TSA contribution.
3. Salary reduction deferrals to a TSA cannot exceed $9,500 per year. If an employee also participates in other elective deferral plans, these other deferrals must be totaled with the TSA deferral to determine whether the $9,500 limit has been exceeded.

Susan participates through elective deferrals in an SEP and a TSA. If she defers $6,000 into the SEP, the maximum deferral for the TSA is $3,500, since salary reduction deferrals cannot exceed $9,500.

TSA regulations also permit a **special election** whereby the $9,500 salary reduction limitation can be increased (usually by an additional $3,000). An employee who has completed 15 years of service with the non-profit organization may increase the contribution limit by the smallest of the following amounts:

- $3,000
- $15,000 reduced by amounts not included as part of income in prior years due to use of the increased limit
- The excess of $5,000 times the number of years of service less the amount of past employer contributions to the salary reduction plan

For example, Harvey has been a school teacher in the Pleasantville System for 20 years. During this period, the system has contributed nothing to his TSA. Harvey has never used this election before.

5,000 x 20 = 100,000 - 0 (employer contributions) = $100,000

Harvey may increase his elective deferral by the least of $3,000, $15,000 or $100,000. In this example, Harvey can increase his TSA contribution by $3,000. Basically, he could continue to contribute $12,500 per year until he reaches a total of $15,000 in special election additions ($3,000 x 5 years).

This special election actually allows the participant to receive monetary credit for past years of service. Frequently, this election is referred to as the catch-up provision. Most often, this catch up provision will permit an additional $3,000 of deductible contributions to the TSA until an aggregate of $15,000 is reached.

TSAs are marketed on an organizational basis. The fact that your neighbor happens to be a school teacher does not automatically mean that you, as an agent, could sell the neighbor a TSA. The concept must be sold to the school system which usually means the school system's officials as well as the school board members. The system, the employer, must make the contribution to the plan; either in the form of an employer contribution or by means of an employee elective deferral. Once the TSA is adopted by the system and a master contract is signed by the school system, then all employees of the system are prospects for a TSA.

Needless to say, this concept of "selling the plan to the system" is not a simple matter. Most hospitals, school systems, etc., will limit the number of TSA carriers with whom they will do business. This limitation is primarily due to the administrative work and detail imposed on the employer when a TSA is adopted. Allowing every company who approaches the employer the right to solicit TSA business could become an expensive administrative nightmare for the employer. Thus, most school systems, for example, will limit the number of TSA carriers to possibly no more than three.

Other alternative contribution limitations are available for employees of most non-profit organizations. These elections were implemented by the IRS to allow certain employees who have low contributions in their early years of employment to catch up by making relatively higher contributions in their later years of employment. An eligible employee may make an **irrevocable election to use one of the following alternative limitations**.

Limitations 1 and 2 permit an overall increased limit. Limitation 3 permits an increased exclusion allowance.

Limitation #1 allows an employee **once in his or her lifetime** to use a special overall limit for the limitation year which ends with the tax year in which the employee terminates employment. The tax year and the limitation year are usually one and the same. The tax year refers to a calendar year. The limitation year is also usually a calendar year unless the employee has elected a different 12-month period. This special one-time limit is equal to the lesser of:

- $30,000
- The smaller of the current year exclusion allowance compared to the exclusion allowance, excluding employer contributions during the 10-year period ending with the date of the employee's separation

An example follows:

> Mrs. White has worked for St. Peter's Home for the Aged for 20 years. She is retiring December 31, 1992. Her compensation is $20,000 per year. St. Peter's has contributed $45,000 to a TSA for her. St. Peter's contributions for the past 10 years have been $35,000. Mrs. White's **current year exclusion allowance** is equal to:
>
> salary x years of service x 20% - employer contributions
>
> $20,000 (20) = $400,000 x 20% = $80,000 - $45,000 = $35,000
>
> Mrs. White's **separation exclusion allowance**, taking into consideration the employer contributions for the **10-year period** ending with the date of the separation, is as follows:
>
> $20,000 (10) = 200,000 x 20% = 40,000 - 35,000 = $ 5,000

Mrs. White may exclude $5,000 (the separation exclusion allowance) since it is the smaller of the two exclusion amounts and of course, is less than $30,000.

A second alternative election permits an employee to use as the overall TSA limit for the tax year, the lowest of:

- The employee's regular exclusion allowance for the tax year
- $4,000 plus 25% of includable compensation for the tax year
- $15,000

Let's assume the following example:

> Jack is about to retire from the Meadowbrook School System after 20 years of service. His current salary is $30,000. The system has contributed $40,000 to a TSA on his behalf. Jack may exclude (deduct) the smallest of the following:
>
> 1. Current year exclusion allowance:
> $30,000 (20) = 600,000 x 20% = 120,000 - 40,000 = $80,000
>
>   or

ELECTIVE DEFERRAL PLANS

2. $4000 + 30,000 (25%) = $11,500

   or

3. $15,000

Jack may exclude $11,500. This amount is an alternative overall limit, not an exclusion allowance. It should be remembered that these first two alternative limitations apply to employer contributions.

Alternative limitation #3 permits an employee to exclude up to $30,000 or 25% of compensation without regard to his or her current year exclusion allowance. When an individual elects to use alternative 3, both the exclusion allowance and maximum overall limit will be the same. When this alternative is elected, the employee must total all employer pension plan contributions and TSA contributions in arriving at the $30,000/25% limitation.

Any election to use these special alternative limits is usually made with regard to the individual's income tax liability for a particular tax year. Any such election will coincide with the exclusion reflected on the individual's tax return.

Taxation

Taxation of TSAs follows that of any qualified plan. Employer contributions and/or employee deferrals are tax deductible as long as these contributions do not exceed the allowable limits discussed above. Investment income on contributions is tax deferred. These tax advantages are of particular value for the TSA participant due to the salary reduction concept.

When the non-profit organization employee elects a salary reduction, he or she will only be taxed on the balance of the compensation. For example, an employee with a salary of $20,000 agrees to a salary reduction of $2,000 thus reducing the taxable compensation to $18,000. Federal, state, and city taxes are only computed on $18,000. However, Social Security taxes are calculated on the full $20,000 of compensation.

When the employee retires, the entire TSA amount is tax basis and thus will be taxed at ordinary income tax rates. Generally, upon the death of an employee, all amounts received by the beneficiary are usually taxable as ordinary income.

Vesting is not the same as with other qualified plans. The individual is always 100% vested in all contributions made to the plan. Graded vesting schedules are not permitted with TSAs. In essence, TSA vesting is similar to that of SEP vesting.

Loans from a TSA are permitted in accordance with IRS regulations. Unless the loan is required to be repaid within five years, it will be taxed as a distribution. If the purpose of the loan is to acquire a principal or main residence of the participant, the loan repayment period may exceed five years.

Penalties which can be imposed on TSA participants include the excess contribution penalty of 6%. The penalty tax is on the amount by which the contribution exceeds the lesser of the exclusion allowance or the overall limitation of the plan plus any other excesses carried over from previous years.

Early distributions prior to age 59½ will result in a penalty of 10% of the premature distribution unless the distribution is due to death, disability or other occurrence as mentioned in Chapter 2.

Distributions in excess of the greater of $150,000 or $112,500 (indexed) are subject to a 15% penalty. The employee is also subject to the 50% tax for delayed distributions. Again, both of these concepts were also discussed in Chapter 2.

CASH OR DEFERRED ARRANGEMENTS (CODA)

Another type of salary reduction plan is a CODA or **401(k) plan**. Under a 401(k) plan, eligible employees have two options. They may take employer contributions in cash or enter into a salary reduction agreement with the employer and defer amounts of their compensation. If the employee elects the cash option, there are no tax advantages as any money paid to the employee will be treated as compensation or a bonus and thus taxable.

Generally, the salary reduction option with the 401(k) plans is very similar to the TSA reductions. The employee will set aside some money on a pretax basis. Administratively, the employer will perform the necessary payroll reduction function and any amounts deferred are not included in the employee's gross income.

The 401(k) plan may be an employer pay all (non-contributory) or it may include provisions for both employer and employee contributions. Most often, 401(k)s provide for employee salary reductions plus some "matching employer contribution".

> Benevolent Benny, an employer, has called a meeting to announce to his 25 employees that he is implementing a 401(k) plan and that each employee can have his or her salary reduced from 1%-5% and have that amount contributed to the plan. He then asks for a show of hands to determine how many employees wish to sign up for this plan. Much to his dismay, only three employees indicate that they want to participate.

Benny's plan is meeting with employee opposition because Benevolent Benny is not contributing anything on behalf of his employees.

> Mary Beth, an employer, calls a meeting of her 25 employees to announce the implementation of a 401(k) plan whereby employees can have their salary reduced from 1%-5% and for every dollar that the employee contributes to the plan, she, the employer, will match it with 50 cents.

In this situation, Mary Beth will probably realize considerable more employee participation than Benny in the previous example. When an employer motivates the employees to participate in the plan through a salary reduction agreement plus some employer contributions, the plan becomes much more attractive and is less likely to be discriminatory in favor of the higher paid employees.

By implementing a 401(k) plan the employer is able to offer some attractive benefits and advantages to the employees. These include:

- A reduction in taxable income and tax deferred growth of these deferrals
- The establishment of retirement benefits
- A flexible method of meeting individual objectives and needs

This last point needs further explanation. First, the 401(k) is a flexible plan in that an employee may elect to participate or not participate. Secondly, the individual can select a salary reduction amount which meets his or her own objectives.

Eligibility

Eligibility for participation in a 401(k) plan is typically that the employee must have completed one year of service or be age 21, whichever is the later of the two. The plan must also satisfy the coverage and participation requirements common to all qualified plans; that is, the percentage test, ratio test or the average benefit test. These were discussed in Chapter 2.

These participation and coverage requirements have possibly increased significance with a 401(k) plan because there is a tendency for more of the higher paid people to become involved in salary reduction plans. Generally, this class of employee can more readily afford a cut in salary in order to participate in the plan.

Due to this fact, there is an additional nondiscrimination test which applies to a 40l(k) plan — the **Actual Deferral Percentage (ADP) test**. Generally, this test only permits the actual deferral percentage of the higher paid employees to exceed that of the lower paid employees by approximately 1%-2%. The higher paid employee generally will want to have a larger percentage of compensation reduced. The ADP test permits this but will place a limitation on this excess percentage. The effect of this requirement can be seen in the following table:

TABLE 6-1

Lower Paid Employees' Deferral Percentage	Maximum Higher Paid Employees' Deferral Percentage
1%	2%
3%	5%
5%	7%
7%	9%
9%	11.25%

ELECTIVE DEFERRAL PLANS

Gus is a businessowner and your client. He has installed a 401(k) plan for the benefit of his 40 employees. There are no employer contributions and only six of the employees have signed up for salary reductions. These six employees include Gus and his managers and department heads.

Gus needs to add some incentive for the other employees to join the 401(k) as very possibly, the plan is top heavy due to the current participants. To remove this discrimination, Gus should probably offer to contribute some percentage or dollar amount to the 401(k) for those employees who participate. If other participation cannot be achieved, the plan will probably continue to have the discriminatory problem.

Contributions

Contribution limits must take into consideration all elective deferral plans in which the individual participates. This would include SEPs and TSAs as well as the 401(k). The employee elective deferral limit is $7,000 as indexed. It should be noted that if an individual is participating in a TSA, the contribution limit is increased to $9,500 for all elective deferral plans in accordance with the TSA rules.

Margaret participates in a 401(k) and a TSA. She currently contributes $6,000 to the 401(k) through a salary reduction agreement. What is the maximum she may contribute to the TSA?

The answer is an additional $3,500 because of the increased limit of $9,500. If Margaret was participating in a SEP and a 401(k), the maximum contribution limit would be $7,000 as indexed. Any amounts which are deferred in excess of these limits are not excludable from the participant's gross income and thus will be included in the participant's gross income for the taxable year, including taxable investment income that any excess contributions may have generated.

Taxation

Taxation of 401(k) plans is similar to that of any other qualified plan. Employer contributions and employee deferrals are tax deductible. Investment income is tax deferred. As such, 401(k) distributions are considered tax basis and are taxed at ordinary income tax rates upon receipt. It should also be noted that taxes can be deferred under a 401(k) distribution by complying with the rollover provisions for qualified plans.

For example, a 401(k) distribution could be rolled into an IRA. Such a rollover may be a total or partial rollover. Any amount which is not rolled over, will be taxed to the employee.

Vesting requirements are similar to those of any other qualified plan. Employee deferrals are always 100% vested. Any matching employer contributions must at least follow the vesting regulations common to all plans — 3/7 or 0/5 employee vesting as discussed in Chapter 2. Thus, depending on the vesting schedule elected, employees must be fully vested in the employer's contributions not later than after five or seven years.

Penalties related to 401(k) plans are similar to those for other qualified plans. Generally, if an employee receives a premature distribution prior to age 59½, a 10% penalty is imposed on the amount received. As is true with most qualified plans, the individual must begin a systematic distribution of the plan benefits by age 70½ or face a 50% tax penalty. Excess distributions are penalized at the rate of 15% of the excess as was discussed in Chapter 2.

There is also a penalty for excess 401(k) contributions. It should be noted that "excess contributions" are the contributions made on behalf of highly paid employees (by the employer) in excess of the maximum amount permitted under the ADP test (mentioned above). Unless the excess contributions are distributed or otherwise corrected within two and a half months following the end of the plan year, the employer will incur a 10% penalty (excise tax). Correction of the excess contributions can simply mean distributing the excess to the employees. When this happens, the contribution is naturally taxable to the employees.

Excess contributions are not amounts contributed in excess of the elective deferral limit ($7,000 indexed). Any such excesses are treated as **excess deferrals**; not excess contributions. Amounts which are deferred in excess of the limits must be included in the employee's gross income for taxation. If the excess deferrals have accumulated investment income, the investment income is also taxable to the employee.

Hardship withdrawals are permitted under 401(k) plan regulations. Hardship withdrawals may only be made from the employee's contributions. Hardship distributions are permitted only if the employee has experienced an immediate, serious financial need and there are no other reasonable financial resources available to meet the need. Financial hardship includes the following situations:

- Medical expenses incurred by the employee or family members
- The purchase of the employee's principal residence
- College tuition payments for family members
- The need to prevent eviction of the employee's principal residence or to prevent foreclosure of a mortgage

Generally, a distribution may be deemed necessary if the employer relies upon the employee's representation that the financial hardship cannot be resolved through reimbursement from insurance contracts, use of the individual's personal assets, or by any other financial means available to the person.

When a financial hardship distribution is made, the plan must provide that the employee cannot make elective contributions for a period of 12 months following receipt of the distribution. In addition, the elective deferral limitation of $7,000 as indexed, will be reduced by the amount of the elective contribution for the taxable year in which the hardship distribution was received.

THRIFT/SALARY SAVINGS PLAN

Thrift or salary savings plans should not be confused with 401(k) plans. Prior to the enactment of 401(k) legislation, salary savings or thrift plans were often offered by employers for the purpose of encouraging employees to save money. Although a thrift plan could be a qualified plan, most often it was simply a payroll deduction savings plan whereby employees could make contributions to the plan with after-tax dollars. The attractiveness of these plans was due to the payroll deduction of contributions and investment earnings accumulated on a tax-deferred basis.

Thus, the principal difference between a salary savings plan and a 401(k) plan is that the employee enjoys a tax-deductible contribution with the 401(k) as well as tax-deferred investment growth. Accordingly, most employee/employer plans being established today will be 401(k) types.

Plan Design

Unlike the 401(k) plan, a savings plan uses **after tax employee contributions**. Employer contributions are tax deductible. Employees voluntarily agree to contribute a certain percentage of compensation to the savings plan. Growth on these amounts is tax deferred until received by the employee.

There is a certain element of investment risk to the employee since the employee is free to direct his or her contributions into a variety of investment vehicles such as bonds, stock accounts, mutual funds, etc.

Generally, a formula is used to determine level of contributions. A plan may specify that the employee may contribute from 1-5% of compensation and the employer will contribute one-half of the amount selected by the employee. Thus, if an employee elects a 3% after tax contribution, the employer matches it with a deductible contribution of 1½.

Generally, many of the features of a salary savings plan are similar to that of most qualified plans, especially a profit sharing plan. Unlike other qualified plans, the salary savings plan usually offers liberal withdrawal or loan features and provisions.

Due to the fact that this plan is voluntary for employees, there is the danger that the plan could become discriminatory in favor of the higher paid employees. Generally, the higher paid employee is more apt to elect a savings program than the lower paid employee.

In order to prevent this, the plan must comply with a separate discrimination test. The plan will not be considered discriminatory (for the higher paid employees) if the average ratio of employee contributions plus employer contributions does not exceed the greater of:

- 125% of the contribution percentage for all eligible employees, or
- the lesser of 200% of the contributions percentage for all eligible employees or 200% plus 2 percentage points.

For example, if a lower paid employee is contributing 4% to a plan, the higher paid employees could not contribute more than 6% (2 percentage points higher) to the plan.

If the plan becomes discriminatory, it can lose its qualified plan status and consequently, its tax advantages.

In many other ways, the two types of plans are similar. The employer may or may not make any contributions to the thrift plan. Often thrift plans, like 401(k) plans, allow employees to select from a variety of investment vehicles with respect to their own contributions. Usually, the amount of employee contributions to either type of plan is fairly flexible. Both types of plans cannot discriminate with regard to employee contribution amounts.

Funding

Funding for elective deferral plans is generally available in a variety of ways. Most often a plan will provide several forms of funding from which a participant may elect. For example, a plan may provide any or all of the following funding vehicles:

- Bond funds
- Stock funds
- Government securities
- Annuities
- Money market funds
- Mutual funds
- Certificates of deposit

The plan participant may direct all contributions into one of these funding sources or may elect to divide these contributions among two or more of these investment products.

For those employees who can tolerate the risks associated with investments, various types of securities, stocks, bonds and mutual funds are available. For those who desire more secure type investments, there are CDs, fixed annuities, and similar guaranteed-type products.

SUMMARY

SEPs, TSAs and 401(k)s are often described as elective deferral plans due to the fact that the individual can elect a salary reduction which provides for certain tax advantages as well as providing a systematic method of saving dollars for retirement purposes. As qualified plans, elective deferral plans must comply with the qualification requirements of any other such qualified plans. These include nondiscrimination requirements, vesting requirements, excess contribution stipulations, etc. The principal characteristics and statutory requirements of TSAs and 401(k)s are identified in Tables 6-2 and 6-3.

TABLE 6-2

PLAN FEATURES

TSA

Eligibility	Must be an employee of a non-profit organization in accordance with IRC 501(c)(3)
	May require one year of service and minimum age 21
Contributions	Employer — the lesser of 25% of compensation or $30,000
	Contributions may be based on the individual's exclusion allowance
	Employee salary reduction deferrals are limited to $9,500
	Catch-up provisions provide an additional $3,000 per year to an aggregate of $15,000
Taxation growth	Tax-deductible contributions and tax-deferred
Vesting	100% vesting in all plan contributions
Penalties	Excess contribution — 6% excise tax on excess
	Excess distribution — 15% penalty on excess over $150,000 or $112,500 as indexed
	Premature distribution — 10% excise tax if prior to age 59½ with certain exceptions
	Delayed distribution — 50% tax on the amount which should have been distributed
Other Comments	Employer sponsored TSAs must comply with non-discrimination requirements
	One time alternative contribution limits can increase contribution amounts
	Loans are permitted — must be repaid within five years unless for the purchase of a home

TABLE 6-3

PLAN FEATURES

401(K)

Eligibility	The later of age 21 or one year of service and is eligible to make an elective deferral
Contributions	Employer — 25% up to maximum of $30,000
	Employee deferrals - $7,000 as indexed
	Employer/employee — combined maximum of $30,000
Taxation	Tax deductible contributions and tax-deferred growth
Vesting	Employer contributions — 0/5 or 3/7 vesting
	Employee deferrals — 100% immediate vesting
Penalties	Excess employer contributions — 10% excise tax
	Excess distribution — 15% penalty on excess over $150,000 or $112,500 as indexed
	Premature distribution — 10% excise tax if prior to 59½ with certain exceptions
	Delayed distribution — 50% tax on the amount which should have been distributed
Other Comments	Plans must satisfy standard non-discrimination tests plus the ADP test
	Maximum aggregate elective deferrals for TSAs and 401(k) plans is $9,500
	Hardship withdrawals are permitted

REVIEW EXERCISES

1. Paula is a kindergarten teacher in the Valley School District. She has been employed for four years and makes $25,000 per year. During the past four years, the school system has contributed $4,000 to a TSA on her behalf. Calculate Paula's exclusion allowance.

2. Mary has been employed as a nurse for St. Luke's hospital for 20 years. During this period, the hospital has contributed $40,000 to a TSA. Mary wishes to take advantage of the special election to increase her normal contribution. She has never used this election before. What are the additional amounts available to Mary and how much can be added to the current contribution?

CHAPTER 7

KEOGH PLANS

By definition, a Keogh plan is a qualified retirement plan for a self-employed businessowner and eligible employees. Congressman Keogh was the sponsor of the so called Keogh Act which amended the Internal Revenue Code to allow the self employed to establish qualified plans. Keogh plans are also referred to as HR-10 plans.

These qualified plans came into existence by means of the Self Employed Individuals Tax Retirement Act of 1962. This initial legislation contained certain restrictions which caused many of the self-employed businessowners to ignore this new law. However, beginning with the passage of ERISA in 1974, Keogh requirements began to become more liberal. By 1983, by means of the Tax Equity and Fiscal Responsibility Act (TEFRA), Keogh plans were finally established on the same basis with most corporate plans. Today, there are only a few differences between a Keogh plan and corporate pension plans. The primary difference is simply that a Keogh plan is for a non-incorporated form of business.

THE SELF-EMPLOYED AS AN EMPLOYEE — ELIGIBILITY

In accordance with tax law, self-employed individuals are not considered employees. A qualified plan must be established by an employer for the benefit of the employees and their beneficiaries. Accordingly, the self-employed businessowner could not participate in a qualified plan since he or she is not an employee. However, Keogh plans permit the owner to participate in the plan as an employee.

For purposes of plan participation, an employee is generally defined as anyone who has earned income. Earned income is distinguished from unearned income by the fact that the individual earns compensation for personal services rendered to an employer or business. Unearned income of course is income derived from investments, interest, rents, royalties, etc.

Thus, a sole proprietor or a partner in a non-incorporated business are treated as employees of the business as long as they have earned income or personal service income. They are then eligible to participate in a Keogh plan as an employee.

In addition, all eligible employees of the sole proprietor or partnership must be included in the Keogh plan. Generally, an employee (common law employee) is usually defined as a person who is compensated, controlled and directed by the employer or business. Another test of an individual's status as an employee is whether Social Security taxes are paid on the employee's behalf.

All employees who then meet the eligibility requirements of the plan (usually the later of age 21 or one year of full time service) must be included as plan participants.

It should also be noted that an individual can be a participant in a qualified corporate retirement plan and an HR-10 at the same time.

> Sally works for General Motors as an automotive engineer. She is an employee of the corporation and is covered under General Motors' qualified retirement plan. In her spare time, she operates a part-time automotive repair business as a sole proprietor. She would be eligible to establish a Keogh plan for a portion of her self-employed income.

Thus, in Sally's situation she could participate as an employee in two qualified plans and enjoy the tax advantages of both. It is even conceivable that Sally could have an IRA since she would qualify for the IRA by having earned income and we will assume that she is less than 70½ years of age. However, she probably would not be able to claim a tax deduction for any IRA contribution due to the fact that she is an active participant in another qualified plan(s) and presumably is making too much money to take the tax deduction.

A life insurance agent would be another example of an individual who participates in the insurer's agent pension plan and as a sole proprietor would be eligible to use a Keogh plan for any self-employed commissions received.

PLAN QUALIFICATION

The self-employed businessowner is eligible for the same type of qualified plans as a corporation. These would include the various forms of pension plans including defined contribution and defined benefit plan, and profit sharing plans. Needless to say, the self-employed businessowner must also satisfy the requirements pertaining to any qualified plan in order to be able to benefit from the tax advantages of such plans.

Eligibility requirements, contribution limitations, vesting and similar requirements must be met including those requirements pertaining to top heavy plans. Generally, the non-incorporated business is relatively small and as such, often the owner is the highest paid person. In addition, there may be only a few other employees. Thus, there is a tendency for these plans to be top heavy.

> Dr. Paine, D.D.S., practices dentistry as a sole proprietor. He employs one receptionist, one dental assistant, and one dental hygienist. Dr. Paine's compensation is $150,000 annually. The total compensation for his other three employees is $50,000.
>
> Dr. Paine wishes to establish a 10% defined contribution Keogh plan. Ten percent of his total payroll ($200,000) will result in an annual contribution of $20,000, of which, $15,000 (75%) will benefit Dr. Paine.

Since more than 60% of the plan contribution will benefit Dr. Paine, the plan is top heavy. As such, the plan must comply with certain top heavy qualification requirements as previously discussed in Chapter 2.

It should be kept in mind that Dr. Paine is entitled to a greater contribution in terms of dollars because of his higher compensation. But if Dr. Paine establishes a 10% plan, he must set aside 10% of compensation for each eligible employee.

In addition, if the sole proprietor controls or owns more than one business, all such controlled businesses must be included for purposes of satisfying the qualification requirements of qualified plans. All of the owner's employees (including the other owned businesses) must be included in the plan for participation and qualification requirements. The plan for the controlled businesses must provide benefits and contributions equal to the contributions and benefits provided for the owner-employee.

Thus, if Dr. Paine maintained a second office with a staff of two or three employees, he must include the employees of the second office in the plan and provide them with comparable benefits and contributions.

> Mary Beth has an HR-10 and earns $100,000 per year as a sole proprietor. She has two full-time employees who each earn $20,000. The plan specifies a contribution of 10% of compensation.
>
> The total of $40,000 of employee compensation times 10% equals a contribution of $2,000 each for the two employees.
>
> Mary Beth's contribution will be equal to her compensation of $100,000/1.10 which equals $90,909 x 10% or $9,090. Her compensation as a sole proprietor equals net earnings less the deductible contribution made on her behalf (thus the need to divide by 1.10 before making the calculation).
>
> Thus the total contribution would be $4,000 + $9,090 = $13,090.

PLAN CONTRIBUTIONS

If the HR-10 is a defined contribution plan, the maximum plan contribution is the lesser of 25% of compensation or $30,000. If the plan is a defined benefit plan, the contributions are limited to an amount necessary to provide the lesser of a $90,000 benefit, as indexed, or 100% of the participant's average compensation for the individual's highest three consecutive years. If the Keogh program is a profit sharing plan, the contribution limitation is 15% of compensation up to a maximum of $30,000 per participant.

It should be noted that these figures are maximum contribution limits. In reality, the average plan will provide benefits or contributions in lesser amounts. Plan contributions represent a fixed liability for the employer and accordingly, a more conservative contribution or benefit limit is usually established.

Conversely, these contribution amounts represent the maximum tax deductible contributions which an employer may enjoy. An employer could contribute greater amounts to any qualified plan, but would lose the tax advantages if these maximums were exceeded. In addition, there is a 10% tax penalty for excess, nondeductible contributions.

Compensation for a self-employed, non-incorporated individual is defined as the net earnings from the business excluding the deductible contribution made on behalf of the owner-employee. The amount of these earnings can be calculated by dividing the self employment earnings by one plus the contribution percentage.

Thus, if we revisit Dr. Paine, we would divide his $150,000 (before contribution earnings) by 1.10 (10% contribution formula) with the result equal to $136,363. This amount would then be multiplied by the contribution percentage (10%) to arrive at the amount to be contributed on behalf of Dr. Paine — $136,363 x 10% = $13,636.30.

Contributions made for the other employees are deductible from gross self employment earnings as a necessary business expense. Thus, the deductible contribution in Dr. Paine's situation becomes 10% of the additional employee payroll of $50,000 which equals $5,000 plus the $13,636.30 which represents his deductible contribution.

If part of the employer contributions are for the purchase of life insurance benefits as part of the Keogh plan, these amounts are not deductible contributions on behalf of the self-employed owner-employee. The cost of the life insurance is subtracted from the plan contributions. The amount to be deducted from the contribution is equal to the P.S. 58 charges for the life insurance. The P.S. 58 charges are the costs of pure life insurance protection which is taxable to the employee under a qualified plan, such as a Keogh.

Once again, let's look at Dr. Paine's situation. Let's assume that there is life insurance included in his Keogh plan and that the P.S. 58 charges for the amount allocated to him is $300. This amount is subtracted from the $13,636.30 Keogh contribution which leaves a total of $13,336.30 as the deductible contribution on behalf of Dr. Paine.

TAXATION AND PLAN DISTRIBUTIONS

As a qualified plan, Keogh plan distributions are subject to the same type of taxation as any corporate qualified plan. Generally, as a qualified plan, contributions are deductible, investment earnings on the contributions are tax deferred and the benefits or distributions received are taxable.

Some qualified plans allow for non-deductible voluntary contributions from plan participants. The individual can recover these amounts without incurring a tax liability as a return of cost basis. The self-employed businessowner may not include any P.S. 58 charges in his cost basis even though these amounts are not deductible.

In the majority of situations, all distributions received from the Keogh plan will be taxable as tax basis. Pre-retirement benefits received due to the death of the participant are fully taxable as are normal retirement benefits. Lump sum distributions received from a Keogh plan provide special tax treatment in much the same way that any lump sum distribution made from a qualified corporate plan does.

However, certain requirements must be met if the distribution is to be identified as a **lump sum distribution**. A distribution will be considered a lump sum distribution if it occurs after the businessowner or any employees have attained age 59½ or died. In addition, the owner-employee may also receive a lump sum distribution due to a total disability. The owner's employees may also be eligible for a lump sum distribution (and its favorable tax treatment) due to termination of employment.

Generally, an individual who receives a lump sum distribution after 1986 may elect to use a **5-year income averaging formula** for calculation of the taxes. Prior to 1986, a 10-year averaging formula could be used. The 5-year averaging formula may be used only once, the taxpayer must have been a plan participant for at least five years and be at least age 59½ when the distribution was received.

Once any cost basis is deducted from the lump sum distribution, the 5-year formula provides that the ordinary income tax will be computed on **1/5 of the total taxable amount** of the lump sum distribution less a minimum distribution allowance. This amount is then multiplied by 5. The formula uses single taxpayer rates.

$$\text{5-Year Formula} = \frac{\text{Taxable Amount} - \text{Distribution Allowance}}{5} \times 5$$

The distribution allowance is the lesser of $10,000 or ½ of the total taxable amount. This amount is further reduced by 20% of the total taxable amount in excess of $20,000.

Casper, age 60, has received a $50,000 lump sum distribution from his HR-10 and has no other lump sum distributions in the current year. He elects to 5-year average his tax liability. All of the distribution is tax basis.

Casper's distribution allowance is $10,000. One-half of the taxable amount is $25,000 less 20% of $30,000 (50,000 – 20,000). Thus, the lesser amount is $10,000.

The total taxable amount is $50,000 – $10,000 or $40,000. The 5-year formula specifies 1/5 of the total taxable amount.

$$\text{Total taxable amount is: } \frac{\$40,000}{5} = \$8,000$$

Referring to 1992 tax tables for a single taxpayer with $8,000 of taxable income, the amount of the tax owed is:

$540 on $3,600 plus 15% of the excess ($4,400) which is $660. Total Tax: $1,200.

This amount is then multiplied by 5 ($1,200 x 5) and the total tax owed is $6,000 on a $50,000 lump sum distribution.

If Casper does not elect to 5-year average, disregarding any exemptions or deductions, the tax due on $50,000 would total $11,212. Thus, if the plan participant elects a lump sum distribution from the Keogh plan, there are some definite tax advantages if the participant 5-year averages his or her tax liability.

If the plan participant elects installment payments from the plan at retirement, these payments will be taxed the same as from any corporate plan. Usually, the entire amount received is taxable at ordinary income tax rates assuming there are no adjustments for any cost basis.

Keogh plans also accept **rollover distributions** from other qualified plans in accordance with the rollover rules applicable to any other qualified plan. A partial distribution of at least 50% of the employee's benefits may also be rolled over if the reason for the partial distribution is due to the individual's death, disability or termination of employment.

Premature distributions (prior to age 59½) are also treated like any similar distribution from other qualified plans. The plan participant is subject to a 10% penalty tax on the amount of the premature distribution in addition to ordinary income tax on the distribution. This penalty applies unless the reason for the distribution is due to death, disability or qualified early retirement in which it can be demonstrated that the individual has retired early (prior to 59½) and the plan benefits will be distributed to him or her for at least a period of five years following early retirement.

Excess distributions incur a 15% penalty on any excess amounts received in much the same manner as any other qualified plan. In addition, an owner-employee is subject to an additional penalty of 10% on excess amounts received.

VESTING OF BENEFITS

Vesting provisions for Keogh plans are the same as with any qualified corporate plan. The employer may establish the 0/5 or 3/7 vesting schedule. However, the employer may also consider 100% immediate vesting as an option.

Frequently, the self-employed businessowner may not employ any full time employees other than him or herself due to the fact that often, the business is relatively small. Consequently, a Keogh plan may be established with only one full time owner-employee as an eligible participant. Thus, 100% immediate vesting may be attractive.

However, it should be remembered that if 100% immediate vesting is specified, any full time employees subsequently hired who become eligible to participate in the plan, will also have 100% immediate vesting.

Funding

As an employer-sponsored plan, a Keogh's funding may take the form of individual or group investment products. Thus, the types of funding available for IRAs, SEPs and CODAs are also available for Keogh plans. In addition, there are group contracts including group fixed and variable annuities available for funding purposes.

Often annuities are choices for funding because by definition, an annuity provides a guaranteed income for the life of the annuitant. Thus, it becomes an ideal retirement vehicle, either as an individual or group contract.

Annuities are basically fixed or variable. A fixed annuity is a fully guaranteed contract in which there is no investment risk to the plan participant. A variable annuity is designed to be a hedge against inflation. As such, variable annuity contributions are normally invested in a common stock portfolio which creates an element of investment risk for the plan participants.

Since this employer-employee plan primarily consists of employer contributions only, it is most often the employer who will make the decision as to the type of plan funding. However, often this is also a choice of the plan participant.

SUMMARY

A Keogh plan (HR-10) is a qualified retirement plan for the self-employed and eligible employees. Generally, a Keogh plan is very similar to any other qualified plan available to corporate entities.

As a qualified plan, a Keogh plan must comply with all qualified plan requirements; i.e., eligibility requirements, vesting, contribution limitations, etc. In addition, Keogh plans must be filed and approved by the IRS and are subject to the requirements of ERISA. Taxation and tax penalties are similar to the taxation and penalties of any other qualified plan.

Table 7-1 summarizes the principal features for Keogh plans.

TABLE 7-1

PLAN FEATURES

KEOGH PLANS

Eligibility	The later of age 21 or one year of service
	Self-employed owner and employees
Contributions	Generally, the lesser of 25% of compensation or $30,000
	The plan may allow non-deductible voluntary employee contributions
Taxation	Tax deductible employer contributions
	Tax deferred investment growth on contributions
	Tax basis fully taxable at ordinary income tax rates upon receipt of benefits
	Special tax treatment for lump sum distributions using 5-year income averaging
Vesting	Employer contributions — 0/5 or 3/7 vesting schedule
	Employee contributions — 100% immediate vesting
Penalties	Excess contribution — 10% penalty tax
	Excess distributions — 15% penalty on excess over $150,000 or $112,500 as indexed Additional 10% penalty for owner-employee
	Premature distribution prior to age 59½ — 10%
	Delayed distributions — 50% tax on the amount which should have been distributed (by age 70½)
Other	Top heavy rules apply
Comments	Owner-employee's compensation = self-employed earnings after a deduction for any owner-employee plan contributions
	Rollover transfers allowed

REVIEW EXERCISES

1. Ralph works for IBM as a computer engineer. He also operates a computer consulting business out of his home in partnership with a business associate. Identify the types of qualified plans Ralph is eligible for and provide an explanation as to why he is eligible for these plans.

2. With reference to the 5-year averaging formula for lump sum distributions from a Keogh, calculate the total taxable amount if an owner-employee has a $20,000 lump sum distribution.

CHAPTER 8

CORPORATE QUALIFIED PLANS

Any of the qualified plans discussed in this text could be implemented by a corporate business entity with the exception of IRAs, TSAs, and Keogh plans. Thus, a corporation could establish an SEP, a 401(k) or any other pension or profit sharing plan. Basically, the decision which has to be made by the businessowner is when to install a qualified plan and which type of plan best meets the needs of the employer and the employees.

THE QUALIFIED PLAN DECISION

Charlie started a training business five years ago when he was 45-years old. He named the business Training Resources Inc. The business provides motivational, sales, and product training including classroom programs and published materials for corporations in need of such services. Charlie began the business by himself but hired a close friend, Fred, to do marketing and sales one month after the business started.

In the first year of operation, Training Resources made a modest profit of $4,000. In each of the succeeding years, the business has earned substantially more money and after five full years of operation, the business had gross earnings of $1.3 million. Due to acquiring an international account at the end of the fifth year, Training Resources expects to have gross sales in excess of $2.5 million by the end of the sixth year.

Over the last five years, in addition to Fred, Charlie has added 13 additional employees and recently added five more at the beginning of the sixth year to help handle the large international account. This brings the total number of employees to 20.

The marketing and sales staff consists of five employees. The firm employs six technical writers, an illustrator, and two editors. In addition there are four permanent seminar instructors. The balance of the staff consists of administrative employees. Training Resources also uses the services of approximately 40 independent contractors who provide instruction for various training seminars held throughout the country.

Charlie provides his 20 full-time employees with group life insurance and disability income as well as a comprehensive group medical plan. Fred and a few of the older employees (including Charlie) have questioned the need for a company retirement plan. Due to the success of the business, especially the expected large increase in company income during the upcoming sixth year, Charlie's accountant has also suggested that he might want to consider some alternatives to paying more in corporate taxes.

Charlie's story may be a bit unusual in that the business has done extremely well in a relatively short period of time. Most new businesses are characterized by a series of good and bad years before they stabilize and show consistent income and profits. Usually at some point during the life of the business a decision must be reached regarding the need to implement a qualified retirement plan. Naturally, this scenario is true not only of corporate entities but of the self-employed and non-incorporated businesses as well.

Thus, the first question to be answered is in reference to timing — when is a business a likely prospect for a pension plan?

QUALIFIED PLAN CONSIDERATIONS

There are basically three factors which help determine the need for implementing a qualified plan — employee considerations, tax considerations and the ability to pay for the plan.

Employee Considerations

Employee considerations usually involve such intangibles as employee morale, productivity and the ability to attract and retain key personnel. Employee morale and productivity generally go hand-in-hand. A happy employee is a productive and loyal employee.

In Charlie's business, he employs some technical people who may be hard to find in the labor force. If this type of employee becomes unhappy and leaves, he or she may not be easily replaced. Frequently employees switch jobs because of employee benefits as well as salary considerations. If the lack of a retirement plan is an important issue, then the employer must weigh the cost of a plan in relation to the cost of not having a plan and possibly not having some key employees. Thus, competitive business situations may motivate the businessowner to seriously consider a qualified retirement plan.

Conversely, the existence of a qualified plan can serve as a device to attract new employees as well as retain them. The unhappy employee from another firm may end up working for Charlie because he has a plan and the former employer did not.

It should also be remembered that the employer-owner is also an employee. He or she may desire a retirement plan for personal reasons. In Charlie's case, we will assume he has worked hard to make the business a success and will continue to work the long hours necessary for continued success. Charlie is now 50 years of age and may want to retire early, say at age 60. His business can serve as his retirement vehicle depending on the disposition of the business at his retirement. But certainly, a qualified retirement plan would be beneficial to him.

Tax Considerations

Naturally, another factor which affects the decision to implement a qualified plan are the **tax considerations**. Needless to say, if the business is not making any money, then it probably does not have a tax problem and a tax deduction is meaningless.

But, let's review Training Resources, Inc. and Charlie's situation. The gross income is expected to double over the next 12 months and there has been a fairly consistent profit picture each year of operation. The accountant has suggested the need for a tax deduction. Thus, there appears to be a business reason for considering the installation of a qualified plan. Added to this, is the fact that Charlie, Fred, and a few of the older employees have also questioned the need for a retirement plan. These factors would certainly seem to indicate that Charlie and Training Resources, Inc. may well be a prospect for a qualified plan.

The deductibility of the plan contributions is often the principal reason why an employer considers implementing a qualified plan. If the employer's attitude is one of paying him or herself first and then paying the government, then tax considerations may well be an important factor in arriving at the decision to embark on a pension plan.

Ability to Pay

The final consideration as to whether to install a qualified plan is simply the **ability to pay** for the plan. Other than a profit sharing plan, the employer is faced with a fixed liability in the form of the plan contributions. Can the employer consistently meet this fixed obligation? There are government penalties for failing to make required plan contributions.

For this reason, often when the decision is reached to install a plan, the employer elects to initially implement a **profit sharing plan**. The contribution formula for a profit sharing plan can be worded so that a contribution is made only if the corporation makes a profit. No profit — no contribution and no fixed liability.

The employer may also have to decide on how large of a contribution he or she can afford. Since most qualified plans will allow the lesser of 25% of compensation or $30,000 as a plan contribution, the employer may be well advised (at least initially) to start a plan with a modest contribution formula such as 5% of compensation.

With regard to Charlie, even though it would appear that his company has experienced a steady increase in profits and the financial picture is very optimistic, it could be recommended that Training Resources consider either a profit sharing plan initially or possibly a defined contribution plan with a modest contribution formula. Plans can always be amended to allow for increased contributions in later years if necessary and warranted by the employer's ability to pay for the plan.

THE TYPE OF PLAN

As previously stated, with the exception of Keogh plans, TSAs, and IRAs, a corporation can install any type of qualified plan or combination of plans. The type of plan selected is frequently tied to the cost of the plan and the employer/employee needs. As was just discussed, frequently employers will initially implement profit sharing plans because of the flexibility of contributions.

Defined Contribution Plan

Most companies with qualified plans will have profit sharing, defined contribution or defined benefit plans. For the employer with a stable business income situation and relatively young employees, often a **defined contribution plan** is utilized. The key to a successful and financially secure retirement is basically, time and money. Thus, if adequate sums of money are set aside in a retirement account for a long enough period of time, there should be adequate sums of money available at retirement for each participant.

The contribution to the defined contribution plan is a fixed liability and thus there is somewhat of an assurance that adequate sums of money will be set aside for plan participants. If the plan participants are relatively young, the time element will be satisfied. In Charlie's situation, he is now 50 years of age. If we assume that the majority of the 20 employees are younger than he, then quite possibly, Training Resources, Inc., may be a prospect for a defined contribution plan.

Some may argue that Charlie is not that young at age 50. However, it should be remembered that Charlie probably is the highest paid employee as the owner and president of the company and thus the corporate contribution for him (in dollars) will probably be considerably higher than for any other employee covered under the plan. This can compensate for his "advanced age of 50".

Defined Benefit Plan

Typically a **defined benefit plan** is considered by an employer with large sums of money to contribute. In a sense, there is no limit as to the size of the plan contribution; only a limit on the size of the plan benefit ($90,000, as indexed).

Even though Charlie's business income picture is very bright, he probably will not be a prospect for a defined benefit plan. Let's assume that Charlie is earning $100,000 per year and a proposed defined benefit plan specifies a retirement benefit of 10% of compensation. To provide Charlie with a benefit equal to 10% of compensation in a relatively short time of 15 years, could be very expensive. In addition, the anticipated large increase in business income may be needed for other purposes, such as expansion, working capital, etc.

Frequently, the type of business which may have an interest in a defined benefit plan will be a professional corporation such as a group of doctors, dentists, lawyers, etc. For example, a group of neurosurgeons forming a professional corporation (P.C.) may well have large sums of money generated which could be used as a contribution for a possible defined benefit plan.

Other Plan Types

Other plan types which could be considered include: SEPs, 401(k)s, stock bonus plans and ESOPs. Because of its administrative simplicity, an employer may want to consider a **Simplified Employee Pension plan**. The use of the SEP provides the employer with relief from some of the administrative details of consulting with an attorney or an accountant and the subsequent expense of installing the plan. Since the IRA used in the SEP plan is already a qualified vehicle, some of the initial administrative detail and expense is reduced. In addition, the SEP provides an easy method to encourage employee contributions to the plan on a tax favorable basis.

Frequently, employers will install a combination of possibly a profit sharing plan and a **401(k)**. The 401(k) may be described as a tax favorable employee savings plan, salary savings plan or supplemental retirement plan. Again the general intent is to encourage employee contributions on a tax favorable basis. This enhances retirement benefits at employee expense. The motivation to participate in the 401(k) is often some form of matching employer contributions.

For example, if an employer announced to the employees that the firm was establishing a 401(k) plan whereby they, the employees, could reduce their compensation by up to 10% on a tax favorable basis, probably few employees would participate, other than possibly some of the higher paid employees who could afford to have their compensation reduced. This then could present a problem of the plan being top heavy. To avoid this, the employer could announce that the corporation would contribute 50 cents for each employee dollar invested in the plan. This would probably motivate more of the employees to participate and thus eliminate the danger of the plan being top heavy while at the same time providing an attractive method of enhancing retirement benefits.

A **stock bonus plan** may serve the interests of the employer well by providing a mechanism which encourages or rewards productivity. A stock bonus plan provides the flexibility of a profit sharing plan in that contributions may vary depending on the profits of the company. Thus, more productivity, more profits, and benefits to be derived from the stock bonus plan.

Plan contributions may be fixed or dependent on profits. Stock bonus plans are often thought of as types of profit sharing plans. Thus, plan contributions are limited to a deductible amount of 15% of compensation. If an employer maintains both a profit sharing and a stock bonus plan, the deductible contribution limit is a total of 15%. Thus, if the profit sharing plan specified 10% of compensation, the maximum deductible stock bonus contribution could be 5%.

In addition, the contributions may be made in cash or in the form of company stock. Each participant has an account used to record the contributions made. If cash contributions are made, the money is then used to purchase company stock on behalf of the participants. If the contribution is in the form of stock, then the amount of the deductible contribution will be equal to the fair market value of the stock as of the date it is contributed to the plan.

As stockholders in the company, the participants generally have voting rights in much the same manner that any stockholder has. By "owning a piece of the company", the stockholder-employee may well feel more involved and important to the overall success of the business.

Another "motivational-type plan" which may be installed by the employer is an **Employee Stock Ownership Plan**. The ESOP concept (as discussed in a previous chapter) makes employees "owner-employees," providing the motivation to better productivity, improved customer relations and satisfaction, as well as increased profitability for the corporation. The ESOP becomes a vehicle by which the employer can sell the company to the employees in the form of a qualified retirement plan.

As was previously discussed, an ESOP permits the borrowing of money for the purpose of purchasing the employer's stock as part of the plan. Any such employer contributions in the form of a loan to purchase stock on behalf of the participants are deductible up to 25% of the compensation paid to the participants.

Thus, the employer enjoys the tax advantages of the qualified plan as the employer while at the same time taking advantage of a plan which enables the company to be purchased by the employees which of course is also beneficial to the employer. The employees are participants in a qualified retirement plan and in addition they become owner-employees of the corporation.

Funding

Depending on the type(s) of plan(s) to be implemented in a corporate situation, there are a number of funding alternatives available, most of which have been discussed in other chapters of this text.

Defined contribution, defined benefit, and profit sharing plans are generally classified as employer-employee plans with contributions being made by the employer only. Accordingly, the type of funding used for these types of corporate plans will be according to the employer's election. In addition, the employer's advisors such as his or her insurance agent will be instrumental in recommending a particular type of funding.

Generally both securities and guaranteed contracts (individual and group) may be used. With ESOPs, the employer's own securities often become funding vehicles.

CORPORATE QUALIFIED PLANS

SUMMARY

With the exception of an IRA, TSA, or a Keogh plan, the corporate form of business and the corporate owner may implement any one or combination of the various qualified retirement plans discussed in this text.

The businessowner must decide when to install a qualified plan, the type of plan to install and related to this, weigh the ability to pay for the plan. In addition to providing tax deductions, a qualified plan can also enable the owner to attract and retain key personnel. Accordingly, the owner may consider the installation of a qualified plan when employee demand is evident and when it becomes important to the business for purposes of retention of key personnel.

Many businesses will initially install a profit sharing plan in which contributions are tied to corporate profits. This provides the new corporation with flexibility and relieves the owner from incurring a fixed liability.

Depending on other employer-employee needs, defined contribution and defined benefits may be the type of plan elected. This decision will be made with regard to the cost facts inherent in these plans whereby the employer will incur a fixed liability.

Other plans which provide both the benefits of any qualified plan plus certain intangible benefits such as company loyalty, improved productivity and enhanced customer satisfaction include stock bonus plans and ESOPs. These plans are sometimes referred to as "owner-employee" plans.

REVIEW EXERCISES

1. Paul owns a tax preparation and consulting firm which employs 15 people. The business has been in existence for 14 years. During this time, it lost small sums of money for nine of those years. It has shown small total profits of approximately $15,000 in three of the past five years.

   Paul employs bookkeepers and accountants. His total payroll is $400,000 annually. The average age of the employees is 47. Paul is 51. Several of the employees have been complaining about a lack of a pension plan.

1A. What type of recommendation might you make to Paul regarding the timing of a plan (is he really a prospect for a qualified plan)?

1B. What type of plan would you recommend and why?

1C. What alternative or additional qualified plans might you recommend to Paul?

CHAPTER 9

POLICY PLANS AND FUNDING ARRANGEMENTS

Once the decision is reached regarding the type of plan to be installed, i.e., profit sharing, defined contribution, etc., another decision must be made regarding how the plan will be funded and what type of funding will be used. This chapter will cover the "how", meaning what form of funding types can be used with qualified plans.

TYPES OF FUNDING A funding organization is an entity which provides for the accumulation and administration of plan assets. These various organizations (banks, insurance companies, trust companies, etc.) have agreements or instruments which govern and regulate the funding of plan benefits. There are basically two types of plans with regard to the form of the funding. They are:

> **Insured Plans** — plans by which plan contributions are made to an insurance company and all benefits are paid by the insurer to the plan participants.
>
> **Trust Fund Plans** — plans by which plan contributions are made to a corporate fiduciary, such as a bank trust department, or an individual fiduciary, acting as a plan trustee. The plan trustee (corporate or individual) administers plan assets and distributes benefits to the participants.

A variation of these two arrangements is sometimes referred to as a combination plan in which part of the plan assets are administered by an insurer and the balance by a trustee. Usually, plan benefits are paid by the insurer. In reality, often the insurer acts as both insurer and plan trustee.

Allocated and Unallocated Funds

The plan may be further classified as an allocated fund or an unallocated fund. An **allocated fund** is one in which plan contributions are allocated to each plan participant in accordance with the plan's contribution formula. Each participant has his or her own account.

An **unallocated fund** is one in which contributions and earnings are simply accumulated for the benefit of plan participants. The plan assets are "pooled" and part of this pool is then later paid to specific participants.

THE FULLY INSURED PLAN — INDIVIDUAL CONTRACTS

A fully insured plan is administered by an insurance company with reference to accumulation of assets and distribution of benefits. Normally, specific funding vehicles will be insurance products. The purpose of a pension plan is to deliver retirement benefits at some later date to plan participants. The plan may also provide a life insurance benefit in the event of premature death.

Plan contributions may be invested in group or individual types of insurance products. An annuity is frequently used as the investment vehicle. By definition, an annuity provides a guaranteed income for the life of the annuitant. Insured plans could use individual annuity contracts or a group annuity contract.

If the plan provides for a pre-retirement death benefit, generally some form of individual permanent life insurance contract is used with the policy's cash value used to provide retirement benefits should the participant reach retirement. Normally, an individual life contract would require individual underwriting and it is possible that some participants may be substandard risks or uninsurable.

The use of annuities and some life insurance to fund fully insured plans has been a "traditional" concept. In the more modern insurance world, the funding vehicles available to the insurance agent are not limited to fixed annuities and life insurance. Contributions to a fully insured plan may be invested in variable annuities and similar equity-based products (securities) other than the traditional products. Thus, if the plan consists of individual contracts, each participant has the opportunity to "direct" plan contributions into a series of individual investment vehicles.

For example, the plan agreement may provide that contributions could be made to a guaranteed Certificate of Deposit fund, a common stock portfolio, fixed or variable annuities, a mutual fund, a government bond fund, etc. Normally, the participant is provided with the flexibility to specify into which fund or funds, his or her plan contributions should be made. As such, specific amounts are allocated to each participant's contract.

Plans using individual plans naturally require that separate contracts be issued to each plan participant. Often an agreement is formulated between the employer and a trustee whereby the trustee serves as the custodian for the individual contracts. Normally, these policies are maintained by the trustee. The trustee pays the premiums and is usually the owner of the contracts. The participant naturally completes and signs the application for insurance, annuities, etc.

The annual contribution to the plan and the subsequent retirement benefit will have a bearing on the types of policies or investment contracts in force among the participants.

> For example, if the plan formula calls for a contribution equal to 10% of compensation for each participant, this amount becomes a fixed liability for the employer. Let's assume two employees of the same age who both earn $10,000 per year. Accordingly, a contribution of $1,000 annually will be made for each employee.
>
> Employee A elects to have his contribution placed in CDs and a fixed annuity. Employee B elects to have her contribution placed in a mutual fund and a variable annuity. Twenty years later, they both are ready to retire. There is the possibility that one of these employees could have considerably more money accumulated at retirement due to the allocation of these funds.
>
> If the stock market did particularly well for the 20-year period, then Employee B who had invested in a variable annuity and a mutual fund may well have more retirement dollars than Employee A. Conversely, it's possible that Employee A who had invested in guaranteed, yet conservative contracts, could have a greater amount of money accumulated if the stock market did not perform very well during the 20-year period.

It should be noted that when the participant can direct the investment of his or her contribution, any losses experienced are at the risk of the participant. The plan trustee or fiduciary is not held liable. Thus, with individual selection as to the investment vehicle, the plan participant must be able to withstand the inherent investment risks associated with securities and equity-based products.

THE FULLY INSURED PLAN — GROUP CONTRACTS

Fully insured plans may use group contracts in lieu of individual contracts as the principal funding mechanism. Most insurers will offer group annuity contracts and group deposit administration contracts as the principal funding vehicles. The group concept basically provides plan coverage of all participants under one policy with no individual policies being underwritten or delivered.

The insurer will normally enforce compliance with certain group requirements: minimum group size requirements, specific participation requirements, and a minimum annual contribution per participant.

Group Annuity Contracts

Group annuity contracts may be fixed or variable (just as individual annuities may be fixed or variable). The fixed annuity will provide guarantees that the variable does not. Individual or group fixed annuities provide for the investment of the plan contributions in the insurer's general account. Typically, the general account consists of a portfolio of fixed, conservative, relatively safe investments such as mortgages, real estate, CDs, etc.

The basic premise behind the variable annuity is that it provides a hedge against inflation by the investment of plan contributions in the insurer's separate account which consists primarily of a common stock portfolio. Thus, there is a certain degree of investment risk to the plan participant as separate account investments are not guaranteed with regard to principal or investment return. If the plan participant is able to withstand the investment risk, he or she will hopefully not experience a loss of purchasing power over the years during which the contributions are made or later, at retirement.

POLICY PLANS AND FUNDING ARRANGEMENTS

Table 9-1 illustrates the principal characteristics of fixed and variable annuities.

TABLE 9-1

FIXED AND VARIABLE ANNUITIES

Fixed Annuities	Variable Annuities
Principal guaranteed	Principal not guaranteed
Interest guaranteed	Interest not guaranteed
The amount of the monthly benefit is guaranteed	The amount of the monthly benefit is not guaranteed
Expenses are guaranteed	Expenses are guaranteed
Mortality is guaranteed	Mortality is guaranteed
Contributions invested in the general account and fully guaranteed	Contributions invested in the separate account and not guaranteed
No investment risk to the participant	The participant bears investment risk

Generally, it is the agent's or trustee's responsibility to advise all plan participants of the principal differences between fixed and variable contracts due to the investment with the variable contract. This disclosure requirement is also necessary with any of the products used to fund the plan.

Deposit Administration Contract

Another group funding device is a group **deposit administration contract** which offers more flexibility than the group annuity contracts. Most individual annuity policies and group annuity contracts represent allocated funds in that specific amounts are allocated to specific participants. Deposit administration contracts are primarily unallocated funds by which deposits or contributions are simply made to a fund on behalf of all plan participants. At retirement, these unallocated funds can then be used to purchase an annuity for the retiring participant.

These contributions may be invested in the insurer's general account (fixed account) or separate account (equity account) thus providing the plan with guaranteed investments and equity investments or any combination of the two. The plan trustee or the employer may transfer funds between the general and separate accounts to achieve the best performance possible. Normally, the insurer will require advance written notice of such transfers.

The fixed account is maintained for each participant in proportion to their contribution as it pertains to the total contribution and the plan formula. These contributions will be invested in the insurer's general account. These amounts become part of the general assets of the insurer and are credited with a guaranteed rate of return.

An equity account is also maintained for each participant in much the same manner as the fixed or general account. In accordance with federal law (the Investment Company Act of 1940), the equity or separate account must be registered with the Securities and Exchange Commission as an investment company. This investment company status will take the form of a unit investment trust or generally an open end investment company.

If the equity account is registered as a unit investment trust, each plan participant's account balance will be determined by means of investment units. Thus, when a contribution is made to the account, the invested dollars will purchase a certain number of units.

If the equity account is registered as an open end investment company, the value of each plan participant's account balance will be measured in terms of shares of the fund. Just like a mutual fund, plan contributions purchase a certain number of shares of the fund.

Naturally, since the contributions are unallocated, the participant's retirement benefit will not be determined until the individual actually reaches retirement in accordance with the plan's provisions, at which time, a portion of the fund will be allocated to the retiring participant relative to the plan's benefit formula and provisions.

TRUST FUND PLANS

The trust fund concept is the oldest of the funding vehicles used for pension plans. As such, there are more participants covered by these arrangements and more plan assets provided through trust funds.

The trust fund plan is one in which the plan contributions are deposited with the plans's trustee who is responsible for the investment and administration of these assets. In addition, the trustee is responsible for the investment income generated by the plan contributions and is normally going to provide benefit payments directly to the retired participants. Typically, the trustee is a corporate trustee.

The duties, responsibilities, and limitations of the trustee are provided for in the **trust agreement**. This agreement is usually drawn up between the employer and the corporate trustee. Among others, the trust agreement will contain the following provisions:

- The investment authority and duties of the trustee
- The payment of legal, trustee and related plan fees and expenses
- Recordkeeping duties and responsibilities
- Reporting responsibilities of the trustee to the employer
- Conditions for the replacement of the trustee
- The payment of benefits by the trustee to plan participants

The trust agreement is thus concerned primarily with the receipt of plan contributions, investment of these contributions, and benefit payments to the participants.

Recordkeeping and administrative duties of the trustee are, to a degree, dependent on the employer's desire to be involved in such administrative details. If the plan is relatively small, the employer may desire to retain this recordkeeping function. On the other hand, if the plan is fairly large, the employer may specify that the trustee will maintain all records.

The principal responsibility of the trustee is the investment of plan contributions for which the trustee charges an investment fee. Needless to say, the plan trustee has a fiduciary responsibility to the employer and the participants. All investments must be in accordance with the trust provisions, the plan contribution requirements and any federal laws which are applicable.

For example, in accordance with ERISA, investment of plan contributions in the employer's own securities are limited to 10% of the fund's value. Of course, this requirement does not apply to stock bonus plans or ESOPs as typically, all funds are invested in the employer's stock with these types of plans.

Generally, corporate trustees (such as a banking institution) have established various trusts with different investment objectives. This provides the employer with a large degree of flexibility with regard to the type of investment vehicle to be used. This flexibility is one of the chief advantages of the trust arrangement.

Since the accumulated funds are not allocated, there is also a great degree of flexibility with regard to plan benefits. The trust plan will typically accommodate just about any type of benefit formula.

Trust fund arrangements usually require the services of an enrolled actuary to determine the amount of contributions and to periodically value the plan assets. To accomplish this, the actuary must use certain actuarial assumptions and a specific actuarial cost method. In accordance with ERISA, any investment assumptions used will be rather conservative and reasonable for the specific plan.

In addition, the employer provides some input regarding the choice of actuarial assumptions and the cost method used by the actuary. The assumptions and the cost method used will impact the plan's cost. The employer must not only budget for the plan's contribution amounts and frequency of these payments but also certain plan expenses such as the trustee's investment fees, recordkeeping fees, legal fees, etc.

THE USE OF LIFE INSURANCE IN A QUALIFIED PLAN

Since the goal of a retirement plan is to accumulate adequate retirement dollars for future delivery, consideration must be given to funding devices. For example, if inflation grows at 5% and a qualified plan earns 4%, the retired plan participant will experience erosion of the purchasing power of retirement dollars.

Life insurance is not an investment contract in the same sense that mutual funds, a variable annuity, stocks and bonds, are considered investments. Life insurance is a fully guaranteed contract whereas these other investments are not. Life insurance does have cash values which may grow at 4-5%, compared to higher return investments. In spite of these apparent drawbacks, there can be situations whereby the use of life insurance in a qualified retirement plan could well be a suitable recommendation. One of principal advantages of using life insurance in a qualified plan is that the employer is using a deductible contribution to pay for the life insurance.

Life Insurance Situations

Following is a discussion of some of the situations when life insurance may be an important consideration for a qualified plan.

Employee Needs: As is often the case, many individuals do not have adequate amounts of life insurance. If this was generally true in a given situation, a recommendation for the use of some life insurance inside of the qualified plan could certainly help these employees to meet their life insurance needs.

In addition, life insurance benefits can serve as a substitute of an otherwise inadequate premature retirement benefit. If a covered employee dies prematurely, his or her plan benefits become immediately vested. However, let's assume that an employee is in a defined benefit plan which specifies that his retirement benefit will equal 10% of pay. Let's further assume that this amount will result in a $5,000 per year benefit. The employee dies after 3 years participation in the plan with possibly a vested benefit of a few thousand dollars. Life insurance in the plan can serve to provide a meaningful benefit for the surviving dependents.

Key Executive Needs: Often key executives are "discriminated against" due to their higher compensation. For example, a group life plan which provides a life insurance schedule equal to one times salary not to exceed $50,000 serves many employees well if they're not making too much money, ie., more than $50,000. For the employees earning in excess of $50,000, they are unable to receive a one times salary life insurance benefit.

Frequently, an employer may utilize a split dollar life insurance arrangement or a deferred compensation plan funded with life insurance to compensate the key executive and provide a meaningful benefit. Another plan available for the key executive is the qualified pension plan. The inclusion of life insurance in the pension plan can fill the gaps left by conventional plans and supplement the key executive's need for life insurance.

Tax Problems: Life insurance benefits are generally federal income tax free. They are also not subject to the 15% excess accumulation tax on plan benefits. Accordingly, the use of life insurance in qualified plan can eliminate the possibility of excess accumulation tax on the plan.

The death proceeds payable from insurance (less any policy cash values) in a qualified plan are not subject to federal income taxation or to the 15% excess accumulation tax. Thus, life insurance proceeds offer specific tax advantages for plan participants.

Life insurance proceeds can also be used to provide liquidity for a participant's estate. Potential federal estate taxation can be resolved in favor of discounted life insurance dollars in lieu of using 100 cent dollars taken from estate assets to provide liquidity. Providing additional life insurance dollars inside the qualified plan, can be an attractive additional benefit of the plan, especially for the key executives.

Safety: Life insurance is a fully guaranteed contract. If the participants or the employer desire a large degree of safety and wish to avoid various types of investment risk, life insurance can be used as a funding device which extremely low risks. In addition to the plan benefits being guaranteed, the life insurance company also guarantees the life insurance benefits.

In addition to the guarantees provided by life insurance, costs (the premium) are also very predictable in that a fixed level premium becomes a known quantity in contrast to other investment vehicles, such as stock or mutual funds. The "costs" associated with stock investments are variable in the sense that if stock values decline, plan benefit levels will also decline and the employer must make a larger contribution to make up for this deficiency in stock values.

POLICY PLANS AND FUNDING ARRANGEMENTS

Life Insurance as an Incidental Benefit

Life insurance can be used in a qualified plan to provide "incidental death benefits." Generally, a non-retirement benefit provided by a qualified plan is considered incidental. The primary purpose of a qualified pension plan is to provide "living benefits" at retirement. The primary purpose of life insurance is to protect against premature death. Thus, the use of life insurance in a qualified plan is considered to be incidental.

The IRS has established two criteria to identify life insurance as an incidental benefit. These are:

- The plan participant's death benefit cannot be more than 100 times the monthly retirement benefit.

- The total premiums paid over the life of the plan must be less than the following percentages of the plan cost for the plan participant:

Ordinary life insurance	50%
Term insurance	25%
Universal life	25%

If a plan uses whole life insurance, the premium must be less than 50% of the plan contribution. Thus, if the total plan contribution was $1,000, the whole life premium could be as high as $499.

Life Insurance Coverage

Life insurance benefits must be provided for all plan participants on a nondiscriminatory basis. The amount of life insurance can be based on the participant's retirement benefit or the plan contribution formula. For example, a life insurance benefit may be specified as an amount equal to 100 times the participant's monthly pension benefit. Thus, an individual expected to receive $500 per month would be entitled to a life insurance benefit of $50,000. All plan participants must be provided the same 100 times benefit. Although all participants would not receive the same amount of life insurance.

A minor exception to the nondiscriminatory aspects of the amount of insurance coverage pertains to those with insurability problems. Since the life insurance used in the plan will probably be some type of individual whole life contract, there will be underwriting involved. If the group is large enough, the insurer may provide limited or modified underwriting, thus permitting those with some insurability problems access to standard life insurance.

However, if underwriting and insurability problems are going to be a consideration, then the plan itself needs to address this issue. Accordingly, the plan may specify that life insurance coverage is conditioned on proving insurability as a standard risk. Participants who cannot prove standard insurability will still be eligible for life insurance but on a reduced basis. The same premium dollars would simply purchase smaller amounts of life insurance due to a substandard rating. For example, a substandard risk may be limited to a life insurance benefit equal to 50 times the retirement benefit instead of 100 times the retirement benefit.

Another consideration regarding the amount of life insurance to be used in the plan will depend in part on the plan type. Life insurance is generally advantageous for use in a defined benefit plan. Remember that a defined benefit plan does not limit the amount of plan contributions. Benefits are limited to $90,000 as indexed.

Using life insurance in the defined benefit plan adds to the overall deductible contributions. A defined benefit plan can be fully funded with investment type products such as mutual funds, stocks, bonds, etc. Then in addition to the plan funding, the cost of the life insurance benefit can be added to the total plan contributions.

In contrast, the life insurance cost is included in the contribution made to a defined contribution plan. Thus, when $1,000 is contributed to a defined contribution plan, this figure includes the cost of the life insurance.

Life Insurance and Defined Benefit Plans

As previously mentioned, the use of life insurance in a defined benefit plan can be viewed as more advantageous due to the fact that the cost of the life insurance is added to the plan contribution and is not included in the plan contribution. There are various methods used to include life insurance in the defined benefit plan.

POLICY PLANS AND FUNDING ARRANGEMENTS

Combination Plans: This method or plan combines some type of whole life (including universal life) policy with an investment or side fund. As previously mentioned, life insurance by itself may be inadequate to meet the plan's retirement benefit. Thus the use of the investment fund permits dollars to be invested in various assets such as stocks or bonds, CDs, etc. in order to meet retirement needs and benefit amounts. In addition, the use of the life insurance provides an insured a death benefit as well as the use of the policy's cash values to provide retirement benefits.

Table 9-2 illustrates this arrangement

Table 9-2

THE COMBINATION PLAN

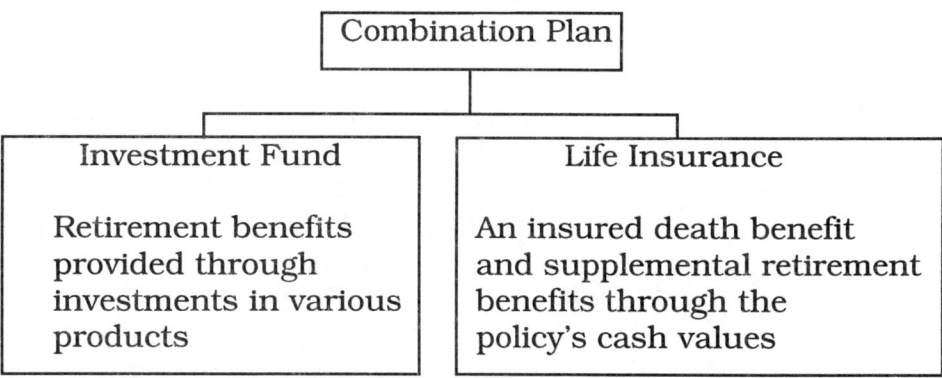

Ideally, the combination plan is best suited for the relatively small employer, for example up to 25 employees. This is due to the need to issue individual policies and the administrative costs associated with these policies.

Generally, the amount of the life insurance benefit will be some factor of the retirement benefit, such as 100 times the retirement benefit. Thus, if the participant's defined benefit equals $5,000 per month, the amount of the life insurance will be $500,000. Let's assume that the total retirement benefit is to amount to $600,000 at age 65. From this amount, we would subtract the life policy's guaranteed cash value at age 65. The result might look like the following:

Monthly pension benefit:	$ 5,000
Life insurance benefit:	$500,000
Age 65 required amount:	$600,000
Age 65 cash value:	$250,000
Net side fund value:	$350,000

Thus, the employer does not have to fund for the entire retirement benefit. The side fund accumulated value will be reduced by the amount of the life policy's guaranteed cash value. Without the life insurance in the plan, the employer must fund to meet the required age 65 amount of $600,000.

In addition, if the policy which is issued is a participating policy in that dividends are declared, the cost of the insurance can be reduced by the dividend payment thus reducing the total cost of the plan.

Provided we stay within the 100:1 insurance ratio, conversely, the dividends could also be used to purchase paid up additional amounts of insurance which will also create additional cash value. This additional cash value would result in a smaller contribution to the side fund.

Insurance Only Plans: This type of plan is also referred to as a fully insured plan in that it is funded only by life insurance and annuity contracts; in other words, "insurance products." There is no investment or side fund with this arrangement. A plan is an insurance only or fully insured plan if:

- It is funded with insurance contracts (life insurance and annuities) which are either group or individual contracts.
- The contracts require a level annual premium to normal retirement age.
- The insurance contracts are equal to the plan's defined benefit amounts.
- All policies are paid currently and have not lapsed.
- No rights under the policies have been assigned to another party.

POLICY PLANS AND FUNDING ARRANGEMENTS

- There are no outstanding cash value loans at any time during the plan year.

Fully insured plans also provide the advantage of not having to comply with the minimum funding requirements common to defined benefit plans. In addition, a fully funded plan is easier to administer than a defined benefit plan with an investment account.

All plan benefits are guaranteed by the insurer since insurance and annuity contracts are being used as the funding vehicles. A exception to this would be the use of a variable annuity instead of a fixed annuity.

Life Insurance and Defined Contribution Plans

Life insurance in a defined contribution plan may be voluntary in that each participant may make a life insurance election. Life insurance may be automatic in that there is no participant election and the plan document specifies a certain amount of life insurance.

The amount of life insurance used must conform with the "incidental limits" imposed by the IRS. If whole life insurance is used, the total premium must be less than 50% of the total plan contribution, ie., 49%. Thus, if the total contributions to a participant's account after 10 years were $20,000, the total amount of insurance premiums paid could not exceed $9,999.

Similar to the defined benefit plan, the life insurance policies will be "cashed in" at retirement to provide additional retirement benefits. If the plan participant dies prematurely, the life insurance benefit serves as a lump sum settlement of "what might have been" - the individual's regular retirement benefit. In addition, upon death, the participant is fully vested in his or her accrued pension benefits.

Taxation for the Plan Participant

The life insurance premiums paid are tax deductible for the employer assuming that the amount of life insurance complies with the incidental limits previously discussed. The tax deductibility of the life insurance premiums is one of the advantages of using life insurance in the qualified plan.

However, the plan participant does incur a tax liability. The **economic value** of the life insurance benefit is taxable to the participant based on the lower of the IRS P.S. 58 table or the insurer's one-year term rates. If the participant makes any contribution to the cost of the life insurance, that amount is deducted from the potential tax liability of the individual.

In essence the participant is being taxed on the economic value of the **pure insurance protection**. This amount is the difference between the policy's face value and its cash value. Thus, if a participant has a $100,000 whole life policy with $25,000 of cash value, the pure insurance protection is equal to $75,000. The P.S. 58 charges would be based on $75,000. For example:

> Bill, age 40, is a participant in a defined benefit plan which provides him with a $250,000 death benefit by means of a whole life insurance policy. The policy's current cash value is $50,000. Using the P.S. 58 charges, Bill will have to claim an additional $884 (200,000 x 4.42) of income for the current tax year.

The higher the policy's cash value the lower will be the additional tax liability although the P.S. 58 rates do increase with age. Thus, a life policy which produces a large amount of cash value early in the life of the contract (such as life paid up at 65) would be more beneficial from a tax standpoint than a regular whole life contract which may not have any cash value during the first 2-3 years.

TABLE 9-3

P.S. 58 Rates
Ages 21-65

Age	Premium	Age	Premium	Age	Premium
21	$ 1.67	36	$ 3.41	51	$ 9.97
22	1.73	37	3.63	52	10.79
23	1.79	38	3.87	53	11.69
24	1.86	39	4.14	54	12.67
25	1.93	40	4.42	55	13.74
26	2.02	41	4.73	56	14.91
27	2.11	42	5.07	57	16.18
28	2.20	43	5.44	58	17.56
29	2.31	44	5.85	59	19.08
30	2.43	45	6.3	60	20.73
31	2.57	46	6.78	61	22.53
32	2.70	47	7.32	62	24.50
33	2.86	48	7.89	63	26.63
34	3.02	49	8.53	64	28.98
35	3.21	50	9.22	65	31.51

Again, the difference between the policy's face amount and cash value is multiplied by the attained age P.S. 58 rate to determine the cost of the pure life insurance which results in additional taxable income for the participant.

Taxation for the Beneficiary

If the participant dies, there are certain tax consequences for the beneficiary.

> The pure insurance of the death benefit (face amount less cash value) is income tax free to the beneficiary as a life insurance benefit.
>
> In addition, another $5,000 of the policy's proceeds may qualify as a death benefit exclusion.
>
> All of the P.S. 58 charges paid by the participant can be recovered tax free from the death benefit.

Let's assume that Mary has died prior to normal retirement. She was a participant in a defined benefit plan which provided a $100,000 death benefit. Upon her death at age 50, the policy's cash value was $25,000. Calculation of the tax would be as follows:

$100,000 - $25,000 (cash value) = $75,000 pure insurance

Death benefit exclusion	$ 5,000
Recovery of P.S. 58 costs	$10,000
Total Tax Free Benefit	$90,000

The remaining $10,000 of the life insurance proceeds will be taxed as a plan distribution in the same way that the non-insurance benefits are taxed.

Even though the death benefit is partially taxable, generally maintaining the life insurance inside the plan is advantageous in that the premiums are paid with deductible dollars.

Federal Estate Taxation

Death benefits received from a qualified plan are includable in the deceased's estate for federal estate tax purposes. This is no different than individual life insurance owned by a decedent being included in the estate.

However, remember, to keep property out of your estate, you can't own it or have any incidents of ownership. It may be possible for an insured death benefit to be excluded from the deceased's estate if the participant has no **incidents of ownership** in the contract. Incidents of ownership means paying premiums, obtaining cash values, naming a beneficiary, etc.

To avoid incidents of ownership, the participant could:

- Have the policies owned by a separate trust under the plan
- Appoint irrevocable trustees (a commercial bank) to manage the assets
- Have all ownership rights exercised by the trustee

As is true with any tax planning strategies, the IRS may or may not view this type of arrangement favorably.

SUMMARY

There are two major types of pension plans with reference to funding. They are the insured plan and the trust fund plan. Contributions may be made on an allocated or unallocated basis.

Allocated funds are those which specifically identify a contribution for each plan participant. An unallocated fund is one in which contributions are made for the benefit of plan participants collectively without regard to specific amounts for each participant.

An insured plan is one in which an insurer receives the contributions and pays plan benefits to participants. Fully insured plans may use individual or group products to fund the plan. Typically, individual products may include fixed annuities, variable annuities, mutual funds, common stock, and other securities.

Group products for a fully insured plan include fixed and variable group annuities as well as group deposit administration contracts. Deposit administration contracts offer flexibility for the employer and the participants and funds contributed are unallocated. These funds may be invested in the insurer's general or separate account.

The general account of the insurer consists primarily of relatively safe, conservative investments such as mortgages, real estate, and CDs. The separate account consists primarily of a portfolio of common stock thus there is considerable investment risk to the plan participant.

Trust fund plans are administered by a plan trustee (usually a corporate trustee) whose duties primarily deal with plan contributions, investment income and benefit payments to the plan participants. The trustee's specific authority, duties, and responsibilities are included in the trust agreement. Typically, these include:

- Investment authority
- Recordkeeping functions
- Payments of certain costs and fees
- Payment of plan benefits

Plan trustees have a fiduciary responsibility to the employer and the plan participants and must act as a prudent person (or entity) in a position of financial trust and in accordance with all federal laws.

REVIEW EXERCISES

1. Identify the various types of individual policies or contracts usually found in a fully insured pension plan.

2. A fully insured plan offers both fixed and variable annuities as funding policies. What are the advantages and disadvantages of each?

3. Identify some of the primary duties and responsibilities of a trustee in a trust fund plan.

CHAPTER 10

EMPLOYER CONSIDERATIONS

Once the need for installation of a qualified plan has been established and the type of plan selected, the employer is then faced with various decisions regarding funding and the cost of the plan. In addition, the employer must also decide on specific plan provisions regarding eligibility, vesting, etc. Due to the requirements of ERISA, many specific plan provisions are more or less predetermined. For example, eligibility requirements for an employer-sponsored plan typically are restricted to one year of full time service and minimum age of 21. Thus, the employer has little to decide.

This chapter will primarily focus on employer decisions regarding funding and cost factors of the plan.

COST CONSIDERATIONS

The primary purpose of a qualified retirement plan is to provide benefits for retired workers. This requires that necessary funds be contributed in order that the plan's benefits will materialize at retirement. In the past, some employers simply elected to pay each retiree a monthly retirement benefit as it became due. This was simply known as **current disbursement funding**. Obviously, the major drawback to this method was the fact that the retired worker was forced to rely on the employer's good intentions and ability to have the necessary monthly payment when it became due.

A similar funding approach was known as **terminal funding**. With this method, the employer set aside a single sum on the date that each employee retired. This single amount was to be adequate for funding the retiree's benefit. This amount of the terminal funding was dependent on the life expectancy of the individual and the assumed rate of return on the single sum. This method too had obvious drawbacks such as the availability of large sums of money when the employee retired and miscalculating interest or investment returns. ERISA has replaced these funding concepts.

In accordance with ERISA, employers must set aside predetermined amounts of money on a systematic basis prior to the participant's retirement. This is referred to as **advance funding**. Periodic contributions are made for the plan participants during their working years. Thus, the required funds will be there when the participant reaches retirement.

In addition, this method also enables the corporation to adequately budget for the expense of the pension plan by "pre-paying" these benefits in advance of the participant's retirement. This concept is analogous to a single premium whole life policy (a large sum similar to terminal funding) verses an annual premium whole life policy. An individual could more easily afford or budget for an annual premium whole life policy than a substantially higher, single premium whole life contract.

Since advance funding of benefits is required under current law, it should be noted that these advance payments are used to fund **benefit estimates**, not necessarily the actual cost of benefits.

> Jan is the owner of a medium size company, ABC Inc., which has 30 employees, all of whom are eligible to participate in the company's 10% defined contribution plan. Total annual payroll for the firm is $600,000. Thus, the annual plan contribution is $60,000. Normal retirement under the plan is age 65 and 10 years of service with the company.

Basically, the example of Jan and ABC Inc. reflects the idea that the annual contribution of $60,000 is an estimate of the amount of money necessary to provide this particular group with a retirement benefit. Naturally, all of the 30 current employees will not be the group that eventually retires at age 65. Some of the present employees will be terminated prior to retirement. Some may die or become totally disabled. Some may continue to work past age 65 and postpone their retirement.

In addition, due to terminations, some employees will forfeit non-vested amounts which will reduce the corporation's out-of-pocket expense. Needless to say, new employees will be added to the plan over time thus possibly increasing the annual cost.

Because of so many variables, the actual cost of the pension plan can only be estimated. The actual cost can only be determined when the last retired participant dies and no further retirement benefits will be paid to anyone thereby terminating the plan. However, this uncertainty regarding the actual cost of the plan can be reduced by actuarial estimates of the ultimate cost of the plan. These estimates are reasonably accurate thus eliminating or reducing the actual cost uncertainty. To accomplish this, assumptions must be made regarding these variables which will affect the final cost of the plan.

COST FACTORS (ASSUMPTIONS)

The final or ultimate cost of the pension plan will be based on the following factors:

- Benefits to be paid
- Expenses
- Investment income or earnings

Thus, by formula, the ultimate cost of a pension plan could be stated as follows:

Ultimate Cost = Benefits + Expenses − Investment Income

The amount of plan benefits will depend on several factors:

- The number of participants actually retiring
- Mortality of the retirees
- The benefit formula

Number of Participants

The **number of participants** who will actually retire under the plan is affected by several factors. As was previously stated, some of the plan participants will quit or otherwise terminate their employment prior to retirement or they may die prematurely. The greater the number of pre-retirement deaths, the lesser the number of retirees and possibly the lower the cost of the plan.

However, if the plan provides incidental life insurance benefits as a pre-retirement death benefit, then premature deaths among participants will not necessarily reduce the cost of the plan as additional benefits are included in the plan in the form of a pre-retirement death benefit.

To predict these premature deaths with some certainty, an actuary will use a standard mortality table. Mortality assumptions used in calculating the cost of the plan will be based on these tables. As mortality increases due to better lifestyles, medical advances, etc., the impact of mortality assumptions on the ultimate cost of the pension plan may well increase.

Another factor which will have an effect on the number of retired participants is the frequency and length of any disabilities among the active participants. If a plan provides disability benefits, then it will have to include a disability assumption regarding the frequency or likelihood of a disability occurring.

Employee terminations and new hires will also have an effect on the number of plan participants. Terminations and layoffs generally result in less or no contribution being made for such employees. Thus, these contingencies represent cost reducing factors for the plan, assuming the terminated employees are not fully vested. Generally, terminations and layoffs are highest for the younger age employees. Naturally, if employees are terminated and replaced with new hires, then there may be no significant impact on the cost of the plan. The plan actuary will normally make an assumption regarding the turnover of employees. A final factor affecting the number of plan participants is the age or rate at which retirement takes place. Due to life expectancy, the later the retirement, the lower the plan cost. Early retirements (i.e., prior to age 65) will result in higher costs. Generally, most actuaries will assume normal retirement — age 65 in their assumptions.

Mortality

The **mortality** of the participants after retirement is another cost consideration. Assuming normal retirement at age 65, the actuary will make an assumption based on a standard mortality of basically, how long benefits will have to be made on the average. The longer the life expectancy the higher the cost. If an actuary notes that a particular employer encour-

EMPLOYER CONSIDERATIONS

ages early retirement, then plan costs will undoubtedly increase.

However, there appears to be a trend to later retirement rather than early retirement. Due to economic reasons, an employee may elect to work beyond age 65. Assuming this individual can still be productive, the employer may encourage this. It not only provides the employer with a veteran, experienced worker but also will probably result in decreased cost of the pension plan.

As an assumption affecting plan cost, the length of the retirement benefit period might decrease due to this need for the senior worker to remain active for economic, emotional or psychological reasons.

Amount of Benefit

The final factor affecting plan benefits is naturally the **amount of benefit** to be paid to each participant. A defined benefit plan is a costly plan. If the plan specifies that all participants will retire with a benefit of $250 per month, then projections and assumptions are relatively easy to make. On the other hand, if the benefit formula provides a benefit related to final average compensation or one which may be offset for Social Security, then assumptions must be made regarding future pay increases and changes in the Social Security system.

Also affecting the ultimate cost of the plan are the **expenses**. Administrative expenses must be included in cost considerations. Some of these expenses include actuarial costs, legal and accounting fees, administrative expenses, etc. The expense assumption used will depend in part on the type of funding used.

A plan which is funded by individual contracts such as individual annuities will be more costly than plans funded by group contracts. This is due to the fact that most individual policies, (i.e., an individual annuity) will also contain a loading for contractual expenses. This expense factor is usually less with group contracts as the cost of administration is reduced. Thus, expense factors with insured plans tend to be more accurate than with trust fund plans since the insurer charges a specific amount for each policy or group contract.

In the case of trust fund plans, the employer often pays plan expenses separate from the actual plan contributions. Thus, actuarial, legal, administrative, accounting, and investment expenses are charged to the plan and are separate from the total contributions.

Another factor affecting the ultimate cost of the plan is the **interest or investment income** assumption. Depending on the actual funding instrument used, this assumption may be fairly accurate or it may need to be adjusted for certain economic conditions, increases or decreases in interest rates, etc. However, the investment income earned on the plan assets generally will reduce the final cost of the plan.

The higher the interest rate assumption, the lower will be the cost of the plan. Conversely, the lower the assumption, the higher will be the plan's cost. Naturally, a plan which uses a high interest rate assumption thus resulting in a lower annual cost may at some point in the future need to have additional funds contributed should the interest assumption used prove to be very inaccurate.

If a plan's contributions are being deposited in a bank account or a Certificate of Deposit which provides a stated return, then any interest assumption used to project the ultimate plan cost will be more predictable and reliable. However, interest assumptions become more difficult if the plan's assets are invested in securities such as common stock or mutual funds. Wide fluctuations in the market can result in problems regarding interest assumptions.

Generally, interest assumptions used account for the size of the pension fund, the investment objectives of the plan trustees, current interest rates, and long-term projections as well as current and long-term economic conditions.

In summary, these actuarial assumptions are then incorporated into an actuarial cost method to arrive at the cost of the plan. An actuarial cost method is a technique for spreading the estimated plan costs over future plan years.

FUNDING CONSIDERATIONS

The type of funding selected by the employer will have an effect on the cost of the plan due to the various assumptions used in calculation of plan costs.

EMPLOYER CONSIDERATIONS

There are a wide variety of funding mechanisms from which to choose. These include insured plans and trust funds, individual and group contract considerations. No one funding vehicle is preferable over any other mechanism. Often, the plan's provisions may indicate the type of funding to be used. The employer's own needs and objectives should be weighed with reference to the selection of a funding device.

Factors affecting the selection of funding involve:

- Cost
- Safety of benefits
- Flexibility
- Service

Cost

Cost factors include:

- The benefits to be paid
- Investment earnings
- Administrative expenses

The cost of benefits in a trust fund is determined by the actual number of participants who survive to retirement and the length of the benefit payments or period. Benefit costs will be determined by the actual experience of the group.

Generally, an insured plan will pool mortality experience and thus this cost is shared by all. The actual cost will be determined by the insurer's experience with the group of individual contracts.

With regard to administrative expenses, an insured plan will have certain types of expenses that a trust fund plan will not have. These include agent commissions, state premium taxes and federal taxes. A trust fund plan usually will have higher actuarial expenses than an insured plan.

As a general rule, insured plans using individual contracts will have a higher administrative cost than group contracts or trust fund plans.

Investment earnings probably result in the most significant factor affecting the cost of a plan. Seemingly insignificant increases in investment return can result in substantial reductions in plan costs. Again, the return on the plan contributions will be based on the type of investment. If the contributions are invested in the insurer's general account, a stated, guaranteed return is usually provided. If the contributions are invested in an equity account without guarantees, then plan costs become more unpredictable due to market fluctuations.

Benefit Safety

Benefit safety or security is a factor of the financial strength of the employer and the investment performance of the plan. Regardless of the form of the plan (insured, trust plan, etc.), there is no assurance that the employer will continue in business. Thus, if the business becomes bankrupt, the safety of plan benefits may be jeopardized.

Defined benefit plans are protected by the Pension Benefit Guaranty Corporation against such a contingency as the failure of the business. However, many plans are not covered by the PBGC. ERISA does stipulate the priority of payment of plan assets with regard to business failures and plan terminations. Thus, employees achieve some benefit security.

However, at any point in time, benefit security depends on the amount of funding in the plan and the value of these assets for which each employee is entitled in accordance with ERISA.

Flexibility

Funding flexibility may be an important factor in selecting a funding product. Of primary concern is the fact that whatever method of funding is selected, it must be adequate in order to provide the benefits as dictated by the plan specifications. Naturally, some funding products offer greater degrees of flexibility than others. Group deposit administration contracts and the trust fund approach provide a greater degree of flexibility than a group fixed annuity, for example.

Depending on the actuarial assumptions used, the trust fund approach provides flexibility with regard to contributions to the plan. Allocated, fully insured plans naturally provide less flexibility as specific contributions must be made with reference to the requirements of the plan and the insurer.

Funding flexibility with regard to changing the funding product may also be an important consideration for the employer. Again, the trust fund approach provides ease and flexibility should the employer desire to change trustees or alter the plan investment. Typically, the trust fund allows for a wider range of investment products than individual or group contracts.

Service

Plan service is another consideration for the employer. It should be remembered that the employer is not in the pension business and thus needs the advice of competent professionals before and following the installation of a qualified plan. Typically, a fully insured plan will provide the employer with competent service "after the sale" by the employees of the insurer.

The trust fund approach often may require the employer to provide his or her own administrative services and support or to pay for such services from third parties. However, insurers may also charge various fees for plan services after the pension plan is installed. Whether these services are included as part of the plan or provided by means of an extra charge, the important factor is the consistency, competency, and quality of the service provided.

Pension plans are heavily regulated by the federal government and as such require proper service in order to comply with various regulations. ERISA requires compliance with regard to various Department of Labor and Internal Revenue Service filings and reports as well as disclosure compliance with regard to plan participants.

SUMMARY

Once an employer has made the decision to install a pension plan, there are other decisions to be made; chief among them are cost and funding considerations.

ERISA requires that qualified pension plans employ advance funding as opposed to terminal or disbursement funding. Advance funding actually only provides funding for the estimated cost of the plan due to several variables. These variables include: the number of participants who actually retire, premature death, disability, and employee turnover.

The ultimate cost of the plan is related to the benefits to be provided, expenses, and investment return. The benefit factor relates to the number of participants who will actually retire and how long benefits will be paid to these retired employees. Plan expense pertains to the administrative expenses, legal expenses, and related costs associated with installation and administration of the plan. Investment return refers to the projected return on the plan contributions. Higher projections result in lower cost factors. However, if the higher returns do not materialize, additional contributions may have to be made to the plan to assure proper level of benefits.

Funding considerations relate to plan costs, benefit safety, flexibility, and plan service. Plan cost can vary depending on the type of plan, i.e., fully insured or a trust plan. Benefit safety pertains to the financial stability of the employer and the ability to continue to make plan contributions. Plan flexibility relates to the ability to make changes and adjustments in plan trustees, contributions, investment products, etc.

Due to federal requirements, administrative service is an important plan consideration. The cost of this service in addition to the competency and consistency of the service is important to the employer. Typically, a fully insured plan will provide necessary administrative services through the insurer's own personnel. Other types of plans may require that the employer pay for the services from a third party.

REVIEW EXERCISES

1. Identify some of the variable factors that contribute to the validity of the statement that pension plan funding is used to fund benefit estimates.

2. Explain the components of the following formula:

   Ultimate Cost = Benefits + Expenses − Investment Income

3. Briefly discuss some of the employer considerations regarding the selection of a funding device.

CHAPTER 11

PLAN DESIGN

The previous two chapters have explored funding considerations and cost factors associated with the selection and installation of an employer sponsored pension plan. The employer must decide, with competent advice from an agent and other professional advisors, whether to implement a fully insured plan or to adopt the trust fund approach. Other decisions include whether to fund the plan with individual or group contracts, guaranteed or equity-based investments, as well as reviewing the anticipated cost of the plan currently and in the years to come.

The overall design of the plan is another important consideration which the employer must address prior to the formal adoption. What type of vesting should be used? Are there any employees who require special consideration with regard to benefits? Should any life insurance be used in the plan? What type of plan provisions are important? These and similar questions are addressed when the employer considers the overall design of the plan.

At the end of this chapter, there is a sample profit sharing plan which covers all of these plan design elements. As you study this material, you should refer to the sample plan as a reference for specifics regarding such design features as vesting, contribution formula, eligibility requirements, etc.

EMPLOYEE CONSIDERATIONS

Once the decisions have been reached regarding the implementation of the pension plan, funding considerations, and cost factors, the employer must then decide which type of plan to install, i.e., defined benefit, defined contribution, profit sharing, etc. These decisions will be influenced by identifying those employees who should realize the greatest benefit from the plan.

As was previously stated, one of the motivations for installing an employer sponsored plan is to attract and retain key personnel. Naturally, this group of employees will probably benefit the most from the plan. Their salaries are higher. Their skills and productivity are important for the continued profitability of the company. Needless to say, one of these key persons is of course the businessowner.

> Cindy, age 36, is the owner of Ajax, Inc., a computer consulting firm which employs 30 full time employees. Cindy started the business eight years ago with considerable help from her long-time friend, Lisa, who is also age 36. Lisa is the vice president in charge of operations. Bill, age 44, is the vice president in charge of sales and marketing. There are several technical-type employees, a few sales representatives and administrative support employees.

The firm has done very well in recent years. There has been a 10%-15% gain in business income in each of the past five years. Cindy was influenced to adopt a plan because of the need for an additional tax deduction and the need to offer a meaningful benefit to the employees, many of whom are highly skilled computer professionals.

Obviously, three of the key people in this scenario are Cindy, Lisa, and Bill. A second group, the technical, highly skilled computer employees are also important. Finally, the administrative support personnel would represent the last group of employees with reference to their degree of importance to the corporation.

There are three principal types of plans which could be recommended for Ajax, Inc.: a profit sharing plan, a defined benefit plan or a defined contribution plan.

Profit Sharing Plan

Most often, a **profit sharing plan** is the "first plan" an employer may undertake as contributions do not represent a fixed liability for the employer. This is particularly true if the corporation has an inconsistent or unstable income picture. Thus, if the employer feels that he or she is unable to commit to a fixed contribution every year due to an unstable business income, then the profit sharing plan may be strongly considered.

However, in the Ajax case, this does not appear to be true as the company has done very well the past several years. There does not appear to be the unstable profit picture associated with most new businesses. It appears as though Ajax is prepared to undertake a fixed annual commitment in the form of the plan contribution. Therefore, the profit sharing plan may not be the most suitable recommendation for Ajax.

Defined Benefit Plan

A **defined benefit plan** is another possible choice for Ajax. Defined benefit plans certainly represent a fixed liability for the employer and retirement benefits are "predetermined" so that the employee knows at least what percentage of his or her compensation will eventually be paid as a retirement benefit. However, this may be a bit misleading as very often, the employee does not retire exactly at age 65 and this predetermined benefit may be less than anticipated due to early retirement or even termination of employment.

Of course an advantage of the defined benefit plan is that it definitely favors the higher paid employees. The employee who earns $12,000 per year and is told that his or her retirement benefit will be 10% of compensation, may not get too excited. However, let's assume that Cindy earns $150,000 per year. A benefit of 10% of compensation may well be more meaningful to her.

Coupled with the defined benefit advantages for the higher paid employees is of course, the higher cost to the employer to provide these benefits. Generally, defined benefit plans are costly and do not have any contribution limitations. Remember, defined benefit plans are limited by benefit amounts of $90,000 as indexed. Although the defined benefit plan can be costly, this may not be a major consideration with regard to Ajax as it appears that the key people are relatively young and thus time becomes an ally in providing a retirement benefit. Generally, the longer the period of time in which to accumulate the retirement funds, the lower the annual cost. Had the key people at Ajax been in their 50s, then the cost of the defined benefit plan may have been prohibitive.

It appears that the defined benefit concept offers the necessary tax advantage and is beneficial to the higher paid key persons as well as the highly skilled computer group provided they too are relatively young. In addition, the cost of the plan may not be out of reach for the company since it appears that the 30 employees are fairly young.

Defined Contribution Plan

Possibly, the principal advantage of a **defined contribution plan** is its simplicity. Although the employees are not provided with a predetermined amount of retirement benefit, they are informed that a predetermined contribution will be made to their accounts plus (or minus) investment return on these contributions. Their retirement benefit will simply be equal to their account balances at retirement. Often, this is a much easier concept to understand (for the employee) than the defined benefit plan.

The defined contribution concept will generally be less costly than the defined benefit as the maximum contribution is limited to $30,000 per participant. Thus, if Ajax were to install a 10% defined contribution plan, 10% of the employees' compensation will represent the annual contribution. Automatically, due to the plan's formula, the largest amount of the contribution will benefit the key personnel since they are presumably the higher paid employees. There is no reference to age or the time of retirement.

Conversely, a defined benefit plan could require a higher contribution for a lower paid employee who happens to be relatively older than the other employees. In Ajax's situation for example, Cindy is 36 years old and makes $150,000 per year. Let's assume that one of the other employees earns $20,000 per year and is age 55. The contribution for a defined benefit plan could be higher than the contribution for Cindy the owner primarily because of the age difference. The same situation with a 10% defined contribution plan would result in a $15,000 contribution for Cindy and a $2,000 contribution for the older employee.

Thus, if a defined contribution plan is to be considered, one of the important factors could be the ages of the employees and the relative cost associated with the plan (generally lower than defined benefit). Of course another consideration will be a meaningful retirement benefit. Remember Ajax felt the need to provide a meaningful plan for their key personnel and highly skilled employees. A token defined contribution plan which results in a relatively small retirement benefit may not achieve the desired purpose.

Combination Plan

Another alternative for the employer is to consider a combination plan. Let's assume that Cindy decides on a 10% defined contribution plan because it does provide the tax deduction that Ajax needed and it does provide a retirement benefit (although unknown) for the employees. To enhance the overall program and to increase the amount of the retirement benefit, let's assume that Cindy decides to combine a 401(k) elective deferral plan with the defined contribution plan.

Further, Cindy agrees to contribute 50 cents for every employee dollar contributed to the plan through the salary reduction agreement. She is now able to enhance the retirement program at a minimal cost to the corporation for those employees who elect to participate. Generally, the participation will come from the higher paid, key personnel. As long as there is adequate participation and the 401(k) does not become top heavy, this combination of plans will satisfy Cindy's objective of providing an attractive program for the key personnel and enjoying the tax deductions inherent with both programs.

BENEFIT FORMULAS

Plan design considerations will also include factors with regard to the plan's formula for providing benefits. Generally, this becomes a cost consideration. Once the employer has selected the type of plan and has made a commitment as to the amount of money to be spent, then a decision will have to be reached regarding the benefit formula.

Generally, there are two basic defined benefit formulas. These two formulas have different variations but essentially, the basic defined benefit formulas are as follows:

Unit Benefit

A **unit benefit** is a benefit formula which provides for an employee's total service with the employer. For example, a unit benefit formula may provide a retirement benefit equal to one percent of the participant's final average compensation times years of service.

> Thus, if Bob retires with average annual compensation of $20,000 and 20 years of service, his retirement benefit is:
>
> $20,000 x 1% = 200 x 20 = $ 4,000 ($333.33 monthly)

Flat Percentage of Compensation

The second basic formula is a **flat percentage of compensation** offset by years of service less than a specific number. For example, this formula may specify 20% of average compensation reduced by 1/25th (4%) for each year of service less than 25.

> Mary's defined benefit plan uses a flat percentage of compensation benefit formula which stipulates that the plan benefit equals 10% of compensation reduced by 2% for each year of service less than 20.
>
> If Mary's average compensation is $25,000 when she retires after 15 years of service, her retirement benefit would be as calculated follows:
>
> $25,000 x 10% = $2,500 less 10% ($250) = $2,250 per year
>
> The 10% reduction is equal to 2% for each year less than 20, in this case five years.

If we revisit Bob, we would now find that his defined retirement benefit would be equal to:

> $20,000 x 20% = $4,000 less 5/25 (20%) = $3,200 ($266.66 per month)
>
> In a sense, Bob is penalized 20% due to having only 20 years of service at retirement.

Another common device used to reduce the amount of the defined retirement benefit is to offset the benefit by the amount of Social Security received. Conceptually, the employer is already contributing to the employee's retirement by the payment of Social Security taxes. Therefore, to reduce plan costs, it may be recommended that the participant's defined retirement benefit be reduced by all or a portion of the Social Security retirement benefit.

Let's give Bob a raise and change the benefit formula slightly. He now has average compensation of $40,000 and the unit benefit formula specifies:

> 2% of compensation times years of service, less 100% of the participant's Social Security retirement benefit.

PLAN DESIGN

Bob's benefit would be as follows:

$40,000 x 2% = 800 x 20 = $16,000 ($1,333 monthly)

The benefit of $1,333 per month would be an expensive benefit to fund under a defined benefit plan. To reduce this expense and liability, let's assume that Bob's Social Security benefit will be $1,000. Thus, the employer would have to fund only a monthly benefit of $333, a considerably less expensive liability.

Naturally, when the plan is to be a defined contribution plan, favoring certain groups of employees is more or less "automatically" taken care of by the contribution formula. Normally, this formula will simply state that a specific percentage of compensation will be used as the amount of the annual contribution. The higher paid participants will naturally realize a higher amount of contribution being allocated to their accounts and conversely, the lower paid employees will have smaller amounts contributed to their accounts.

Factors which can reduce the employer's cost due to the formula used are the plan forfeitures and excess interest or investment income. Participants who leave the plan prior to being fully vested will forfeit non-vested portions of their account balances. Normally, these amounts will be distributed among the remaining participants as additional contributions or as part of the formula contributions. If part of the formula contributions, then the employer's expense is correspondingly reduced by the amount of these forfeitures.

It is also possible to reduce some of the employer's cost if excess interest is credited to the participants' accounts. These amounts can be used to reduce employer costs or they may be used to enhance the account values of the participants in which case the employer would not realize any savings.

PLAN CONDITIONS

The next employer consideration will be with regard to specific conditions of the plan. There are certain plan provisions which need to be considered which have an effect on the plan participants and the cost of the plan. These conditions or provisions include:

- Eligibility requirements

- Vesting provisions
- The definition of compensation
- Disability and death benefits
- Normal and early retirement provisions
- Plan distributions

Eligibility

Eligibility refers to when an employee may become a participant in the plan. In past years, it was not uncommon for an employer to establish an eligibility condition which held an employee out of a pension plan for a period of three to five years or longer. Over the years, eligibility requirements have been modified by law so that the practice of prolonged eligibility is no longer possible.

Generally, participant eligibility requires that full time employees with at least one year of full time service and attained age of 21 must be admitted to the plan. An exception to this requirement occurs when the plan provides 100% immediate vesting. With this liberal vesting stipulation, eligibility requirements can be extended to three years of service.

An employer could eliminate an entire group of employees from a plan on occupational criteria such as the plan being identified as a non-union plan. This would make all union employees ineligible for the employer sponsored plan. However, usually when this occurs, the employer may be required to contribute to a separate union-sponsored plan for these union employees.

As has been discussed in other chapters, eligibility requirements cannot result in the plan being top heavy and accordingly benefiting the key employees to a greater degree than allowed by law.

Once eligibility has been achieved, the employee must enter the plan at a specific time also stated in the plan. Most often, this stipulation will indicate that an employee is eligible to join the plan on the plan anniversary following compliance with the eligibility requirements. However, once eligibility has been achieved, the employee must be included in the plan within **six months**. Because of this six month restriction, most plans will have two enrollment periods per year, usually six months apart.

PLAN DESIGN

The ABC Inc. Pension Plan provides that eligible employees must enter the plan on the plan anniversary nearest the date on which the individual satisfies the eligibility requirements. The plan's anniversary is July 1. Enrollment periods are July 1 and January 1.

Lucy satisfied the eligibility requirements on August 15, 1992. Ted satisfied eligibility requirements on January 10, 1993.

In this example, Lucy will join the plan on January 1, 1992. Ted enrolls in the plan on July 1, following compliance with the eligibility criteria. Both employees are joining the plan within six months of completion of the eligibility requirements.

Eligibility provisions are basically imposed on the employer to protect the interests of the employee so that an otherwise eligible participant is not excluded from participation in the plan any longer than the limits of the law allow. From the employer's perspective, the longer an employee can be held out of the plan, the lower the contribution to the plan. Thus the maximum length of time that an employee can be withheld from a plan is normally the 12 month eligibility period plus the maximum of six months for enrollment.

Sample eligibility requirements appear on page 11-22.

Vesting

Vesting provisions are another important consideration for the employer. However, as discussed in a previous chapter, current law basically allows three different vesting provisions:

- 100% immediate vesting
- The 0/5 vesting schedule
- The 3/7 vesting schedule

Most employers will not usually consider 100% immediate vesting. From the employer's viewpoint, not all employees will remain with the employer until retirement. Some employees may not remain employed with the employer beyond a few months or a year or so. Accordingly, why should a contribution be made for very short-term employees?

A vesting schedule will limit the amount of contributions for these short-term employees. Keep in mind that when an employee terminates employment, any vested contributions belong to the terminated employee. Any amounts not vested remain in the plan for the benefit of the remaining plan participants. These forfeitures can decrease the amount of the annual employer contribution. Frequently, it is in the employer's best interest to possibly elect the 3/7 vesting schedule whereby 100% vesting does not occur until the end of the seventh year of plan participation thus allowing for short-term employee terminations and forfeited non-vested amounts being used to reduce plan costs (contributions).

Conversely, if an employer has just a few, very loyal employees and the company has experienced hardly any employee turnover, then a more liberal vesting schedule may be beneficial to both the owner and his or her long-term employees. Even if an employer decides to adopt a very liberal vesting schedule due to loyal employees and no turnover, it must be remembered that any future employees will also be subject to this liberal schedule and they may not exhibit the same long-term loyalty as current employees.

A typical vesting schedule appears on page 11-22.

Definition of Compensation

One of the many definitions found in a pension trust agreement is the **definition of compensation**. This is naturally an important definition because plan contributions and benefits are normally based on some factor of the participant's compensation. In particular, the definition of compensation has added significance with regard to a defined benefit plan.

Often, defined benefit plans base benefits on some factor of the participant's average compensation. Average compensation frequently is defined as the average of three or possibly the highest five years of the individual's employment. Often, it may also be defined as the highest three years of compensation in the last five years of employment prior to retirement. In defined benefit plans, restrictive definitions of compensation can drastically change the amount of benefit to be received and the amount of the contribution to be made.

Regardless of the type of plan, it is important to have the term compensation defined in such a way as to meet the needs and objectives of the employer. For example, if compensation is defined as an hourly rate or annual amount while excluding bonuses, this may be detrimental to those employees whose compensation usually includes substantial bonuses such as the employer and other key executives. Also, the definition of compensation should address the fact that frequently employees receive commissions in addition to a base salary. Will compensation include both salary and commissions or exclude the commissions?

A sample pension plan definition of compensation appears on page 11-23.

Premature Death or Disability

Another issue to be considered with regard to plan design is what to do, if anything, in the event of premature **death or the disability of a participant**. Most plans automatically provide that in the event of death or disability of a participant, that individual's account balance becomes 100% vested. Thus, it could be said that the participant's pre-retirement death benefit equals his or her account balance. This amount could be $1,000 or $101,000. It may be desirable to provide some other form of death benefit.

Often, an employer may simply elect to provide an adequate death benefit by means of the firm's group life plan. Using this vehicle, plan participants may exclude up to $50,000 of group term insurance from income and taxation. However, if the employer wants to provide a larger death benefit, this can be achieved through the pension plan.

If the plan is a defined benefit plan, each participant may have life insurance protection up to **100 times** the anticipated monthly retirement benefit. Thus, if a participant's monthly retirement benefit is to be $250, then that individual may have life insurance to fund a pre-retirement death benefit in the amount of $25,000.

For defined contribution plans, up to **50%** of the employer's contribution may be used to pay life insurance premiums for whole life contracts; and up to **25%** of the contribution may be used for term insurance premiums.

Thus, if a plan participant dies before retirement and the plan provides for a life insurance benefit, the total pre-retirement death benefit would equal the life insurance amount plus the participant's current account value. However, the value of the life insurance protection must be included in the individual's taxable income each year.

The cost of the life insurance protection is considered a distribution from the qualified plan. Thus, when the premiums are paid by the employer, the employee must report the value of the life insurance benefit as taxable income. The value to be reported as income is the cost of the pure death protection in accordance with the IRS's P.S. 58 table. This table reflects one year term rates per $1,000 of face value. These rates are determined by the IRS. If the insurer's one-year term rates are lower, they may be used to calculate this taxable benefit.

> Mary has a $20,000 life insurance benefit included in her pension plan. The economic value of this benefit must be reported as taxable income by Mary. At the end of the year, Mary will receive the P.S. 58 values for this amount of insurance as additional income for tax purposes.
>
> Mary is 48 years old and the P.S. 58 charge is $7.89/$1,000. Mary's additional taxable income is:
>
> 20,000 x $7.89 = $157.80

If the insurer's one-year term rates were less than $7.89 per $1,000, then these rates could be used for this calculation in lieu of the P.S. 58 rates.

It should be noted that the $50,000 exclusion for group term plans is not available when individual or group life insurance is provided within the pension plan.

Generally, **disability benefits** are not provided by the plan other than if disability occurs, the participant is considered 100% vested and could receive these amounts as a "disability benefit". Frequently, the employer may provide for disability income benefits by means of individual or group disability contracts and this benefit is separate from the pension plan.

However, for those plans which may specify some form of disability benefit, one of the key questions to ask is, "What constitutes total disability?" If this benefit is to be provided by a disability income policy, then the definition of total disability contained in the policy will answer the question. However, if this is not the case, some other means will have

PLAN DESIGN

to be utilized to determine when a participant is totally disabled and thus eligible for the disability benefit.

One method used is to employ the Social Security definition of total disability. This definition is very restrictive. Approximately only one of three Social Security claimants can qualify for disability benefits due to the government's definition of total disability.

This definition requires that the claimant be unable to perform the duties of any occupation within the national economy and the disability must be expected to last at least 12 months and/or end in death.

Possibly, using the Social Security definition of disability may simply be too restrictive. Another method used to determine disability is a board or committee established by the employer to review such cases in accordance with some criteria also established by the employer.

Typically, if the pension plan begins to pay benefits due to the disability of the participant, these benefits are normally taxed since the cost basis of a qualified plan is always zero and all amounts received are thus taxable. There have been some court decisions made whereby these benefits, as disability benefits, have been excluded from taxation. However, generally the benefits will be taxed.

One other provision which will have to be included if the plan design does provide a disability benefit, is how to treat benefits paid to a disabled employee who recovers and returns to work. Will that individual's eventual retirement benefit be reduced by the amount of disability benefits paid prior to retirement? This is a decision which the employer must make and incorporate in the plan design.

Retirement Age

One final major decision which must be made is the **retirement age and/or early retirement** provided by the plan. Traditionally, in the United States, it is presumed that an individual retires at age 65. There are situations in which an individual may retire early due to possibly the physical inability to continue to work or simply due to a lack of financial necessity.

On the other hand, there is a growing tendency in this country for employees to continue to work beyond age 65. People are living longer due to medical advances and healthier lifestyles. As a result, many of these individuals may desire to work beyond normal retirement at age 65. Part of the plan design and provisions must address this fact.

The concept of normal retirement is covered by IRS regulations. These regulations specify that an individual must have a nonforfeitable right (fully vested) to the plan's normal retirement benefit upon reaching normal retirement age. Normal retirement age is then defined as the normal retirement age specified in the plan or the later of age 65 or the fifth anniversary of the effective date of the employee's participation in the plan. Most plans will specify that normal retirement is age 65. The plan will further provide provisions for early retirement. This provision normally states that an employee is eligible for early retirement if he or she:

> "has attained age 55 and has at least 10 years of full time service."

Naturally, the early retirement provision could be more liberal than this if the employer so elected.

In addition, those employees who may retire early must be informed that their retirement benefit will be less (regardless of the type of plan) since contributions and investment growth are limited to a shorter period of time. The monthly benefit paid will also be smaller due to the fact that actuarially and statistically, the benefit will have to be paid for a longer period of time thus reducing the amount of benefit to be paid. Finally, the plan participants must also be informed that early retirement, prior to age 59½ may create a 10% tax penalty.

The issue of late retirement may simply be covered by an additional statement associated with normal retirement provisions. For example, such a statement may be:

> "Normal retirement under this plan is age 65 unless the employee elects to continue employment and the employer provides such employment, then retirement may be extended beyond age 65 up to a maximum retirement age of 70."

Naturally, a later retirement with presumably fewer years of retirement payments can result in a higher monthly benefit than normal retirement benefits.

An additional issue related to later retirement which may also have to be addressed in the plan design is the situation whereby an employee retires and then resumes employment with the employer. In these cases, the employer may want to include a provision in the plan which stipulates that if an employee returns to full time employment after retirement, then retirement benefits will be suspended.

Distributions of Plan Benefits

Distributions of plan benefits are regulated by the IRS. Thus, the employer may have little choice. Retirement benefits which are the result of employer and/or employee contributions, as well as rollover contributions, must provide a **qualified joint and survivor annuity option** as a means of distributing benefits to the participant. Under this option, plan benefits are paid to the retired employee for life and upon the participant's death, benefits are paid to the surviving spouse for life.

A qualified joint and survivor annuity option provides benefit payments for the life of the participant with a survivor annuity for the life of the spouse which is not less than one-half of the amount of the benefits payable during the lives of the participant and the spouse. In addition, the benefits paid must be equal to the actuarial equivalent of a single annuity for the life of the plan participant. Thus, a joint and 50 percent or a joint and two-thirds survivor option would qualify.

A qualified plan is not required to provide a qualified joint survivor annuity option in any situation whereby the participant and the spouse were not married for one full year ending on the earlier of the participant's retirement date or death. In addition, the plan participant may waive the joint survivor annuity option with the written consent of the spouse. In addition, this required joint survivor annuity option is not mandatory for defined contribution plans (except target benefit and money purchase plans) and certain forms of ESOPs.

In reality, regardless of any exceptions to this IRS requirement, most employers will include a joint survivor option as a means of plan distribution as well as other annuity options such as straight life, life with period certain, etc. These various options are more or less automatic with fully insured plans using individual or group annuities provided by an insurer.

SAMPLE PROFIT SHARING PLAN

00

Internal Revenue Service

Plan Description: Prototype Standardized Profit Sharing Plan

Department of the Treasury

Washington, DC 20224

Person to Contact:

Telephone Number:

Refer Reply to:

Date:

Dear Applicant:

In our opinion, the form of the plan identified above is acceptable under section 401 of the Internal Revenue Code for use by employers for the benefit of their employees. This opinion relates only to the acceptability of the form of the plan under the Internal Revenue Code. It is not an opinion of the effect of other Federal or local statutes.

You must furnish a copy of this letter to each employer who adopts this plan. You are also required to send a copy of the approved form of the plan, any approved amendments and related documents to each Key District Director of Internal Revenue Service in whose jurisdiction there are adopting employers.

Our opinion on the acceptability of the form of the plan is not a ruling or determination as to whether an employer's plan qualifies under Code section 401(a). An employer who adopts this plan will be considered to have a plan qualified under Code section 401(a) provided all the terms of the plan are followed, and the eligibility requirements and contribution of benefit provisions are not more favorable for officers, owners, or highly compensated employess than for other employees. Except as stated below, the Key District Director will not issue a determination letter with regard to this plan.

Our opinion does not apply to the form of the plan for purposes of Code section 401(a)(16) if: (1) an employer ever maintained another qualified plan for one or more employees who are covered by this plan, other than a specified paired plan within the meaning of section 7 of Rev. Proc. 89-9, 1989-6 I.R.B. 14; or (2) after December 31, 1985, the employer maintains separate accounts for key employees as defined in Code section 419(e), which provides postretirement medical benefits allocated to separate accounts for key employees as defined in Code section 419A(d)(3). In such situations, the employer should request a determination as to whether the plan, considered with all related qualified plans, and if appropriate, welfare benefit funds, satisfies the requirements of Code section 401(a)(16) as to limitations on benefits and contributions in Code section 415.

If you, the plan sponsor, have any questions concerning the IRS processing of this case, please call the above telephone number. This number is only for use of the plan sponsor. Individual participants and/or adopting employers with questions concerning the plan should contact the plan sponsor. The plan's adoption agreement must include the sponsor's address and telephone number for inquiries by adopting employers.

If you write to the IRS regarding this plan, please provide your telephone number and the most convenient time for us to call in case we need more information. Whether you call or write, please refer to the Letter Serial Number and File Folder Number shown in the heading of this letter.

You should keep this letter as a permanent record. Please notify us if you modify or discontinue sponsorship of this plan.

Sincerely yours,

Chief Employee Plans Qualifications Branch

PART 1: **Fill in the required information.** Part 2 contains provisions not requiring elections that complete the operational features within each Section of the Adoption Agreement.

FOREWORD

The undersigned Employer adopts the _____ Simplified/Standardized Profit Sharing Plan for those Employees who shall qualify as Participants hereunder, to be known as the

A1 _____
(Enter Plan Name)

It shall be effective as of the date specified below. The Employer hereby selects the following Plan specifications:

CAUTION: The failure to properly fill out this Adoption Agreement may result in disqualfication of the Plan. This Plan may be used in combination only with (Insurance Company) Standardized or Simplified/Standardized Plans.

EMPLOYER INFORMATION

B1 NAME OF EMPLOYER _____
_____

B2 ADDRESS _____

_____ _____ _____
City   State   Zip

TELEPHONE _____

B3 EMPLOYER IDENTIFICATION NUMBER
   a. ☐ _____ - _____
   b. ☐ Applied For

B4 TYPE OF ENTITY (Check one)
   a. ☐ S Corporation
   b. ☐ Professional Service Corporation
   c. ☐ Corporation
   d. ☐ Sole Proprietorship
   e. ☐ Partnership
   f. ☐ Other _____

B5 DATE BUSINESS COMMENCED _____

B6 EMPLOYER IS A MEMBER OF (Check applicable item(s)):
   a. ☐ A controlled group
   b. ☐ An affiliated service group
   c. ☐ Neither of the above

PLAN DESIGN 11—19

B7 NAME(S) OF TRUSTEE(S)

a. _____

b. _____

c. _____

B8 TRUSTEE'S ADDRESS

a. ☐ Use Employer Address

b. ☐ _____
        Street

   _____ _____ _____
   City   State   Zip

B9 LOCATION OF EMPLOYER'S PRINCIPAL OFFICE:
a. ☐ state of _____

b. ☐ commonwealth of _____

and this Plan and Trust shall be governed under the laws of same.

B10 EMPLOYER FISCAL YEAR means the 12 consecutive month period ending on _____.
                                                                              month   day

PLAN INFORMATION

C1 EFFECTIVE DATE

This Adoption Agreement of the (Insurance Company) Simplified/Standardized Profit Sharing Plan and Trust shall:

a. ☐ establish a new Plan effective as of _____ (hereinafter called the "Effective Date").

b. ☐ constitute an amendment and restatement in its entirety of a previously established qualified plan of the Employer which was effective _____ (hereinafter called the "Effective Date"). Except as specifically provided in the Plan, the effective date of this amendment is _____.

C4 PLAN NUMBER assigned by the Employer (select one):

a. ☐ 001   b. ☐ 002   c. ☐ 003   d. ☐ Other _____.

C7 IS THIS A PAIRED PLAN?

a. ☐ Yes. Name the plan(s) with which this Plan is paired.

_____
(Plan Name)

b. No or N/A.

NOTE: This Plan can only be paired with (Insurance Company) plans listed on page 9 of this Adoption Agreement.

Copyright © 1996 The Merritt Company   LHPP/4-96

ELIGIBILITY, VESTING AND RETIREMENT AGE

D3 CONDITIONS OF ELIGIBILITY (Plan Section 3.1)
(Elect a, or elect b and complete)

Any Eligible Employee shall be eligible to participate in the Plan if such Eligible Employee has satified the attained age and service requirements specified in a or b below:

a. ☐ FOR NEW PLANS

    ATTAINED AGE REQUIREMENT: Age 21
    SERVICE REQUIREMENT: 1 Year of Service

b. ☐ FOR AMENDED AND RESTATED PLANS

    1. ☐ ATTAINED AGE REQUIREMENT: Age 21
        SERVICE REQUIREMENT: 1 Year of Service

    2. ☐ ATTAINED AGE REQUIREMENT: Age 20½
        SERVICE REQUIREMENT: ½ Year of Service
        (An Employee shall not be required to complete any specified number of Hours of Service to receive credit for such fractional year.)

NOTE: These elections must be completed in a manner which reflects the provisions of the Plan in effect immediately prior to adoption of this amended and restated Plan. If the eligibility conditions of the prior plan differ from these choices, a standardized adoption agreement must be used.

D4 EFFECTIVE DATE OF PARTICIPATION (Plan Section 3.2)
(Elect a, or elect b and complete)

An Eligible Employee shall become a Participant as of the Effective Date if he has satisfied the conditions of eligiblity in D3 above as of such date or, if later, as of the date specified in a or b below:

a. ☐ FOR NEW PLANS

Semi-Annual Entry: The earlier of the first day of the seventh month of the Plan Year or the first day of the seventh month of the Plan Year coinciding with or next following the date on which he met such conditions.

b. ☐ FOR AMENDED AND RESTATED PLANS

    1. ☐ Semi-Annual Entry: The earlier of the <u>first</u> day of the Plan Year or the first day of the seventh month of the Plan Year

    2. ☐ Semi-Annual Entry: The earlier of the <u>last</u> day of the Plan Year or the last day of the sixth month of the Plan Year

    3. ☐ Annual Entry: The <u>first</u> day of the Plan Year

    4. ☐ Annual Entry: The <u>last</u> day of the Plan Year

coinciding with or next following the date on which he met such conditions.

NOTE: These elections must be completed in a manner which reflects the provisions of the Plan in effect immediately prior to adoption of this amended and restated Plan. A semi-annual entry date option must be elected if D3b1 above is elected.

ADMINISTRATIVE NOTE: Although the Plan may provide for annual entry as of the first day of the Plan Year or for semi-annual entry, actual Plan administration and insurance purchases will be completed annually in conjunction with the Anniversary Date (last day of the Plan Year).

PLAN DESIGN

D8 VESTING SERVICE EXCLUSIONS (Plan Section 6.4(g))

In determining Years of Service for vesting purposes, Years of Service attributable to the following shall be EXCLUDED (check all applicable):

a. ☐ Service prior to the Effective Date of the Plan or a predecessor plan.

b. ☐ Service prior to the time an Employee attained age 18.

c. ☐ No exclusions.

D12 EARLY RETIREMENT DATE (Plan Section 1.11)
(Elect a, or elect b and complete)

a. ☐ No early retirement provision is provided.

b. ☐ Early Retirement Date means, prior to a Participant's Normal Retirement Date, the Anniversary Date coinciding with or next following the date on which a Participant attained his _____ birthday and has completed at least _____ Years of Service.

NOTE: A Participant's right to his Participant's Account shall become nonforfeitable on the date he satisfies the specified age and service requirements if he is still employed on such date.

CONTRIBUTIONS, ALLOCATIONS AND DISTRIBUTIONS

E3 CONTRIBUTION ALLOCATIONS (Plan Section 4.3 and E3 of Part 2 of this Adoption Agreement)

a. ☐ NON-INTEGRATED

b. ☐ INTEGRATED (Complete 1)

    1. The "Integration Level" is equal to (elect one and complete, if applicable):

        A. ☐ the Taxable Wage Base. (The Taxable Wage Base, "TWB," is the maximum amount of earnings that may be considered wages for a year under Code Section 3121(a)(1) in effect as of the beginning of the Plan Year.)

        B. ☐ $ _____ (a dollar amount less than the Taxable Wage Base).

        C. ☐ _____ % of the Taxable Wage Base (not to exceed 100%)

TOP HEAVY REQUIREMENTS

F3 PRESENT VALUE OF ACCRUED BENEFIT (Plan Section 2.2) for top heavy purposes where the Employer maintains a defined benefit plan in addition to this Plan, shall be based on:

a. ☐ N/A. The Employer does not maintain a defined benefit plan.

b. ☐ Interest Rate: _____

       Mortality Rate: _____

EXECUTE AND DATE SIGNATURE PAGE AT END OF ADOPTION AGREEMENT

End of Part 1

PART 2: No entries required.

In addition to the elections made in Part 1, the following provisions shall apply:

PLAN INFORMATION

C2 PLAN YEAR means the 12 consecutive month period ending on the last day of the fiscal year of the Employer.

  NOTE: This Adoption Agreement cannot be used if the Plan Year is being amended or if there is a Short Plan Year.

C3 ANNIVERSARY DATE of Plan (Annual Valuation Date) means the last day of the Plan Year.

C5 PLAN ADMINISTRATOR shall be the Employer.

C6 PLAN'S AGENTS FOR SERVICE OF LEGAL PROCESS shall be the Trustee(s) and the Administrator.

ELIGIBILITY, VESTING AND RETIREMENT AGE

D1 ELIGIBLE EMPLOYEES (Plan Section 1.15) shall mean all Employees who have satisfied the eligibility requirements except employees whose employment is governed by a collective bargaining agreement between the Employer and "employee representatives", provided retirement benefits were the subject of good faith bargaining and provided less than two percent of the Employees of the Employer who are covered pursuant to that agreement are professionals as defined in proposed Regulations Section 1.410(b)-9(g). For this purpose, the term, "employee representatives" does not include any organization more than half of whose members are employees who are owners, officers, or executives of the Employer.

  NOTE: For purposes of this Section, the term Employee shall include all Employees of this Employer and any Affiliated Employer and any Leased Employees deemed to be Employees under Code Section 414(n) or 414(o).

D2 HOURS OF SERVICE (Plan Section 1.30) shall be determined on the basis of actual hours for which an Employee is paid or entitled to payment.

D5 VESTING OF PARTICIPANT'S INTEREST (Plan Section 6.4(b))

  The vesting schedule, based on number of Years of Service, shall be as follows:

Years of Service	Vesting
0-1 year	0%
2 years	20%
3 years	40%
4 years	60%
5 years	80%
6 years or more	100%

D6 AMENDMENTS TO VESTING SCHEDULE (Plan Section 8.1(f))

  This section is not applicable to this Adoption Agreement because Simplified/Standardized Adoption Agreements cannot be used if the vesting schedule has previously been or is being amended to a schedule which is less favorable in any year and vesting for any current Participant is to be determined under such prior vesting schedule.

D7 TOP HEAVY VESTING (Plan Section 6.4(c))

  This section is not applicable to this Adoption Agreement since a vesting shedule which satisfies top heavy vesting requirements is specified in D5.

D9 PRIOR SERVICE RECOGNITION (Plan Section 1.75)

  Years of Service with any predecessor employer shall be recognized for the purpose of this Plan, whether or not the predecessor ever maintained this Plan. In addition, Years of Service with any Affiliated Employer shall be recognized.

PLAN DESIGN

D10 NORMAL RETIREMENT AGE ("NRA") (Plan Section 1.42) means the date a Participant attains his 65th birthday.

D11 NORMAL RETIREMENT DATE (Plan Section 1.43) means the Anniversary Date coinciding with or next following the Participant's "NRA".

CONTRIBUTIONS, ALLOCATIONS AND DISTRIBUTIONS

E1 COMPENSATION (Plan Section 1.8) with respect to any Participant means such Participant's wages as defined in Code Section 3401(a) for purposes of income tax withholding at the source, but determined without regard to any rules that limit the remuneration included in wages based on the nature or location of the employment or the services performed. In addition, Compensation and 414(s) Compensation (Plan Section 1.25) shall include compensation which is not currently includable in the Participant's gross income by reason of the application of Code Sections 125, 402(a)(8), 402(h)(1)(B), or 403(b). Compensation shall be measured over the Plan Year.

NOTE: The Limitation Year shall be the same as the Plan Year.

E2 BASIS FOR DETERMINING EMPLOYER'S CONTRIBUTION (Plan Section 4.1)

Employer contributions shall be discretionary and in an amount to be determined by the Employer. Contributions shall not be limited to net profits.

E3 CONTRIBUTION ALLOCATIONS (Plan Section 4.3 and E3 of Part 1 of this Adoption Agreement)

a. If the Employer contribution shall be allocated on a non-integrated basis, as elected in E3a of Part 1 of this Adoption Agreement, the Employer contribution for the Plan Year shall be allocated to all Participants eligible to share in the allocations in the same proportion that each eligible Participant's Compensation bears to the total Compensation of all eligible Participants.

b. If the Employer contribution shall be allocated on an integrated basis, as elected in E3b of Part 1 of this Adoption Agreement, the following additional provisions regarding the "Maximum Disparity Rate" and the Allocation Basis shall apply:

<u>MAXIMUM DISPARITY RATE</u>

The "Maximum Disparity Rate" shall be determined as follows:

If the "Integration Level"

		the applicable percentage is:	
is more than	but not more than	Top Heavy Plan Years	Non-Top Heavy Plan Years
$0	X*	2.7%	5.7%
X*	80% of TWB	1.3%	4.3%
80% of TWB	Y**	2.4%	5.4%
If the "Integration Level" used is equal to the TWB		2.7%	5.7%

*X = the greater of $10,000 or 20% of the TWB.

**Y = any amount more than 80% of the TWB but less than 100% of the TWB.

ALLOCATION BASIS

The Employer contribution for a Plan Year shall be allocated to the Participant's Account of each Participant eligible to share in the allocation for such Plan Year on the following basis:

Top Heavy Plan Year	Non-Top Heavy Plan Year	Allocation Basis
Step 1	N/A	The Employer contribution shall be allocated to each eligible Participant's Account in the ratio that each eligible Participant's total Compensation bears to all eligible Participants' total Compensation, but not in excess of 3% of each eligible Participant's Compensation.
Step 2	N/A	Any Employer contribution remaining after the allocation in Step 1 shall be allocated to each eligible Participant's Account in the ratio that each eligible Participant's "Excess Compensation" bears to the "Excess Compensation" of all eligible Participants, but not in excess of 3% of an eligible Participant's "Excess Compensation."
Step 3	Step 1	Any Employer contribution remaining after the allocation in Step 2, or the total Employer contribution in non-Top Heavy Plan Years, shall be allocated to each eligible Participant's Account in the ratio that the sum of each eligible Participant's total Compensation and "Excess Compensation" bears to the sum of all eligible Participants' total Compensation and "Excess Compensation." Any allocation under this step shall be limited to the "Maximum Disparity Rate" applied to the sum of an eligible Participant's total Compensation and "Excess Compensation."
Step 4	Step 2	Any remaining Employer contribution shall be allocated to each eligible Participant's Account in the ratio that each eligible Participant's total Compensation bears to all eligible Participants' total Compensation.

For purposes of the above, an eligible Participant's "Excess Compensation" is his Compensation in excess of the "Integration Level" described in E3 of Part 1 of this Adoption Agreement.

E4   FORFEITURES (Plan Section 4.3(f)) shall be used to reduce the Employer's contribution under the Plan.

E5   ALLOCATIONS TO ACTIVE PARTICIPANTS (Plan Section 4.3(c)(1))

A Participant who has not terminated employment during the Plan Year shall share in the allocation of Employer contributions, regardless of Hours of Service.

E6   ALLOCATIONS TO TERMINATED PARTICIPANTS (Plan Section 4.3(c)(2)(i))

Any Participant who terminated employment during the Plan Year for reasons other than death, Total and Permanent Disability or retirement shall share in the allocations of Employer contributions and Forfeitures, provided such Participant compeleted 501 or more Hours of Service.

E7   ALLOCATIONS TO RETIRED PARTICIPANTS, ETC. (Plan Section 4.3(c)(2)(ii))

Any Participant who terminated employment during the Plan Year for reasons of death, Total Permanent Disability or retirement shall share in the allocation of Employer contributions and Forfeitures, regardless of Hours of Service.

PLAN DESIGN

E8 LIMITATIONS ON ALLOCATIONS (Plan Section 4.5)

NOTE: If the Employer maintains at any time or has ever maintained another plan covering some of the same Participants, except in the case of a combination of paired plans, the Employer may not rely on the opinion letter issued by the Internal Revenue Service that this Plan is qualified under Code Section 401, and this Adoption Agreement may not be adopted.

a. If any Participant is or was covered under another qualified defined contribution plan maintained by the Employer which is paired with this Plan as specified in C7 of Part 1 of this Adoption Agreement, or if the Employer maintains a welfare benefit fund, as defined in Code Section 419(e), or an individual medical account, as defined in Code Section 415(1)(2), under which amounts are treated as Annual Additions with respect to any Participant in this Plan, the provisions of Section 4.5(b) of the Plan shall apply.

b. If the Participant is or ever has been a Participant in a defined benefit plan maintained by the Employer which is paired with this Plan as specified in C7 of Part 1 of this Adoption Agreement, the rate of accrual in the defined benefit plan shall be reduced to the extent necessary so that the sum of the Defined Contribution Fraction and the Defined Benefit Fraction shall not exceed 1.0.

E9 CONDITIONS FOR DISTRIBUTIONS UPON TERMINATION

Distributions upon termination of employment pursuant to Section 6.4(a) of the Plan may be made immediately at the Participant's election.

NOTE: For amounts of $3,500 or less, the Plan requires immediate distributions.

TOP HEAVY REQUIREMENTS

F1 TOP HEAVY DUPLICATIONS (Plan Section 4.4)

When a Non-Key Employee is a Participant of this Plan and another plan maintained by the Employer, top heavy minimum benefits shall be provided in the following manner to avoid duplication:

b.1 Not applicable for Simplified/Standardized Plans.

b.2. If this Plan is paired with a defined benefit plan: The top heavy minimum benefits shall be provided in the defined benefit plan specified in C7 of Part 1 of this Adoption Agreement. The Administrator shall verify that the Top Heavy minimum has been provided under the defined benefit plan to Non-Key Employees of this Plan. To the extent a Non-Key Employee of this Plan does not receive a required minimum benefit under the defined benefit plan, a minimum nonintegrated contribution of 3% of such Non-Key Employee's "Top Heavy Compensation" (as defined in Plan Section 4.4(d)) shall be provided in this Plan as specified in Section 4.4(c)(2) in Top Heavy Plan Years.

c.1. Not applicable for Simplified/Standardized Plans.

c.2. If this Plan is paired with another defined contribution plan: The top heavy minimum benefits shall be provided in the other defined contribution plan specified in C7 of Part 1 of this Adoption Agreement. The Administrator shall verify that the top heavy minimum has been provided under the other defined contribution plan. To the extent a Non-Key Employee participating in this Plan does not receive the required benefit under the other defined contribution plan, the top heavy minimum benefit specified in Section 4.4(a) shall be provided in this Plan to such Non-Key Employee in Top Heavy Plan Years.

F2 NON-KEY EMPLOYEES (Plan Section 4.4(a))

For purposes of providing top heavy minimum benefits, Key Employees shall be treated as Non-Key Employees.

MISCELLANEOUS

G1 LOANS TO PARTICIPANTS (Plan Section 7.4) may not be made.

G2 DIRECTED INVESTMENT ACCOUNTS (Plan Section 4.10) are permitted for the Participant's entire interest in any account.

G3 TRANSFERS FOR QUALIFIED PLANS (Plan Section 4.7)

Transfers from qualified plans (and rollovers) shall be accepted in this Plan. Such transfers (and rollovers) shall be permitted for any Employee, even if not a Participant.

G4 HARDSHIP DISTRIBUTIONS (Plan Section 6.11) are not permitted.

G5 PRE-RETIREMENT DISTRIBUTION (Plan Section 6.10) may not be made.

G6 INSURANCE PURCHASES (Plan Section 7.2)

Assets under this Plan shall be invested in life insurance as follows, subject to Plan Section 7.2:

a. Life insurance Contracts shall be purchased at the option of the Participant.

b. No conditions other than the provisions of Section 7.2 shall apply to the purchase of life insurance Contracts.

NOTE: The percentage of aggregate Employer contributions and Forfeitures used to purchase life insurance must not exceed 49.99% for whole life products and 25% for non-whole life products.

End of Part 2

GENERAL INFORMATION

An Employer who has ever maintained or who later adopts any plan in addition to this Plan (including a welfare benefit fund, as defined in Code Section 419(e), which provides post-retirement medical benefits allocated to separate accounts for Key Employees, as defined in Code Section 419A(d)(3), or an individual medical account, as defined in Code Section 415(1)(2), other than paired plan #01-004, #01-005, #01-008, #01-009, #01-010, #01-012, #02-003, #02-004, #02-005, or #02-006) may not rely on the opinion letter issued by the National Office of the Internal Revenue Service as evidence that this Plan is qualified under Code Section 401. If the Employer who adopts or maintains multiple plans wishes to obtain reliance that the Employer's plan(s) are qualified, application for a determination letter should be made to the appropriate key district director of Internal Revenue.

This Adoption Agreement may be used only in conjunction with basic Plan document #01. This Adoption Agreement and the basic Plan document shall together be known as (Insurance Company) Simplified/Standardized Profit Sharing Plan #01-011.

(Insurance company) shall notify the Employer of any amendments made to the Plan or of the discontinuance or abandonment of the Plan provided this Plan has been acknowledged by (Insurance Company) or its authorized representative. Furthermore, in order to be eligible to receive such notification, the Employer agrees to notify (Insurance Company) of any change in address.

SUMMARY

Once an employer elects to establish a pension or profit sharing plan, there are certain decisions which have to be made regarding plan design. Probably the first decision to be made is which type of plan to install. This decision will in part be based on identifying which employees should benefit the most from the plan.

Usually, the key employees are identified as the group to be favored by the plan. The employer will then decide among the available qualified plans such as a defined contribution plan, defined benefit plan, profit sharing plan, or some combination of qualified plans.

Once the type of plan is established, the type of benefit formula must be determined. This decision will in part be influenced by cost factors relative to the type of plan. Under a defined benefit plan, a unit benefit formula provides for the employee's total service with the employer and thus would be more costly than a flat percentage of compensation formula which usually discounts or offsets the plan's benefit for years of service less than a specified number of years.

Benefit formulas may also be used which require the benefits to be offset by Social Security retirement benefits thus providing a lower contribution on the part of the employer. Generally, defined contribution plans provide a formula based on a percentage of the participant's compensation and a profit sharing plan provides for contributions based on compensation only if profits are realized.

Other plan design factors include eligibility requirements such as one year of service and attainment of age 21. Vesting requirements are regulated by law and are normally 100% immediate, 0/5 or 3/7 schedules. The definition of compensation is also an important consideration since plan contributions are usually factors of compensation. If commissions or bonuses are to be included as compensation, this will result in increased employer contributions.

Disability and pre-retirement death benefits are important cost factors as well. Normally, upon death or disability, the participant's pension benefits become 100% vested and thus payable as benefits. In the event that the employer wishes to provide additional death benefits, this can be achieved by adding life insurance to the plan. Both the defined benefit and defined contribution plans provide limits as to how much life insurance benefits and premiums may be.

Defined benefit plans limit the amount of life insurance to 100 times the participant's benefit. Defined contribution place limitations of 50% and 25% on whole life and term insurance premiums respectively.

A final consideration which relates to cost are the retirement age provisions. Normal retirement is usually age 65 but a plan may provide for early retirement or later retirement. Each of these options has an effect on the total cost of the plan.

REVIEW EXERCISES

1. George is age 56 and the sole owner of a small manufacturing business which employs seven other employees, ages 20-36. Annually, the company's profits have been very stable for the past 10 years. George intends to retire in about 10 years and his son, age 33, will take over the operation of the business. What type of pension plan might you recommend to George?

2. Discuss the effects of the vesting schedule and the plan's definition of compensation with regard to the cost of a pension plan.

CHAPTER 12

PLAN ADMINISTRATION

Once the type of plan is decided upon and other plan considerations are addressed, it will then be time to "give birth" to this pension plan and administer it throughout its life. This chapter will cover the following principal concepts:

- Plan installation and administration
- Plan fiduciaries
- Plan reporting requirements
- Plan termination

PLAN INSTALLATION

Acme Inc., holds a Board of Directors meeting on April 30, the last day of its fiscal year. At the meeting, the board of directors approves the adoption of a qualified pension plan for the firm. The plan's documents are signed at the meeting and a small deposit of $1,000 is issued by the Treasurer.

The IRS specifies that a pension plan will be considered in force if it is put into effect by the last day of the business' fiscal year. The formal adoption by the Board of Directors, signing the plan documents and the deposit of $1,000 constitutes placing a plan in effect. Thus, Acme Inc., on the last day of its fiscal year has put a pension plan into effect and it will be considered that the plan has been in force for the entire business year. Accordingly, the business will be entitled to a tax deduction for the $1,000 deposit and the subsequent plan contributions it makes for the initial plan year.

The next step is for Acme to obtain a determination letter from the IRS stating that the plan is qualified in accordance with IRS requirements. Obtaining the determination letter is not necessary in order for the plan to be qualified. However, it is in the firm's best interest to have such a letter on file.

Often a business will use a **prototype plan** which basically means that the pension plan has been pre-approved by the IRS as a qualified plan. Usually these plans are provided by insurers and similar organizations who market pension plans. A copy of a prototype plan is included in Chapter 11 of this text. The advantage of using a prototype plan is its administrative simplicity. The employer generally "fills in the blanks" by providing answers to certain questions and indicating certain information regarding vesting, contributions, retirement age, etc.

If the determination letter is to be requested, the plan must be submitted to the IRS prior to the date on which the company files its business tax return (usually within 2½ months after the end of the firm's fiscal year). There are several forms which must be filed. These include:

- Form 5300, "Application for Determination for Employee Benefit Plans"
- Form 5302, "Employee Census Form"

At the time the application for the determination letter is made, a notice must be provided to all employees informing them of the pending determination letter. The form of this notice is specified by the IRS. In addition a prescribed submission fee is also required. Depending on the type of plan, the fee could be in excess of $800.

Once the forms and application are reviewed, assuming everything meets IRS specifications, a favorable determination letter will be issued to the corporation. This letter simply states that the plan complies and is qualified.

This process involves not only the Board of Directors but a group of professional advisors including input from the firm's insurance agent, attorney, and accountant. In addition, every qualified plan must have a plan administrator. The administrator could be an individual or a group of persons. Generally, it will not be the employer.

The administrator's job is to oversee the operation of the pension plan including providing participants with plan information, filing required forms with the IRS and the Department of Labor, benefit calculation, recordkeeping, etc. This is normally not the employer's function. A third party, the firm's attorney or CPA, may function in this position.

PLAN ADMINISTRATION

Frequently, the administrator is a third party administrator (TPA). The TPA is an organization which employs accountants, actuaries and various administrative people whose primary task is to administer qualified pension plans on behalf of the employer. In some states, TPAs need to be licensed and their function and activities are regulated by the state insurance department.

FIDUCIARY RESPONSIBILITIES

Generally, a fiduciary is defined as a person in a position of financial trust. ERISA carefully regulates and defines the duties of plan fiduciaries. ERISA provides that a plan fiduciary must act for the exclusive benefit of the plan's participants and their beneficiaries by means of prudent conduct and by adhering to the investment objectives and provisions of the plan.

An individual is considered a fiduciary with reference to the plan to the extent that the person exercises discretionary authority or control regarding plan management, provides investment advice and/or has the responsibility to provide plan administration. Accordingly, if the employer or the company retains any type of authority or control over the plan, then the employer could be identified as a fiduciary. If the employer delegates all authority and plan responsibilities to a TPA, then certainly the TPA would have a fiduciary responsibility with regard to the operation of the plan. ERISA requires that fiduciaries be named in the plan documents.

A plan fiduciary who violates any of his or her duties and responsibilities is personally liable to correct any investment losses resulting from the violation. Also, the courts may impose other penalties including removal from the plan as a fiduciary.

Naturally, if as part of his or her fiduciary responsibilities, a plan fiduciary recommends an investment which goes sour and a loss occurs, the fiduciary will not be held liable for this loss so long as there is no violation of his or her fiduciary duties. It is only when a loss may occur as the result of a violation that the fiduciary becomes personally liable.

In addition to recovering any loss due as the result of a fiduciary violation, the Secretary of Labor may prosecute the individual in court. If an out of court settlement is reached or a court so orders, the fiduciary may also be penalized up to 20% of the amount of the loss.

In summary, it is clear that not just "anyone" should be identified as a plan fiduciary. An employer who maintains any discretionary control over the plan and is thus identified as a fiduciary can be personally liable for anything which may go wrong with the plan. Since a fiduciary is held to be in a position of financial trust; is knowledgeable and competent with regard to plan matters; must exercise prudent judgement, etc., it is wise to use a person who fits this description. The employer who owns a manufacturing concern or who operates a group of retail stores, probably knows little regarding the operation of a pension plan.

A former U.S. Supreme Court Justice, Justice Cardozo, defined the role of a fiduciary as follows:

> "Many forms of conduct, permissible in a work-a-day world for those acting at arm's length, are forbidden to those bound by fiduciary duty. A trustee is held to something stricter than the morals of the market place. Not honesty alone, but the punctilio of an honor the most sensitive, is then the standard of behavior."

One of the more important duties of a plan fiduciary is to avoid certain **prohibited transactions**. Prohibited transactions are certain transactions between a plan fiduciary and specific individuals. These individuals include:

- Other plan fiduciaries, attorneys or employees of the plan
- A TPA servicing the plan
- The employer
- Another business controlled (more than 50%) by the employer
- A person who owns 10% or more of the corporation

This group of people are referred to as parties in interest or disqualified persons. A plan fiduciary is prohibited from entering into certain transactions with these disqualified persons. These transactions include:

- Sale or leasing of any property
- Lending money
- Providing goods or services
- Transferring of any plan assets to a disqualified person

PLAN ADMINISTRATION

It is also a violation if a plan fiduciary uses any of the plan's assets for his or her personal account or gain. Further, a violation will occur if a plan (other than an ESOP or stock bonus plan) invests in more than 10% of the employer's own stock or bonds.

Needless to say, not every transaction between a plan fiduciary and a disqualified person is considered a prohibited transaction. There are specific statutory and administrative exemptions provided by ERISA. It is beyond the scope of this text to provide specifics regarding these exemptions. Some of these exemptions include:

- The loan of plan assets to plan participants
- Provisions whereby an insurance agent may receive commissions on the sale of annuities used to fund the plan
- Provisions whereby life insurance and annuity contracts may be transferred to or from a plan
- Allowing loans from the plan to pay operating expenses

Violation of these regulations governing prohibited transactions include personal liability on the part of the plan fiduciary for any losses plus a specific tax levied by the IRS on the disqualified person who participates in the transaction.

PLAN REPORTING REQUIREMENTS

Once the plan has been installed, the plan administrator appointed, fiduciaries identified, and related matters completed, the next requirement to be fulfilled by the plan administrator will be the annual reporting to the federal government.

Annual Return/Report

Annually, the plan administrator will prepare and file the **Annual Return/Report (form 5500)** with the IRS and the Department of Labor. This annual report will provide the IRS and the Department of Labor with the following types of information:

- The number of plan participants including any who have terminated employment with vested benefits
- Any plan amendments
- Plan asset information including the funding arrangements used

- Whether the plan is subject to the Pension Benefit Guarantee Corporation (PBGC) termination insurance or if the plan requires a fidelity bond
- A balance sheet reflecting the assets and liabilities of the plan
- The plan's vesting schedule
- Whether the plan had any prohibited transactions
- Whether the plan is integrated with Social Security

Form 5500 includes various attachments or schedules which also need to be included in this annual submission. These attachments require insurance information, actuarial information and information about the plan's trustees.

Defined benefit plans must be covered by PBGC termination insurance. Form PBGC-1 must also be filed each year with that year's premium not later than 8½ months after the close of the plan year.

Tax forms (Form W-2P) must be provided for participants who have retired and are receiving monthly benefits. Any participant who has received a lump sum distribution must also be provided with the appropriate tax form (1099-R)

Summary Annual Report

A **Summary Annual Report** must be given to each plan participant annually. This report basically summarizes most of the information contained in the form 5500 and must be given to the participants not later than nine months following the close of the plan year.

Summary Plan Description

When the plan is initially installed, each participant must receive a **Summary Plan Description** within 120 days following the effective date of the plan. Subsequent new participants must also be provided with this form within 90 days of becoming eligible to participate in the plan. Copies of the Summary Plan Description and any plan modifications must also be filed with the Department of Labor.

The Summary Plan Description generally provides full disclosure of the plan provisions and benefits. This information includes:

- Identification of the plan itself, the plan administrator, and any plan trustees (fiduciaries)
- Eligibility and participation requirements
- The plan's vesting schedule
- The method of funding
- How benefits are determined and paid
- Information regarding plan termination and the disposition of plan assets
- A disclaimer which states that the actual plan provisions govern the information contained in the Summary Plan Description

Any plan reporting documents must be provided to current plan participants and should also be given to retired participants and/or their beneficiaries unless all plan benefits have been paid to the participant.

An annual benefit statement is not required by law. Most plan administrators will automatically include such information with the annual reports provided participants. In addition, a participant may request such a statement and it will have to be provided within 30 days of the request.

The plan administrator will also be responsible for establishing benefit claims procedures to include how a claim is to be filed as well as appeal procedures if a claim is denied. A claim which is denied must be reviewed by a plan fiduciary.

Failure to properly administer a qualified plan will result in penalties being imposed. For example, a late filing of form 5500 and any required schedules can result in a penalty of $25 per day up to a maximum of $15,000. There are additional monetary fines for similar violations.

Many employers who establish a pension plan will procure the services of a TPA to take care of these various reporting requirements. Again, the employer has a business to manage and is not in the pension administration business. Naturally, a fee is charged for these plan administrative services provided by TPAs.

PLAN TERMINATION

Upon installation, a pension plan is normally viewed as having an unlimited life. However, due to business problems, economic conditions, etc., a qualified plan may have to be terminated. Such termination can be initiated by the employer or the federal government.

The PBGC is authorized to enforce termination of a defined benefit plan if it is not properly funded or if the plan is unable to provide retirement benefits. In addition, it may be terminated if an owner has received a distribution in excess of $10,000 and the plan is left with considerable unfunded vested liabilities or the PBGC has reason to believe that if the plan continues, the PBGC will experience considerable losses.

A terminated plan results in the following:

- All participants become 100% vested as of the date of termination
- A determination letter must be received from the IRS indicating that the termination has not adversely affected the qualification of the plan
- If the plan is a defined benefit plan, the PBGC must approve of the termination
- Plan participants must be notified of the termination

When the plan was initially approved by the IRS as a qualified plan, one of the factors considered was the permanency of the plan. Generally, the IRS will deem a plan to have been permanent if it has been in force for **10 years**. Thus, if an employer terminates a plan a couple of years after it was established and the IRS can prove that the employer only intended that the plan would be temporary, it can disqualify the plan retroactively. This has serious consequences for the employer who took tax deductions for plan contributions and now is informed that the plan never qualified.

Normally, the IRS will accept the following as reasons for plan termination:

- Bankruptcy, insolvency, or business merger
- Substitution of another type of qualified plan
- Changes in pension laws which adversely affect the existing plan

If the question of the permanency of the plan is not at issue, the IRS will then review the plan to determine that the benefits to be paid are not discriminatory (in favor of the key persons). Normally a defined contribution plan is not discriminatory in that the participant's account balances usually reflect the employer's contributions as approved by the IRS in the determination letter.

On the other hand, defined benefit plans present special problems at termination. Rarely would the plan's funds equal the participants' defined benefit. The sum of the present values of all benefits will be compared to the current market value of the plan assets. If the current plan assets exceed the present value of the benefits to be paid, the plan can be terminated and the excess amounts may be allocated to the plan participants or refunded to the employer.

If the plan assets are less than the present value of the plan's benefits, the PBGC must approve the termination. This is known as a distress termination. To terminate a plan under a distress termination, one or more of the following factors must be present:

- The business is bankrupt, insolvent, or in liquidation proceedings
- The business is unable to pay its obligations
- Bankruptcy court approves the termination
- Pension plan costs have become burdensome due to the financial condition of the business

The plan administrator must prove at least one of these points, file necessary forms and obtain a detailed statement from an enrolled actuary certifying the amount of plan assets, the present value of benefit liabilities and the present value of benefits guaranteed by the PBGC. In summary, termination of a defined benefit plan is much more troublesome than a defined contribution plan.

If the PBGC determines that the plan can qualify for a distress termination, the plan administrator may distribute plan assets to the participants. If the plan cannot qualify for a distress termination, the PBGC will appoint a trustee to manage the plan termination. The employer will be held liable for the guaranteed benefits provided by the PBGC.

Once the termination is approved and the participants have been notified, distribution of plan benefits can take place. The plan must provide paid-up deferred annuity contracts or distribute all assets in cash to the participants or provide a system of distribution which combines these two alternatives.

If the plan contains life insurance contracts, upon termination, the normal procedure is to distribute these policies to the participants who will assume the premium payments. The participant will be taxed on the value of the policy. This value is usually the cash value less the P.S. 58 costs (paid by the participant).

For example if a policy's cash value is $4,500 and the participant has paid a total of $2,000 in P.S. 58 charges over the years, the taxable value to the participant is $2,500.

If the participant is not to assume ownership of the policy, the policy may be cashed in for its available cash value and this amount will be included in the employee's taxable distribution. It should be remembered that the cost basis of a qualified plan distribution is always equal to zero. Thus, the entire distribution is subject to federal income tax when received unless the participant elects to roll this amount into an IRA, in which case, the taxation will be postponed until received at a later date.

Alternatives

Termination of a qualified plan produces serious economic impact on all of the parties involved. To avoid these consequences, an employer might consider **alternatives to plan termination**.

One such alternative would be to **amend the plan** in such a way as to reduce the employer's expense and liability. A plan could be amended to reflect a change in the level of benefits to be paid or the contribution formula. If this is done, the employer's cost will be reduced. ERISA does not permit present participant accruals to be reduced. A change in the benefit formula will result in a change in the amount of the annual contribution and future participant accruals.

Another alternative is to petition the IRS to **waive the plan's minimum funding requirements** if a severe financial hardship occurs. The IRS may waive such funding for up to three years in any 15 consecutive plan year period. In other words, the inability to pay the annual contribution can result in a postponement of this liability. Notice, the obligation is merely put off until another time. The annual contribution must eventually be paid.

A final alternative to plan termination is to **freeze the plan** and current account values and amend the plan to prohibit any future new participants. Plan distributions can occur but no further contributions will be made to the plan. In essence, the plan has not been terminated, it has merely been "suspended". A plan utilizing this alternative to termination still must comply with all ERISA requirements including administration and the annual reporting to the IRS, the Department of Labor and the plan participants.

SUMMARY

Once a qualified plan is established by an employer, there are certain administrative and reporting requirements which must be satisfied. The first of these concerns plan installation. Normally, a plan can be established by a resolution of the firm's Board of Directors and a minimum deposit for the plan. The balance of the plan contribution must be made within 2½ months following the end of the business' fiscal year. Certain forms will be filed with the IRS in order to obtain a letter of determination which generally specifies that the employer's plan is qualified. This entire process involves the employer and the services of an insurance agent, an attorney and the firm's accountant.

Administration of a qualified plan is a complicated matter. Often the employer will obtain the services of a TPA to provide necessary administrative services. These services include the annual reporting to the IRS and the Department of Labor as well as disclosure information for plan participants. Such reports include the Annual Report, reports to the PBGC, Summary Annual Reports and tax reporting forms for plan participants.

By definition, a plan fiduciary is a person in a position of financial trust who has specific plan responsibilities and also faces certain liabilities for breach of conduct. A fiduciary may offer investment advice but always must perform with the welfare of plan participants in mind. As such, a plan fiduciary is prohibited from becoming involved in certain transactions with disqualified persons. Some of these prohibited transactions include lending money, the sale of property, and transferring plan assets to a disqualified person.

One of the reasons that the IRS identifies a plan as qualified is because of its permanency. If a plan has been in force for 10 years, it will normally be deemed as permanent. However, if a plan is terminated after a relatively short period of time, it may lose its qualification and its preferred tax status.

When a plan is terminated, all participants become 100% vested as of the date of termination. Reasons for plan termination include bankruptcy, insolvency, or liquidation of the business. Before a plan can be terminated, such termination must be approved by the IRS or in the case of defined benefit plans, the PBGC. Once approval is obtained, the plan's assets, including any life insurance cash values can be distributed.

Plan participants can normally elect to become owners of any life insurance policy and assume the premium payment responsibilities. When this occurs, the participant is subject to taxation on the value of the policy which is usually equal to the policy's cash value less the P.S. 58 charges paid by the participant.

Alternatives to plan termination include amending the plan's benefit formula which results in a smaller contribution requirement. The employer may also seek a waiver with regard to plan funding. The IRS can waive (temporarily suspend) funding for up to three years in any 15 year consecutive period of time. Finally, the plan may be frozen which results in no new participants being allowed to enter the plan and no further plan contributions being made. In all other matters, the plan continues including the need for annual administration and filing with the government as well as distributions to plan participants.

REVIEW EXERCISES

1. Sam is independently wealthy and the owner of a business which employs 30 people. His business profits have been substantial for many years and he is now seeking tax relief by means of establishing a qualified pension plan.

    He indicates that he intends to have this plan for only two or three years after which he won't need the tax write off any longer. What potential liabilities or problems can be created in this situation if he attempts to terminate the plan after two or three years?

2. Discuss some of the specific duties and liabilities of a plan fiduciary.

3. Explain some of the alternatives available to an employer in lieu of seeking plan termination.

FINAL COURSE REVIEW

> The following questions cover the course material and answers are provided on page A-9*. When you have completed this review you are ready to take the final exam for continuing education credit on page CE-1.

1. A company's fiscal year ends June 30. If it is to establish a qualified pension plan for its current tax year, a Board of Directors resolution adopting the plan and a minimum deposit must be made by:

    A. July 1.
    B. June 30.
    C. January 1.
    D. June 1.

2. Which of the following is (are) true regarding a determination letter?

    I   A determination letter is mandatory if the plan is to be qualified.
    II A determination letter must be received by the employer before a plan can be established.
    III If a determination is requested, the plan must be submitted to the IRS not later than 2½ months after the end of the company's fiscal year.
    IV At the time the application for a determination letter is made, all employees must be notified of the pending request for the determination letter.

    A. I only
    B. III and IV
    C. I and II
    D. II and IV

---

*If you are missing page A-9, this review may count as your final exam. Contact your course provider for complete instructions.

Copyright © 1996 The Merritt Company

LHPP/4-96

3. Post-retirement employment opportunities for the retiree are usually limited due to:

   A. the retiree's physical inability to perform work tasks.
   B. the retiree's desire not to work.
   C. penalties on earnings imposed by the Social Security system.
   D. all of the above.

4. ERISA requires compliance with certain reporting and disclosure requirements on behalf of:

   I   plan participants.
   II the IRS.
   III the Department of Labor.
   IV the Department of Health and Human Services.

   A. I only
   B. II and IV
   C. I, II and III
   D. II, III and IV

5. An employer has a fixed liability to contribute 15% of employees' compensation to a qualified plan. This best describes a:

   A. defined contribution plan.
   B. defined benefit plan.
   C. profit sharing plan.
   D. deferred compensation.

6. A plan administrator is attempting to maintain the qualified status of a pension plan. In accordance with coverage and participation requirements, what percentage of lower paid employees must benefit from the plan?

   A. 50%
   B. 60%
   C. 70%
   D. 80%

7. Usually the maximum amount of an employee's voluntary contribution to a qualified plan is limited to:

   A. 5%.
   B. 10%.
   C. 15%.
   D. 20%.

8. Which of the following is true regarding early retirement?

   A. Qualified plans do not permit early retirement.
   B. Early retirement usually results in a higher monthly retirement benefit.
   C. Due to the longer life expectancy, the retirement benefit will be increased.
   D. Early retirement will result in a reduced retirement benefit.

9. A defined contribution plan specifies a contribution of 10% of employees' compensation. Total compensation is $100,000. Due to plan participant terminations, there is a total of $2,000 in non-vested accruals. How much must the employer currently contribute to the plan?

   A. $12,000
   B. $10,000
   C. $ 9,000
   D. $ 8,000

10. A key employee may be all of the following **except** a:

    A. company officer.
    B. 1% owner-employee with a salary of $50,000.
    C. highly compensated employee.
    D. 5% owner.

11. The tax penalty created by an excess contribution to an IRA may be resolved by:

    A. removing the excess amount in the current tax year.
    B. obtaining a letter of clearance from the IRS.
    C. 5-year income averaging.
    D. all of the above.

12. A salary reduction SEP permits an employee to make a:

    A. pre-tax salary deduction of up to $7,000, as indexed.
    B. non-deductible contribution of up to $7,000, as indexed.
    C. deductible contribution of $2,000, not indexed.
    D. deductible contribution of $12,000, as indexed.

13. Which of the following is correct regarding the catch-up provision of a TSA?

    A. The catch-up provision allows an additional contribution to the TSA not to exceed $9,500.
    B. To take advantage of the provision, an employee must have at least 15 years of service.
    C. The aggregate of all catch-up contributions cannot exceed $9,500.
    D. The catch-up amount is limited to the greater of $3,000 or the exclusion allowance.

14. An IRA owner dies before any account distributions have been made and has named his spouse as a beneficiary. IRA distributions must begin not later than:

    A. December 31 of the year of death.
    B. the year in which the owner would have been 70½ or December 31 following the year of death.
    C. the fifth year following the year of death.
    D. none of the above.

15. Which of the following would **not** be considered a reason for a 401(k) hardship distribution?

    A. The purchase of the employee's principal residence
    B. College tuition for an employee's dependent child
    C. Debt consolidation to permit personal bankruptcy
    D. Medical expenses due to open heart surgery of an employee's spouse

16. A single sum of money is set aside on a plan participant's retirement date to fund his or her retirement benefit. This best describes:

    A. advance funding.
    B. terminal funding.
    C. current disbursement funding.
    D. post active funding.

17. All of the following would be considered duties of a plan fiduciary **except**:

    A. exercising prudent conduct.
    B. enforcing the provisions of the qualified plan.
    C. avoiding prohibited transactions.
    D. guaranteeing the investment results of the plan assets.

18. The maximum fine for failure to file a form 5500 is:

    A. $ 5,000.
    B. $ 7,500.
    C. $10,000.
    D. $15,000.

19. Most qualified plans must provide a:

    A. straight life annuity option.
    B. joint survivor annuity option.
    C. cash refund annuity option.
    D. life with period certain annuity option.

20. All of the following are true regarding the use of life insurance within a qualified plan **except**:

    A. up to 50% of the contribution for a defined contribution plan can be used for whole life insurance.
    B. the defined contribution plan death benefit cannot exceed 100 times the full retirement benefit.
    C. up to 25% of the contribution for a defined contribution plan can be used for term life insurance.
    D. the death benefit provided for a defined benefit plan cannot exceed 100 times the monthly retirement benefit.

21. Once an employee satisfies the plan's eligibility requirements, he or she must enroll in the plan within:

    A. 3 months.
    B. 6 months.
    C. 9 months.
    D. 12 months.

22. Which of the following vesting schedules would probably not be considered by an employer who is attempting to control plan costs?

    A. 100% immediate
    B. 0/5 schedule
    C. 3/7 schedule
    D. none of the above

23. A benefit formula which provides for an employee's total service with an employer, best describes a(n):

    A. flat percentage of compensation.
    B. 401(k) formula.
    C. offset formula.
    D. unit benefit formula.

24. The key employees for XYZ Inc., are between the ages of 50-57. Which type of pension plan would probably be most beneficial to these key persons?

    A. A defined contribution plan
    B. A profit sharing plan
    C. A defined benefit plan
    D. A 401(k) plan

25. With the exception of stock bonus plans and ESOPs, investment of plan contributions in the employer's own securities are:

    A. unlimited.
    B. limited to 15% of the plan's assets.
    C. limited to 10% of the fund's value.
    D. prohibited under ERISA.

26. Contributions to the XYZ qualified plan are invested in the stock market. The ABC qualified plan invests its contributions in bank certificates of deposit. Which of the following is true regarding interest assumptions relative to these two plans?

    A. The assumptions used for the ABC plan will be more realistic and accurate than the assumptions for the XYZ plan.
    B. The assumptions used for the ABC plan will be less realistic and accurate than the assumptions for the XYZ plan.
    C. The assumptions used for the XYZ plan will be more accurate than the assumptions used for the ABC plan.
    D. None of the above.

27. Which of the following entities would be eligible for an HR-10 plan?

    A. A corporate manufacturing business
    B. A non-profit school system
    C. A sole proprietor
    D. An author who has only unearned income

28. A similarity between a stock bonus plan and an ESOP is that:

    A. contributions are not a fixed liability.
    B. both plans are non-qualified.
    C. retirement benefits are determined well before retirement.
    D. none of the above.

29. Rank order the following plans with regard to probable contribution costs from the most expensive to the least expensive.

   I   Stock bonus plan
   II Defined benefit plan
   III Defined contribution plan
   IV Target benefit plan

   A. II, IV, III and I
   B. IV, II, III and I
   C. II, I, IV and III
   D. I, II, IV and III

30. The risks of old age and retirement years include:

   I   outliving one's financial resources.
   II loss of purchasing power due to inflation.
   III increased taxation by federal and state governments.
   IV limited post-retirement job opportunities.

   A. I and II
   B. II and IV
   C. I, III and IV
   D. I, II and IV

31. In accordance with ERISA, which of the following are required disclosure reports for plan participants?

   I   The summary annual report
   II The summary plan description
   III The determination letter
   IV The PBGC statement

   A. III only
   B. II and IV
   C. I and II
   D. I, II, III and IV

32. Which of the following statements is correct regarding an employer sponsored qualified plan?

   A. Employer contributions are tax deductible.
   B. Contributions are currently taxable to employees.
   C. The plan's investment earnings grow tax free.
   D. The plan's cost basis is taxable at retirement.

33. Generally, the purpose of coverage and participation requirements for a qualified plan is to:

   A. increase revenue for the IRS.
   B. safeguard against plan discrimination.
   C. protect employees from employer insolvency.
   D. none of the above.

34. Which of the following are true regarding vesting?

   I   A plan with an eligibility requirement of three years of service must provide 100% immediate vesting.
   II   A five year vesting schedule requires 20% vesting per year.
   III   Forfeitures from terminated participants will stay in the plan to benefit the remaining plan participants.
   IV   The longest vesting schedule permitted is five years.

   A. I and III
   B. II and IV
   C. I and II
   D. II, III and IV

35. John has an account value in his pension plan of $120,000. This total includes $20,000 in voluntary contributions. At retirement, John's tax basis will be:

   A. 0.
   B. $60,000
   C. $100,000.
   D. $120,000.

36. Charlie, age 40, is in a 25% tax bracket. He receives a $10,000 pension distribution. His total tax liability, including any penalties, will be:

   A. $ 250.
   B. $2,500.
   C. $3,500.
   D. none of the above.

37. Employee compensation used in the calculation of plan contributions is limited to:

   A. $100,000.
   B. $150,000.
   C. $300,000.
   D. $500,000.

38. All of the following are eligible for a TSA **except** a:

   A. college professor.
   B. high school principal.
   C. college student.
   D. high school cafeteria worker.

39. An employee elective deferral plan requires:

   A. a written agreement between the employee and employer.
   B. the employee to elect a salary reduction amount.
   C. that the employee satisfy the plan's eligibility requirements.
   D. all of the above.

40. An individual has a $1,000 excess contribution to an IRA. The excess amount is removed from the account in the current tax year. Which of the following is true?

    A. The penalty tax still must be paid.
    B. The excess amount withdrawn will be considered a premature distribution.
    C. Any investment income earned by the excess contribution is taxed and subject to a premature distribution penalty.
    D. Any investment income earned by the excess contribution is subject to ordinary income tax only.

41. Which of the following would be classified as a type of profit sharing plan?

    A. A target benefit plan
    B. A stock bonus plan
    C. A money purchase plan
    D. None of the above

42. Higher than expected investment income on plan contributions to a defined benefit plan will:

    A. increase the ultimate cost of a plan.
    B. decrease the ultimate cost of a plan.
    C. have no effect on the ultimate cost of the plan.
    D. none of the above.

43. All of the following are alternatives to plan termination **except**:

    A. skipping the annual contribution but keeping the plan in effect with IRS approval.
    B. freezing the plan.
    C. applying for a waiver of funding requirements with the IRS.
    D. amending the plan to reduce plan costs.

44. Form 5500, the Annual Return/Report must be filed with:

    A. the IRS.
    B. the Department of Commerce.
    C. both the Department of Commerce and the IRS.
    D. both the IRS and the Department of Labor.

45. Which of the following is true regarding plan termination?

    A. The PBGC must approve termination for profit sharing plans.
    B. All participants become 100% vested.
    C. Business mergers are not acceptable reasons for termination.
    D. A distress termination is automatically approved by the IRS.

46. Life insurance benefits provided in a defined benefit pension plan may not exceed:

    A. 100 times the retirement benefit.
    B. 50 times the retirement benefit.
    C. 100 times the annual contribution.
    D. 25 times the annual contribution.

47. Which of the following would reduce an employer's plan contribution costs?

    I   Plan forfeitures
    II Excess interest earnings
    III Younger age employees entering the plan
    IV Benefit safety

    A. I and II
    B. II and III
    C. I and IV
    D. I, II and III

48. If a plan containing life insurance is terminated, the value of the policy will be taxed to the participant. This value equals the:

    A. premiums paid less the cash value.
    B. premiums paid less the P.S. 58 charges paid.
    C. cash value less the P.S. 58 charges paid.
    D. P.S. 58 charges plus the premiums paid.

49. Which of the following is true regarding a Summary Annual Report?

    A. It must be filed with the IRS within 90 days of the close of the firm's fiscal year.
    B. It must be given to each plan participant not later than nine months following the close of the plan year.
    C. It must be filed with the Department of Labor within 9 months of the close of the firm's fiscal year.
    D. It must be given to each new plan participant within 30 days of the effective date of participation.

50. Plan eligibility which requires three full years of full time service is:

    A. illegal and a violation of IRS requirements.
    B. permissible if the plan provides 100% immediate vesting.
    C. permissible if the plan provides a 0/5 vesting schedule.
    D. permissible if the plan is a profit sharing plan and all participants are fully vested after one year of plan participation.

ANSWERS

1	Ⓐ Ⓑ Ⓒ Ⓓ	26	Ⓐ Ⓑ Ⓒ Ⓓ
2	Ⓐ Ⓑ Ⓒ Ⓓ	27	Ⓐ Ⓑ Ⓒ Ⓓ
3	Ⓐ Ⓑ Ⓒ Ⓓ	28	Ⓐ Ⓑ Ⓒ Ⓓ
4	Ⓐ Ⓑ Ⓒ Ⓓ	29	Ⓐ Ⓑ Ⓒ Ⓓ
5	Ⓐ Ⓑ Ⓒ Ⓓ	30	Ⓐ Ⓑ Ⓒ Ⓓ
6	Ⓐ Ⓑ Ⓒ Ⓓ	31	Ⓐ Ⓑ Ⓒ Ⓓ
7	Ⓐ Ⓑ Ⓒ Ⓓ	32	Ⓐ Ⓑ Ⓒ Ⓓ
8	Ⓐ Ⓑ Ⓒ Ⓓ	33	Ⓐ Ⓑ Ⓒ Ⓓ
9	Ⓐ Ⓑ Ⓒ Ⓓ	34	Ⓐ Ⓑ Ⓒ Ⓓ
10	Ⓐ Ⓑ Ⓒ Ⓓ	35	Ⓐ Ⓑ Ⓒ Ⓓ
11	Ⓐ Ⓑ Ⓒ Ⓓ	36	Ⓐ Ⓑ Ⓒ Ⓓ
12	Ⓐ Ⓑ Ⓒ Ⓓ	37	Ⓐ Ⓑ Ⓒ Ⓓ
13	Ⓐ Ⓑ Ⓒ Ⓓ	38	Ⓐ Ⓑ Ⓒ Ⓓ
14	Ⓐ Ⓑ Ⓒ Ⓓ	39	Ⓐ Ⓑ Ⓒ Ⓓ
15	Ⓐ Ⓑ Ⓒ Ⓓ	40	Ⓐ Ⓑ Ⓒ Ⓓ
16	Ⓐ Ⓑ Ⓒ Ⓓ	41	Ⓐ Ⓑ Ⓒ Ⓓ
17	Ⓐ Ⓑ Ⓒ Ⓓ	42	Ⓐ Ⓑ Ⓒ Ⓓ
18	Ⓐ Ⓑ Ⓒ Ⓓ	43	Ⓐ Ⓑ Ⓒ Ⓓ
19	Ⓐ Ⓑ Ⓒ Ⓓ	44	Ⓐ Ⓑ Ⓒ Ⓓ
20	Ⓐ Ⓑ Ⓒ Ⓓ	45	Ⓐ Ⓑ Ⓒ Ⓓ
21	Ⓐ Ⓑ Ⓒ Ⓓ	46	Ⓐ Ⓑ Ⓒ Ⓓ
22	Ⓐ Ⓑ Ⓒ Ⓓ	47	Ⓐ Ⓑ Ⓒ Ⓓ
23	Ⓐ Ⓑ Ⓒ Ⓓ	48	Ⓐ Ⓑ Ⓒ Ⓓ
24	Ⓐ Ⓑ Ⓒ Ⓓ	49	Ⓐ Ⓑ Ⓒ Ⓓ
25	Ⓐ Ⓑ Ⓒ Ⓓ	50	Ⓐ Ⓑ Ⓒ Ⓓ

*If you are missing page A-9, this review may count as your final exam. Contact your course provider for complete instructions.

Copyright © 1996 The Merritt Company

ANSWERS TO REVIEW EXERCISES

CHAPTER 1

1. The question of an ethical work-related responsibility may be raised with Archie. In addition, to the tax advantages that Archie will realize as the employer, there are intangible benefits to be reaped including improved employee morale which usually results in increased productivity and company loyalty. In addition, a qualified plan can help Archie attract and retain key employees.

2. It has been shown that a person's standard of living frequently doesn't decrease after retirement but remains the same. Normal expenses continue and those that are eliminated (such as a home being paid off) are frequently replaced by travel and recreation expenses incurred during retirement years. Social Security by itself may be inadequate to meet these requirements and conditions.

3. The primary factors affecting the growth of employer sponsored plans has been the impact of the labor unions and the need to compete for skilled key employees. In addition, a plan is a more efficient means of providing retirement benefits and taking care of older, loyal employees. Finally, employees simply expect their employer to offer a retirement plan as a condition of employment.

CHAPTER 2

1. There are certain advantages to providing for voluntary employee contributions to a qualified employer sponsored plan. These include: employee contributions can reduce the employer's cost; a higher retirement benefit can be realized; and the employees will be able to enjoy tax-deferred investment growth on their contributions.

2. If a plan is top heavy the employer must provide 100% vesting after three years of participation or 100% vesting after six years of participation if the plan uses a 0/7 schedule. More liberal vesting is required in order to offset the plan's top heavy quality and provide more benefits to the lower paid employees.

CHAPTER 3

1. Principal advantages to the employee include the deferral of current taxation, an additional source of retirement income as well as a survivor's benefit and disability income protection.

   Employee disadvantages include the risk that the deferred compensation may not be available when promised, especially if the plan is unfunded. If the corporation becomes bankrupt, the employee gets in line with the rest of the creditors.

   The primary employer advantage is attracting and retaining key executives in accordance with the deferred compensation agreement plus providing an additional retirement benefit. If the plan is unfunded, there is no current liability for contributions to the plan.

   Employer disadvantages include the fact that there is no current tax deduction for the plan and the employer has a long term liability to satisfy in the future. It should be noted that the employer will receive a tax deduction when the deferred compensation is paid to the employee.

2. The corporation does not receive a current tax deduction for any amounts of money set aside to fund the plan. A tax deduction will be realized when the deferred amounts are paid to the employee as compensation. Federal unemployment tax may also have to be paid at a later date.

The employee has no current federal income tax liability but will pay taxes on amounts received at a later date. Upon the death of the employee, the present value of the deferred compensation amounts are includible in the decedent's gross estate for federal estate tax purposes. In addition, when the deferred compensation is received, Social Security taxes will have to be paid on the first year's distribution.

CHAPTER 4

1. One of the advantages of a defined benefit plan is that this type of plan can provide a substantial retirement benefit as there is no limitation to the amount of plan contribution, although retirement benefits are limited to $90,000 per year, as indexed. This type of plan favors highly paid individuals and those situations where the key personnel are older.

   Disadvantages include a relatively higher cost. The employer's responsibility is to fund for a specified future benefit and this can be costly depending on the amount of benefit and the ages of the participants. In contrast to a profit sharing plan, a defined benefit represents a definite fixed liability for the employer.

2. Contribution limits are the same for both plans — 25% of compensation not to exceed $30,000 per year per participant. The amount of retirement benefit is not predetermined with either plan. Contributions are accumulated and the account balance at retirement represents the individual's benefit.

   Naturally, other common features include the fact that both are qualified plans, both have certain tax advantages, both must comply with ERISA requirements, etc.

CHAPTER 5

1. As a businessowner, Ralph may be eligible to establish an SEP plan which will overcome his objection of only being able to contribute $2,000 per year to the IRA. The SEP program will allow a maximum contribution of 15% of compensation up to $30,000 per year plus the plan will also allow elective deferrals of up to $7,000 as indexed.

2. The tax penalties associated with most qualified pension plans including IRAs and SEPs include the following:
   - Excess contributions — 6% on the excess amount
   - Premature distributions (prior to age 59½) — 10% on the amount withdrawn
   - Delay distributions (beyond age 70½) — 50% of the amount which should have been distributed
   - Excess distributions — 15% on the excess amount (the amount will vary by plan)

CHAPTER 6

1. The formula for calculating the exclusion allowance for Paula is as follows:

   20% x salary x years of service less employer contributions

   20% x $25,000 x 4 = $20,000 less $4,000 = $16,000

2. The additional contribution must be the smallest of:
   - $3,000
   - $15,000 less amounts used in a prior election
   - Excess of $5,000 x years service less past employer contributions

   Mary may contribute an additional $3,000 as the other two alternatives are greater than this amount. For example:

   $15,000 less amounts used (0) = $15,000
   $5,000 x 20 years of service = $100,000 less
   $40,000 of employer contributions = $60,000

CHAPTER 7

1. Ralph of course would be eligible to be a participant in the IBM plan assuming he meets all eligibility criteria.

   He has earned income and we'll assume that he is under age 70½, thus he qualifies for an IRA. Any contribution made to the IRA may or may not be deductible depending on his participation in the IBM plan and his compensation.

ANSWERS TO REVIEW EXERCISES

Ralph could probably also qualify for a Keogh plan to use for the compensation he receives from his non-incorporated business which he operates with his partner.

2. The calculation would be as follows:

    $20,000 - $10,000 (distribution allowance) divided by five years which would equal $2,000 as the taxable amount.

CHAPTER 8

1A. A strong argument could be made that Paul is not a very good prospect for a qualified plan because he may not be able to afford it. He has lost more money than he has probably made over 14 years.

On the other hand, maybe he has turned the corner in that he has made a profit in three of the last five years and thus maybe he is a prospect.

1B. The obvious answer to this question is the profit sharing plan due to the instability of the business income and profits.

1C. Possibly a 401(k) plan could be used with little or no employer contributions. The plan could be amended in later years to allow for employer contributions. In the mean time, the employees could participate in a tax favorable program which would enhance their future retirement and Paul will not be held liable for current contributions.

CHAPTER 9

1. A fully insured plan would normally be funded with any of the following products:
    - Fixed or variable annuities
    - Stocks and bonds
    - Some amounts of life insurance
    - Mutual funds

2. The fixed annuity provides a fully guaranteed contract so that the participant does not have to be concerned about principal or investment return — it is fully guaranteed. On the down side, the principal disadvantage is loss of purchasing power from these guaranteed dollars due to inflation.

   The variable annuity is designed to be a hedge against inflation which is its principal advantage compared to a fixed annuity. Unfortunately, this protection against inflation involves investments in a common stock portfolio, thus eliminating most of the guarantees found with a fixed annuity. There may be considerable investment risk to the participant including loss of principal and investment return.

3. Some of these duties and responsibilities include prudent investment of plan contributions, payment of certain fees and expenses, recordkeeping and the payment of retirement benefits to plan participants.

CHAPTER 10

1. Some of these variable factors include early termination of plan participants, premature death and disability of the participants, early and late retirement, variable amounts of investment return and the forfeiture of nonvested amounts. Because of these factors plan funding can only be considered estimates of the actual cost.

2. There are three factors which affect the ultimate cost of a pension plan. They are: benefits, expenses, and investment income. The benefit factor includes the variable number of participants who actually retire, the mortality of these retirees, and the benefit formula used in the plan.

   Expenses may vary from one plan year to the next. These expense factors include: legal fees, accounting fees, actuarial expenses, administrative expenses, etc.

   The final element in this formula is the amount of investment income earned on the contributions made to the plan. Depending on the funding vehicles used, investment return can vary widely. Fixed investments such as certificates of deposit will normally provide a stable return but using variable annuities may provide a very unpredictable return. A higher amount of investment return can reduce the ultimate cost of the plan.

3. Factors to be considered include cost, safety, flexibility, and service. Cost consideration refers to the benefits to be paid, investment earnings, and plan expenses.

   Safety of the plan and its values are important for all plan participants so that the ultimate benefit at retirement can be realized. Thus, an employer would not want to invest contributions in extremely high risk securities.

   Funding flexibility refers to the fact that the type of investment or the mix of investments and contribution dollars should be able to be altered in the future to meet changing needs.

   The employer is not in the pension business. Thus, the employer needs adequate service for the plan from a group of professionals such as an insurer, the agent, the attorney, etc.

CHAPTER 11

1. Possibly a defined benefit plan might be recommended to George. There are only five other employees, all relatively young, so that the cost related to these factors should not be too expensive. George only has about 10 years to retirement and due to his age and the short period of time in which to accumulate money, the defined benefit plan might be in George's best interest.

2. The cost of a plan can be affected by the vesting schedule and the plan's definition of compensation. An extremely liberal vesting schedule (100% immediate for example) will not allow for many non-vested forfeitures which can reduce the annual employer contribution.

   If the definition of compensation used in the plan excludes bonuses and commissions for example, then the annual contributions would necessarily be lower especially if a considerable amount of some employee's compensation includes bonuses and commissions. However, most of the employees likely to receive these additional forms of compensation are the key persons including the employer and this may not be the intent of the employer when he or she established the plan.

CHAPTER 12

1. Sam is exposing himself and his business to some serious reactions by the IRS if it can be determined that there was never any intention to establish this plan on a permanent basis. Plan permanency is normally considered 15 years by the IRS. Attempting to establish a plan for only two years to gain some tax relief could result in the plan being disqualified retroactively which would mean loss of the tax deduction already taken and tax penalties.

2. The plan administrator or any plan fiduciary would have the following duties and responsibilities:
   - To act for the exclusive benefit of the plan participants
   - To make prudent and sound investment decisions
   - To refrain from any prohibited transaction
   - To generally act in a prudent and professional manner.

   Violation of a fiduciary duty will result in the individual being held personally liable for any losses sustained by the plan.

3. Alternatives to plan termination would include:
   - Amending the plan to reduce contributions and plan costs
   - Requesting from the IRS a waiver of the plan's minimum funding requirements
   - The plan can be frozen thus requiring no further contributions.

FINAL COURSE REVIEW ANSWER KEY

1.	B	26.	A
2.	B	27.	C
3.	D	28.	A
4.	C	29.	A
5.	A	30.	D
6.	C	31.	C
7.	B	32.	A
8.	D	33.	B
9.	D	34.	A
10.	B	35.	C
11.	A	36.	C
12.	A	37.	B
13.	B	38.	C
14.	B	39.	D
15.	C	40.	C
16.	B	41.	B
17.	D	42.	B
18.	D	43.	A
19.	B	44.	D
20.	B	45.	B
21.	B	46.	A
22.	A	47.	D
23.	D	48.	C
24.	C	49.	B
25.	C	50.	B

- VOID -
PLEASE USE ALTERNATE
PENSION & PROFIT SHARING
EXAM ENCLOSED.

CONTINUING EDUCATION CANDIDATES

The Final Examination that follows should be completed only if you ordered this manual as a correspondence course for continuing education, and have prepaid your grading fee.

In most states this is an open book test, but you must work alone without assistance from any other person.

Carefully complete the steps below to ensure your Final Exam will be processed as quickly as possible.

- A. Your blank answer sheet is attached to your grading coupon. Use this to "bubble in" your exam answers.
- B. Be sure to fill in your test identification number on the answer sheet. The test ID number for this exam is <u>2730200</u>.
- C. When you have finished your exam, send us:
    1. Pages CE-1 through CE-28 (tear them out of the book).
    2. Your completed answer sheet.
    3. Your grading fee coupon.
    4. The information requested below.
    5. Affidavit of Personal Responsibility (only if you are in Colorado, Georgia, Indiana, Nevada, Oregon, or Rhode Island.)

Attn: Continuing Education Credit & Grading
The Merritt Company
P.O. Box 955
1661 Ninth Street
Santa Monica, CA 90406

IMPORTANT:

- Merritt will be responsible for lost answer sheets only if sent by registered, certified, or express mail and the official receipt contains an authorized Merritt signature.
- Your grading fee coupon must accompany your final examination and answer sheet. The coupon is your only proof of having prepaid for grading services, and can only be replaced by purchasing it at full price.
- You need a score of 70% or higher to pass this course.
- Normal turnaround time for grading is 7 to 10 days (1st Class Mail). Express grading service is available for an additional fee of $30.00.
- Please submit your materials for grading within one year of ordering this manual.

Soc. Sec.# _____ License # _____

Name _____

Home Address _____
                            Street

_____ Phone ( ) _____ DOB _____
City   State   Zip

☐ Check here if this is a new address

Firm Name _____

Address _____
                       Street

_____ Phone ( ) _____
City   State   Zip

☐ Check here if this is a new address

Renewal Date _____ Type of License(s) ☐ Property ☐ Casualty
                                                         ☐ Life   ☐ Health/Disability

State(s) for which I wish to receive continuing education credit*: _____
*There is an additional charge of $10 per state for this service.

Please mail my results to:

I hereby certify that I worked alone in completing this examination.   ☐ Firm ☐ Home

THE ABOVE MUST BE COMPLETED IN FULL IN ORDER FOR US TO PROCESS YOUR EXAM

_____
Signature

- VOID -

PLEASE USE ALTERNATE PENSION & PROFIT SHARING EXAM ENCLOSED.

FINAL EXAM FOR CONTINUING EDUCATION

PENSION & PROFIT SHARING

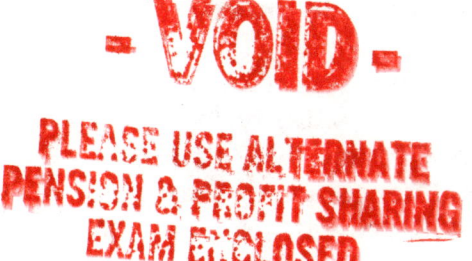

1. Which of the following are considered advantages of a formal employer sponsored pension plan?

   I Employee morale is enhanced.
   II Employer contributions are tax deductible.
   III The employer may be able to attract and retain key personnel.
   IV Employee productivity is often increased.

   1. I and III
   2. II and IV
   3. I, II and III
   4. I, II, III and IV

2. A person in a position of financial trust best describes a(n):

   1. plan fiduciary.
   2. plan participant.
   3. IRS employee.
   4. none of the above.

3. Which of the following factors are considerations with regard to the selection of a funding mechanism for a plan by the employer?

   1. Safety of benefits
   2. Cost of the funding vehicle
   3. Flexibility and service
   4. All of the above

- VOID -

PLEASE USE ALTERNATE PENSION & PROFIT SHARING EXAM ENCLOSED.

4. Which of the following is (are) correct regarding tax penalties for qualified plans?

　　I　Premature distributions prior to age 59½ can result in a penalty of 10% of the amount withdrawn.
　　II　Failure to begin a systematic distribution from a qualified plan following the individual's retirement.
　　III　There is no tax penalty for plan distributions prior to 59½ due to death or disability.
　　IV　Usually distributions prior to age 59½ which are the result of divorce decrees are not subject to the penalty for early withdrawal.

　1. II only
　2. I and III
　3. II, III and IV
　4. I, II, III and IV

5. Ted, age 72, has failed to begin a systematic distribution of his IRA account. The amount which should have been withdrawn is $5,000. The tax penalty for this will be:

　1. $1,000.
　2. $1,250.
　3. $2,000.
　4. $2,500.

6. Which of the following is not true regarding a 401(k) plan?

　1. Employees may take employer contributions in cash.
　2. Employees may elect a salary reduction amount.
　3. Salary reduction agreements offer certain tax advantages for the employee.
　4. Any contributions taken in cash by the employee are not taxed.

FINAL EXAM FOR CONTINUING EDUCATION

7. A series of periodic contributions made on behalf of participants during their working years best describes:

    1. advance funding.
    2. terminal funding.
    3. current disbursement funding.
    4. periodic funding.

8. Qualified plans are required to provide a(n):

    1. straight life annuity option.
    2. joint-survivor annuity option.
    3. installment refund annuity option.
    4. life with period certain annuity option.

9. Which type of qualified plan might an employer consider who has experienced considerable variation in company profits for several years?

    1. A defined contribution plan
    2. A defined benefit plan
    3. A combination plan
    4. A profit sharing plan

10. Setting aside a sum of money when an employee retires to fund the individual's retirement benefit is known as:

    1. advance funding.
    2. terminal funding.
    3. retirement funding.
    4. advance disbursement funding.

11. A 50% partial distribution may be rolled into an IRA if the reason for the distribution is due to:

    1. the total disability of the participant.
    2. the death of the participant.
    3. termination of employment.
    4. all of the above.

12. A qualified plan which is designed primarily as an investment vehicle for the employer's own securities, best defines a(n):

    1. defined benefit plan.
    2. profit sharing plan.
    3. employee stock ownership plan.
    4. stock redemption plan.

13. The primary purpose of ERISA is to protect:

    1. employer interests.
    2. governmental interests.
    3. plan participant interests.
    4. legislative groups.

14. Bud is covered by a qualified plan which uses a 0/5 vesting schedule which specifies 20% vesting at the end of each plan year. He terminates employment after 2½ years of plan participation with an account balance of $10,000. His vested benefit is:

    1. $4,000.
    2. $4,500.
    3. $5,500.
    4. $6,500.

15. An IRA rollover contribution may occur no more frequently than:

    1. once per calendar quarter.
    2. once every six months.
    3. once per year.
    4. once every 60 days.

16. Vicki participates through elective salary deferrals in an SEP and a TSA. If she defers $5,000 in the SEP, the maximum deferral for the TSA is:

    1. $1,500.
    2. $3,000.
    3. $3,500.
    4. $4,500.

17. Sean satisfies his company's pension plan eligibility requirements for participation on March 1, 1992. He must be enrolled in the plan not later than:

    1. June 1, 1992.
    2. September 1, 1992.
    3. December 1, 1992.
    4. March 1, 1993.

18. XYZ Inc. requires that all employees complete two years of service to be eligible for the company's pension plan. Full vesting must occur:

    1. immediately.
    2. within three years.
    3. within two years.
    4. within one year.

19. Jan earned $325,000 in 1992. How much of this amount can be used in the calculation of her pension contribution?

    1. $100,000 as indexed
    2. $200,000 as indexed
    3. $300,000 as indexed
    4. The full amount

20. All of the following are true of an SEP except:

    1. an SEP is a qualified individual plan.
    2. employer contributions are limited to 15% of compensation not to exceed $30,000 per participant.
    3. SEPs use individually owned IRAs for employer contributions.
    4. SEPS offer administrative simplicity.

21. Salary reduction deferrals to a TSA are usually limited to:

    1. $9,500.
    2. $7,500.
    3. $5,000.
    4. $2,500.

22. Cindy, an employer, pays $12 per $1,000 for a life insurance benefit of $20,000 for a plan participant. What are the tax consequences for the plan participant?

　　1. The participant's income is increased by $1,000.
　　2. The participant's income is increased by $240.
　　3. The participant's income is increased by the smaller of the P.S. 58 charges or the life insurance premium.
　　4. There are no tax consequences; only the proceeds are taxed.

23. A stock bonus plan limits the amount which may be invested in the employer's own securities to:

　　1. 10% of the fund's value.
　　2. 10% of the plan contribution.
　　3. 20% of the fund's value.
　　4. none of the above.

24. Which of the following are correct regarding taxation of distributions received from a Keogh plan?

　　I　Pre-retirement distributions due to death are tax free.
　　II　A participant will recover any cost basis tax free.
　　III　Lump sum distributions may qualify for five-year income averaging.
　　IV　Voluntary employee contributions constitute the plan's cost basis.

　　1. I and III
　　2. II and IV
　　3. II, III and IV
　　4. I, II, III and IV

25. A self-employed person would be eligible for which of the following plans?

   I   An IRA
   II A corporate profit sharing plan
   III A Keogh plan
   IV A corporate defined contribution plan

   1. III only
   2. II and IV
   3. I and III
   4. I, II and IV

26. A defined contribution plan specifies a contribution of 10% of compensation. Total participant compensation is $150,000 annually. Currently, there are plan forfeitures amounting to $20,000. This year's contribution will be:

   1. $15,000.
   2. $13,000.
   3. $10,000
   4. none of the above.

27. Jack and Jill, husband and wife, both work and earn in excess of $50,000 each. Which of the following is (are) true?

   I   They both may contribute $2,000 into separate IRAs.
   II They are eligible for a spousal IRA.
   III They may contribute up to $4,000 to an IRA.
   IV They both will enjoy tax deferred investment income on their IRA contributions.

   1. I only
   2. I and IV
   3. II and III
   4. II, III and IV

28. A relatively secure retirement can be achieved by:

    1. regularly investing in the stock market.
    2. systematic savings for a prolonged period of time.
    3. investing in junk bonds with high possible returns.
    4. implementing a savings plan not later than age 55.

29. Which of the following is true regarding non-qualified plans?

    1. Non-qualified plans may not discriminate.
    2. Non-qualified plans do not offer current tax deductions for employer contributions.
    3. Non-qualified plans need not be in written form.
    4. None of the above.

30. IRAs may be funded with all of the following except:

    1. mutual funds.
    2. variable annuities.
    3. life insurance.
    4. fixed annuities.

31. Increased mortality after a participant retires will:

    1. increase the ultimate cost of a plan.
    2. decrease the ultimate cost of a plan.
    3. have little effect on the cost of a plan.
    4. none of the above.

32. A qualified plan in which contributions and investment earnings accumulate or are pooled for the benefit of all participants, best defines a(n):

    1. general asset fund.
    2. unallocated fund.
    3. allocated fund.
    4. separate account fund.

FINAL EXAM FOR CONTINUING EDUCATION

33. Which of the following would not be a major employer consideration with regard to establishing a pension plan?

    1. Cost considerations
    2. Employee considerations
    3. Tax considerations
    4. Employee dependent considerations

34. The maximum employer contribution to a defined contribution plan is:

    1. 10% of compensation up to a maximum of $10,000.
    2. 15% of compensation up to a maximum of $15,000.
    3. 25% of compensation up to a maximum of $30,000.
    4. 15% of compensation up to a maximum of $25,000.

35. A salary reduction SEP permits an employee to make a:

    1. deductible contribution up to $7,000 as indexed.
    2. non-deductible contribution up to $7,000.
    3. deductible contribution up to $30,000 as indexed.
    4. deductible contribution of any amount not to exceed $30,000.

36. Which of the following is true regarding a participant's early retirement from a qualified plan?

    1. Due to longer life expectancy, the retirement benefit will be higher than normal.
    2. The IRS does not allow early retirement provisions.
    3. Early retirement will result in a reduced retirement benefit.
    4. The Department of Labor must approve of any early retirement plan provision.

37. Margaret turned age 70½, September 1, 1990. She must begin a systematic withdrawal from her IRA by:

    1. January 1, 1991.
    2. April 1, 1991.
    3. September 1, 1991.
    4. September 1, 1992.

38. Which of the following is (are) true regarding the pre-retirement death of a plan participant?

    I   The deceased participant's account balance is automatically 100% vested.
    II The deceased participant's death benefit may equal the account balance plus any additional life insurance benefits.
    III Life insurance benefits revert to the surviving plan participants.
    IV Without life insurance, the deceased's death benefit is equal to the account balance as of the date of death.

    1. I only
    2. II and III
    3. I, II and IV
    4. I, II, III and IV

39. Excess contributions to an HR-10 will result in a penalty of:

    1. 10% of the excess amount.
    2. 15% of the excess amount.
    3. 10% of the total contribution.
    4. 15% of the total contribution.

40. Employer contributions to a TSA are limited to:

    1. 15% of compensation up to $30,000.
    2. 25% of compensation up to $30,000.
    3. $9,500 annually.
    4. $12,500 annually.

41. The Pension Benefit Guarantee Corporation:

    I   is part of the IRS.
    II guarantees all pension benefits for all types of plans.
    III requires employer premiums be paid to the PBGC.
    IV is a requirement of ERISA.

    1. I and II
    2. II and IV
    3. II, III and IV
    4. I, II, III and IV

42. All of the following would be considered duties of a plan fiduciary except:

    1. exercising prudent and ethical conduct.
    2. guaranteeing the investment results of the plan.
    3. adherence to plan provisions.
    4. avoiding certain prohibited plan transactions.

43. The ultimate cost of a pension plan equals:

    1. plan benefits plus expenses plus investment income.
    2. plan benefits less expenses plus investment income.
    3. plan benefits plus expenses less investment income.
    4. plan benefits less expenses less investment income.

44. In accordance with 401(k) requirements, a distribution of an excess contribution to an employee:

    1. will cause the employee to pay taxes on the distribution.
    2. will create a tax penalty for the employee.
    3. is illegal and subject to a tax penalty.
    4. is not permitted under a 401(k) plan.

45. Which of the following organizations qualify for a TSA?

   I   The Chamber of Commerce
   II The state government
   III The community chest
   IV A non-government operated hospital

   1. I and III
   2. III and IV
   3. II, III and IV
   4. I, II, III and IV

46. The Summary Plan Description must initially be given to plan participants within:

   1. 120 days of the effective date of the plan.
   2. 30 days of the effective date of plan participation.
   3. 90 days following the close of the plan year.
   4. 60 days of the plan's anniversary.

47. Which of the following is (are) true regarding taxation of qualified plans?

   I   Five year income averaging allows a person to spread a tax liability over a five year period of time.
   II Five year income averaging can be used for lump sum distributions.
   III Rollover contributions provide a method of avoiding federal income tax.
   IV Non-contributory qualified plans have a zero tax basis.

   1. II only
   2. I and III
   3. II and IV
   4. I, III and IV

FINAL EXAM FOR CONTINUING EDUCATION

48. Post retirement employment opportunities are usually very limited for the retiree due to:

    1. the retiree's physical inability to continue to work.
    2. the retiree's desire not to work.
    3. penalties imposed by the Social Security Administration on post-retirement earnings.
    4. all of the above.

49. Which of the following individuals could be excluded from a qualified plan?

    I   John, who has worked for the employer for only three months
    II Mary, age 18, with six months of service with the employer
    III Charlie, age 20, who works a couple of hours each day while attending college
    IV Nancy, who is a union worker covered under her own union plan

    1. I and II
    2. II, III and IV
    3. I, II and III
    4. I, II, III and IV

50. A qualified plan will be considered top heavy if:

    1. key employee benefits exceed 60% of the value for all plan benefits.
    2. non-key employee benefits are not at least 60% of key employee benefits.
    3. key employee benefits exceed 40% of the value for all plan benefits.
    4. non-key benefits are less that the key employee benefits.

51. Which of the following is true regarding group deposit administration contracts?

    1. They are less flexible than group annuities.
    2. Deposit administration contracts consist primarily of unallocated funds.
    3. Deposit administration contracts may be invested in the insurer's general account only.
    4. All of the above.

52. The separate account of an insurer funding the plan's contributions provides:

    1. a guaranteed rate of return.
    2. a guarantee of premiums received.
    3. investment risk borne by the insurer.
    4. investment risk borne by the plan participant.

53. A fully insured pension plan provides for a pre-retirement death benefit. Which of the following types of life insurance policies would most likely be used to fund this benefit?

    1. Group whole life
    2. Individual whole life
    3. Individual 10-year endowments
    4. Group term

54. An employer's primary motivation in providing a qualified plan is to improve employee loyalty, motivation, and productivity. The employer might consider a:

    1. defined benefit plan.
    2. stock bonus plan.
    3. profit sharing plan.
    4. defined contribution plan.

55. An employer employs seven people with an average age of 49 and a total payroll of $250,000. Which of the following plans is likely to be the most costly?

    1. Defined benefit
    2. Defined contribution
    3. Profit sharing
    4. Simplified Employee Pension

56. With regard to IRAs, active participation in other qualified plans:

    1. may reduce the deductibility of IRA contributions.
    2. results in IRA ineligibility.
    3. reduces the amount of the IRA contribution.
    4. results in a tax penalty.

57. Who would be eligible to participate in an HR-10?

    1. An 18 year old part-time employee
    2. An employee-partner with only unearned income
    3. A 25-year-old full time employee with one year of service
    4. None of the above

58. The penalty for an excess contribution to a 401(k) plan is:

    1. 6%.
    2. 10%.
    3. 15%.
    4. 20%.

59. When a qualified plan is identified as top heavy by the IRS, the maximum length of the vesting schedule can be:

    1. one year.
    2. three years.
    3. six years.
    4. seven years.

60. Under the "50/40 rule":

    1. 50 employees or 40% of the workforce, whichever is the greater of the two, must benefit from the plan.
    2. 40-50 employees must benefit from the plan.
    3. the lesser of 50 employees or 40% of the workforce must benefit from the plan.
    4. 40-50% of the workforce must benefit from the plan.

61. One of the principal characteristics of a profit sharing plan is:

    1. flexibility of contributions.
    2. no current tax deduction for contributions.
    3. mandatory contribution amounts.
    4. flexible contribution allocations to plan participants.

62. Specific conditions that an employee must satisfy to become a plan participant best defines:

   1. eligibility requirements.
   2. vesting requirements.
   3. service requirements.
   4. discriminatory requirements.

63. Rank in order the following plans from the most expensive to the least expensive in terms of employer contributions.

   I   Profit sharing plans
   II Defined contribution plans
   III Defined benefit plans

   1. I, II and III
   2. II, I and III
   3. III, II and I
   4. II, III and I

64. Which of the following funding vehicles can be used with a fully insured plan?

   1. Variable annuities
   2. Mutual funds
   3. Fixed annuities
   4. All of the above

65. A plan funded by individual annuity contracts is:

   1. less costly than a group annuity policy.
   2. the least expensive way to fund a qualified plan.
   3. more costly than a group annuity policy.
   4. the most cost effective way to fund a qualified plan.

66. Which of the following is (are) correct regarding the purchase of life insurance benefits as part of a Keogh plan?

    I   Insurance premiums on the life of the businessowner are tax deductible.
    II   P.S. 58 charges are deductible from the plan contributions for all employees.
    III The self-employed owner may not include P.S. 58 charges in the calculation of his or her cost basis.
    IV P.S. 58 charges are deductible from the businessowner's plan contribution.

1. I only
2. II only
3. II and III
4. III and IV

67. With regard to the five year average formula, the distribution allowance is:

1. the greater of $10,000 or 100% of the total taxable amount.
2. the lesser of $10,000 or 50% of the total taxable amount.
3. the lesser of $20,000 or 100% of the total taxable amount.
4. the greater of $20,000 or 50% of the total taxable amount.

68. Which of the following is correct regarding non-qualified deferred compensation?

    I   Deferred compensation plans should be in writing.
    II   Deferred compensation may be an unfunded plan.
    III The deferred compensation benefits are guaranteed to the participant.
    IV Funded deferred compensation plans provide current tax deductions for employer contributions.

1. I and IV
2. II and III
3. I and II
4. II, III and IV

69. A key employee includes all of the following except a:

   1. company officer.
   2. 1% owner-employee with a salary of $50,000.
   3. highly compensated employee.
   4. 5% owner.

70. Which of the following is characteristic of a qualified pension plan?

   I   The plan may not discriminate.
   II The plan must be in writing and communicated to the employees.
   III The plan must be permanent.
   IV The employer is considered a plan fiduciary.

   1. I and II
   2. II and III
   3. I, III and IV
   4. I, II, III and IV

71. Employee status with regard to a TSA is usually determined by:

   1. salary and hours worked.
   2. the payment of employee benefits.
   3. the individual's occupational classification.
   4. the payment of Social Security taxes and workers compensation by the employer.

72. A trustee of a trust fund plan has all of the following duties and responsibilities except:

   1. determining which actuarial cost method to use.
   2. investment of plan contributions.
   3. payment of plan benefits.
   4. recordkeeping functions.

73. In accordance with ERISA, the annual report must be filed with the:

   1. IRS within 120 days of the end of the plan year.
   2. Department of Labor within 210 days of the end of the calendar year.
   3. IRS within 120 of the end of the calendar year.
   4. Department of Labor within 120 days of the end of the plan year.

FINAL EXAM FOR CONTINUING EDUCATION

74. All of the following factors have impacted the growth of private pension plans except:

    1. labor unions.
    2. increases in employee compensation.
    3. employee expectations.
    4. the necessity to compete for key employees.

75. A high interest assumption for a qualified plan will usually result in:

    1. a higher ultimate cost.
    2. increased expense considerations.
    3. a lower ultimate cost.
    4. an average ultimate cost.

76. The tax penalty created by an excess contribution to an IRA may be resolved by:

    1. removing the excess amount in the current tax year.
    2. obtaining a letter of clearance from the IRS.
    3. five year income averaging.
    4. not making a contribution in subsequent years.

77. Which of the following are correct regarding rollover contributions?

    I   Rollovers must be completed within 60 days of a qualified plan distribution.
    II The limitation on rollover amounts is $30,000.
    III Non-qualified plan distributions may be rolled into an IRA.
    IV A rollover may be a 50% partial rollover.

    1. I and IV
    2. II and III
    3. I and II
    4. I, III and IV

78. The tax penalty for an excess pension distribution is:

    1. 15% of the distribution.
    2. 10% of the distribution.
    3. 50% of the excess amount.
    4. 15% of the excess amount.

79. Annual additions to a qualified plan include:

   I   employer contributions.
   II employee contributions.
   III investment income.
   IV forfeited contribution amounts for terminated employees.

   1. I and III
   2. I and II
   3. I, III and IV
   4. I, II and IV

80. As a general rule, a defined benefit plan would be most beneficial to the:

   1. older employees only.
   2. younger, higher paid employees.
   3. older, higher paid employees.
   4. younger, lower paid employees.

81. A corporation could establish any of the following qualified plans except a:

   1. defined contribution plan.
   2. defined benefit plan.
   3. Keogh plan.
   4. profit sharing plan.

82. For most pension plans, investment of plan contributions in the employer's own securities is limited to:

   1. 10% of the fund's value.
   2. 20% of the fund's value.
   3. 10% of the plan contributions.
   4. 20% of the plan contributions.

83. Employee advantages of participation in a 401(k) plan include:

   1. a reduction in taxable income.
   2. tax-free investment income.
   3. a method of avoiding taxation.
   4. all of the above.

84. All of the following are eligibility requirements for participation in an SEP except:

    1. minimum age of 21.
    2. one year of service.
    3. ownership of an IRA.
    4. the employee must have been employed by the employer in three of the preceding five years.

85. Which of the following funding mechanisms would probably have the highest administrative expense?

    1. A group annuity contract
    2. A deposit administration contract
    3. An individual annuity contract
    4. A group variable annuity contract

86. Alice's employer makes a specified 10% contribution to a qualified pension plan for each participant, and Alice's account balance will be used to purchase an annuity for her when she retires. What type of pension plan does Alice have?

    1. A target benefit plan.
    2. A money purchase pension plan.
    3. An employee stock ownership plan.
    4. A defined benefit plan.

87. To avoid having death benefits received from a qualified plan included in the deceased's estate for federal estate tax purposes, the participant must avoid having incidents of ownership in the plan's life insurance. This may be done by:

    1. Having any life insurance policy owned by a separate trust.
    2. Naming a beneficiary for the life insurance proceeds.
    3. Paying part of the premiums due for the insurance.
    4. Designate that part of the life insurance cash values be paid to the participant's estate.

88. Which of the following provisions would typically be found in a deferred compensation agreement?

   I   Forfeiture provisions.
   II Disability provisions.
   III Retirement provisions.
   IV Employment provisions.

   1. I and IV
   2. I and III
   3. II, III and IV
   4. I, II, III and IV

89. Alan and Dedra each want to open individual retirement accounts. Alan is 71 years of age and Dedra is age 62. Both Alan and Dedra have substantial income from rental apartments and stock dividends. Can Alan and Dedra open IRAs?

   1. Yes, both Alan and Dedra may open IRAs.
   2. No, but Dedra may alone because she is under age 70½.
   3. Yes, because both Alan and Dedra have enough income to qualify.
   4. No, because neither have qualifying earned income.

90. The ultimate cost to the employer of a qualified pension plan can be reduced by:

   1. Replacing terminated employees with new hires.
   2. Payment of early or pre-retirement benefits.
   3. A higher interest rate assumption.
   4. Using individual annuity contracts, as opposed to group contracts.

91. An outdated method of retirement funding where the employer simply paid the monthly retirement benefit as it came due, leaving the retired employee completely dependent of the employer's ability to pay at that time, is known as:

   1. Terminal funding.
   2. Current disbursement funding.
   3. Advance funding.
   4. Benefit estimate funding.

FINAL EXAM FOR CONTINUING EDUCATION

92. According to the eligibility requirements of a Keogh pension plan, the persons that may participate in the plan are:

    1. Only the corporate officers that participate on an equity basis in the business.
    2. All employees, but not including the self-employed business owner.
    3. All employees, including the self-employed business owner.
    4. All employees that do not otherwise participate in another pension plan.

93. What are the advantages of using life insurance benefits within a pension plan?

    1. Life insurance benefits are received income tax free.
    2. Life insurance proceeds can provide liquidity for federal estate taxes.
    3. Life insurance can provide surviving dependents a meaningful benefit in the case of a plan participant's premature death.
    4. All of the above.

94. One of the factors contributing to the growth of private pension plans is that it is more efficient to accumulate money for retirement through:

    1. Individual savings accounts.
    2. Group savings.
    3. Labor unions.
    4. Competitive non-union business.

95. Ernestine, as an employer, has set up a pension plan that states she will contribute 10% of each employee's compensation to the plan. However, as a new company owner, she also set up the plan so that she does not have a fixed liability for the contributions. What kind of plan does Ernestine have?

    1. A defined contribution plan.
    2. A defined benefit plan.
    3. A profit sharing plan.
    4. A discriminatory plan.

96. As an incidental benefit, the IRS regulates the amount premiums that can be paid in relation to the plan cost for each participant. If the plan uses term life insurance as an incidental benefit, the premium must be less than what percentage of the plan contribution?

    1. 15%.
    2. 25%.
    3. 50%.
    4. 75%.

97. Howard is a key employee for Combo Inc., and his employer is setting up a funded deferred compensation agreement specifically for Howard. What must be included in the agreement to avoid having this money currently taxed to Howard as income?

    1. Include a provision for early retirement.
    2. Require a plan administrator to oversee the plan.
    3. Include a forfeiture provision.
    4. Include a provision requiring post-retirement consulting services.

98. Jennifer, as a business owner, has decided to start a pension plan for her employees. She has chosen to use an allocated fund type of plan, which means that:

    1. Jennifer will allocate a certain amount of money to the fund each year.
    2. Jennifer will designate a certain amount of money to be paid into the fund at some future date.
    3. The fund will accumulate all assets into a pool for the benefit of all plan participants.
    4. Plan contributions will be allocated to each plan participant's own account according to the plan's contribution formula.

FINAL EXAM FOR CONTINUING EDUCATION

99. The primary **difference** between a 401(k) plan and a thrift or salary savings plan is that:

    1. The 401(k) plan also allows the employee to make a tax-deductible contribution.
    2. The 401(k) plan allows investment earnings to accumulate on a tax deferred basis.
    3. The thrift plan also allows the employee to make a tax-deductible contribution.
    4. The thrift plan allows investment earnings to accumulate on a tax deferred basis.

100. Once a pension plan has met the requirements for qualified plan status, certain tax advantages include:

    1. A current tax deduction for the employer on any plan contributions.
    2. Tax-deferred growth on plan contributions, although employees are taxed on the employer's plan contributions.
    3. Investment earnings received by the employee at retirement are received tax-free.
    4. Lump sum benefit payments may be rolled into a non-qualified plan and continue to grow tax deferred.

ABBREVIATED GLOSSARY OF INSURANCE TERMS

NOTE: A completely separate bound edition of this glossary, with many more insurance terms, is available from Merritt. Please write for information concerning the "Glossary of Insurance Terms" to:

The Merritt Company
P.O. Box 955
1661 9th Street
Santa Monica, CA 90406

Copyright 1996
The Merritt Company

The copyright is not intended to prevent full quotation by any writer on insurance subjects, providing that credit is given to the source. It is intended to prevent duplication of a sequence of definitions in any glossary, vocabulary, or dictionary of insurance terms to be offered for sale or private distribution to any group of persons.

Advance Funding — Periodically, setting aside a predetermined sum of money to fund future retirement benefits of a pension plan.

Allocated Funds — Qualified plan funds which are identified in the name of specific plan participants.

Annual Additions — The total of employer contributions, voluntary employee contributions, and forfeited additions which equal the annual contribution to a qualified plan.

Annual Return/Report (Form 5500) — A required annual report reflecting the pension plan's operation for the year; to be submitted to the IRS and the Department of Labor.

Average Benefit Test — A coverage test for a qualified plan which states that at least 50% of the lower paid employees must benefit from the plan and the average benefit provided must be at least 70% of the benefit provided the higher paid employees.

Contributory Plan — A qualified pension plan which requires some contributions from the plan participants.

Cost Basis — A tax term which means an amount of money which has already been taxed.

Current Disbursement Funding — A method of funding a retirement benefit which consists of simply paying the benefit to the retiree as it becomes due; usually on a monthly basis.

Deferred Compensation — A non-qualified plan, usually used for key persons in a corporation whereby an employee defers receipt of current compensation until a later date such as retirement, death, or disability.

Defined Benefit Plan — A qualified pension plan in which a definite benefit is determined and the employer's responsibility is to fund for this benefit over the life of the plan.

Defined Contribution Plan — A qualified pension plan in which the amount of the annual contribution is definitely determined but the retirement benefits will simply be the amounts accumulated in the participant's account at retirement.

Elective Deferral Plan — A type of qualified plan (401(k) or TSA) whereby participants voluntarily elect to defer current amounts of compensation and these amounts are placed in a retirement plan on a tax favorable basis.

Employee Retirement Income Security Act (ERISA) — A federal law which is designed to protect the interests of participants in a qualified pension plan by requiring specific reports to be filed with the IRS and the Department of Labor as well as disclosure information to all plan participants.

Employee Stock Ownership Plan (ESOP) — A qualified plan which is a type of profit sharing plan whereby the plan is used as an investment vehicle for the employer's own stock. The plan participants' contribution is in the form of the employer's stock.

401(k) Plan — A qualified elective deferral plan whereby participants elect a salary reduction with the amount of the reduced compensation placed in a variety of investment vehicles. The plan may or may not include some form of matching contributions by the employer.

Fiduciary — A person in a position of financial trust such as an attorney, a bank trustee, the employer and plan administrator of a qualified retirement plan. Such person is to act in a prudent and ethical manner on behalf of plan participants.

Five Year Income Averaging — A tax device for lump sum distributions from a qualified plan whereby the individual is enabled to pay a smaller tax on such distributions by using the five-year income averaging formula.

Fully Insured Plan — A qualified plan whereby contributions are made to an insurer and benefits and plan administration are provided by the insurance company on behalf of plan participants.

General Account — A relatively safe, conservative investment portfolio of an insurance company consisting of such investments as real estate, mortgages, government bonds, etc., and such investments are used to help fund qualified plans. The general account normally contains no equity-based investments.

Group Deposit Administration Contract — A funding contract for a qualified plan whereby contributions are accounted for on an unallocated basis for the benefit of all plan participants.

Individual Retirement Account (IRA) — An individual qualified plan established by ERISA whereby individuals who have earned income and are less than age 70½ may set aside up to $2,000 per year on a tax favorable basis for retirement purposes.

Joint-Survivor Option — A required retirement or annuity option whereby retirement benefits are paid for the life of both the plan participant and his or her spouse (survivor). The plan participant may accept or reject the use of this option.

Keogh Plan — A qualified plan for the non-incorporated self employed business owner and eligible participants. Also known as an HR-10.

Money Purchase Plan — A qualified plan which is a type of defined contribution plan in which the participant's account values are used to purchase a lifetime retirement benefit.

Non-Contributory Plan — A plan in which no contributions are required from plan participants. All contributions are made by the employer.

Non-Qualified Plan — A plan (often a retirement plan) for certain key persons which does not meet the IRS requirements of a qualified plan whereby selected individuals are covered under the plan and others are purposely excluded from the plan. Deferred compensation is a common type of non-qualified plan.

Pension Benefit Guaranty Corporation (PBGC) — An organization which is part of the Department of Labor which guarantees pension benefits for certain types of qualified plans. Employers offering these plans must pay an annual premium to the PBGC.

Percentage Test — A coverage test for a qualified plan in which a formula is used to determine if a plan benefits at least 70% of the lower paid employees.

Profit Sharing Plan — A type of qualified plan established by an employer whose business profits have been unstable. A profit sharing plan does not represent a fixed liability as contributions are made to the plan from realized profits; no profits, no contribution.

Qualified Plan — A plan which meets IRS requirements for eligibility, participation, vesting and contributions and is filed and approved by the IRS as a qualified plan with specific tax advantages for the employer and plan participants.

Ratio Test — A coverage test for a qualified plan in which a percentage of lower paid employees benefiting from the plan must equal 70% of the higher paid employees benefiting from the plan.

Rollover Contribution — A contribution which consists of a distribution from a qualified plan which is deposited (rolled) in another qualified plan to postpone current taxation of the distribution.

Separate Account — An investment portfolio of an insurer which primarily consists of investments in equity-based securities such as common stock. The separate account is used to fund variable contracts and provide the participant with a hedge against inflation.

Simplified Employee Pension (SEP) — A type of qualified plan which uses individuals IRAs as a vehicle for accepting employer contributions to the plan. An SEP also permits individual contributions to the plan on a tax favorable basis.

Stock Bonus Plan — A type of profit sharing plan whereby contributions to the plan and benefits derived from the plan are in the form of the employer's own stock.

Summary Annual Report — A summary of a qualified plan's operation which is required to be given to each participant annually.

Summary Plan Description — A summary of a qualified plan's principal provisions which must be provided to all participants within a certain period of time after becoming eligible for plan participation.

Target Benefit Plan — A qualified plan which is a combination of a defined benefit and defined contribution plan whereby an employer is required to fund a specific targeted benefit for plan participants. Target benefit plans impose defined contribution limitations for plan funding.

Tax Basis — A sum of money such as a qualified plan benefit or distribution which has yet to be taxed. Most qualified plan distributions are considered fully taxable.

Tax Sheltered Annuity (TSA) — A qualified plan for employees of certain non-profit organizations as identified by the IRS. TSAs normally provide for an employee to take a salary reduction on a tax favorable basis as a means of setting aside money for retirement.

Terminal Funding — A form of retirement funding by which an employer sets aside a single sum of money when the participant retires. This sum will fund the individual's retirement benefit.

Third Party Administration (TPA) — Organizations who administer qualified plans by providing accounting and actuarial services as well as filing of various reports required by the IRS and the Department of Labor.

Trust Fund Plans — A type of qualified plan in which contributions are made to a plan trustee or a corporate trustee. The trustee in turn will provide retirement benefits for plan participants.

Unallocated Funds — Plan contributions are made or pooled for the benefit of all plan participants collectively.

Variable Annuity — An individual or group contract issued by an insurance company to fund retirement benefits by investing in the insurer's separate account which consists primarily of a common stock portfolio. As a hedge against inflation, the variable annuity presents investment risks to the annuitant.

Vesting — Vesting means ownership; ownership of the employer contributions to a qualified plan by the plan participants. Vesting schedules must be complied with in accordance with ERISA.